THE IMMORTAL TRUTH

Numa Jay
Pillion

T
H
E

IMMORTAL

T
R
U
T
H

*The Akashic
Records Read
by Saints and
Mystics*

The Immortal Truth: The Akashic Records Read by Saints and Mystics

Published by Wheatmark®
610 East Delano Street, Suite 104
Tucson, Arizona 85705 U.S.A.
www.wheatmark.com

International Standard Book Number: 978-1-60494-192-0
Library of Congress Control Number: 2008937280

CONTENTS

A special thank you is extended to Joseph Rickard
for his kindness in proof reading this manuscript.
Joseph Rickard's devotion to the Virgin Mary is the force that
introduced me to the visions of the Venerable Anne Catherine
Emmerick, and is, without a doubt, reflected in this work.
I also express appreciation to Tan Books and Publishers, Inc.,
P.O. Box 424, Rockford, Illinois, 61105,
for allowing me to quote freely from Anne Catherine's visions
as revealed in *The Dolorous Passion of Our Lord Jesus Christ*.

My appreciation to the Reverend Theodore Breslin, D.P., director of The Saint Martin de Porres Guild, 141 East 65th Street, New York, N.Y., For permission to quote from MEET BROTHER MARTIN, By Reverend Norbert Georges, D.P.

The Edgar Cayce readings are on file at
The Association for Research and Enlightenment,
215 67th Street, Virginia Beach, Virginia 23451-2061

Appreciation is extended to The Religious Research Foundation, P.O. Box 350208, Grand Island, Florida, 31735-0208, Phone (352) 460-0266; www.religiousresearch.org - for permission to quote from the Life Readings of spirit guide and counselor, Dr. John Christopher Daniels.

I express deep appreciation for the spiritual guidance given to me from within.

I was not alone.

ABOUT LIFE READINGS

A Life Reading is a record of a soul's history on Earth. It is not fortune telling. There are readings and there are readings. You can be given a reading, listen to a reading, even read a reading. The word "reading" can mean many things. I capitalize Life Readings to clarify any confusion of the purpose of the words.

It is my preference to distinguish Life Readings from readings of other types. If a person is told their fortune with a deck of cards, they are being given a reading by cards. There are numerology readings, astrological readings, psychic readings of various shapes and sizes, so to speak.

A Life Reading includes a person's present and past lifetimes on Earth, and their purpose in those incarnations. This becomes a book of a soul's history on Earth. And in capitalizing Life Reading, I wish to set the Reading apart to give it the distinction it deserves.

Thomas Sugrue capitalized Life Readings in *There Is A River*, his biography of Edgar Cayce. Thomas Sugrue was a native of Connecticut. I came from Connecticut. In that regard I feel a contact with Thomas Sugrue.

THE IMMORTAL TRUTH

A NEW UNDERSTANDING

It is possible, but not very probable, to write about the Immortal Truth without mentioning the great Edgar Cayce.

Edgar Cayce achieved local fame in the 1920s and 30s due to his miraculous medical cures. His name attained national recognition in the 1940s after publication of his biography, *There Is A River*, by Thomas Sugrue, a book sure to nourish the hearts and minds of spiritual seekers for centuries to come.

It was inevitable that Cayce's fame would increase, and in the 1960s his name entered the international hall of fame with Jess Stearn's popular book, *Edgar Cayce: The Sleeping Prophet*. He is justifiably regarded as America's greatest psychic and the father of modern holistic medicine.

Edgar Cayce's ability was of biblical proportions. He is now a legend in the New Age community and his fame will continue into the centuries. Cayce entered into the trance state, but he was not a spiritualist. He did not use trumpets or other paraphernalia associated with spiritualist mediums. His was a case of pure, unadulterated, self-induced trance wherein he would enter into an altered state of consciousness for anyone to witness. There were no gimmicks. His gift was capable of changing the world—but although his name is occasionally mentioned on television and books are still published on his spectacular work, he is presently unknown to a large portion of more recent generations.

So – who was Edgar Cayce? He was a deeply religious gentleman from Kentucky who was raised as a Southern Presbyterian, a self-taught biblical scholar who read the Bible once a year for every year of his life; a man gifted with extraordinary clairvoyant ability who became the originator of modern day Life Readings. While in a hypnotic trance Cayce's consciousness could see into the human body and accurately diagnose the causes and cures of physical ailments. He was responsible for healing the hopelessly sick many, many times. His clairvoyance gave new meaning to the term "the power of the mind."

Cayce's psychic diagnoses were called "physical readings." But his clairvoyance went beyond physical readings. He was able to raise his consciousness above the realm of time and space and see into the timelessness of the past to former life times on Earth; he could assess karmic causes and vocational abilities for an individual's present Earth life. These readings were termed Life Readings to differ from readings of medical diagnoses. *There Is A River* and Gina Cerminara's *Many Mansions* provide in-depth testimony to the inspirational results of Cayce's work. Edgar Cayce died January 3, 1945, at the age of sixty-seven, but, fortunately, Life Readings did not die with him.

It takes more than a lot of prayer, meditation, and devotion to spiritual ideals to be able to expand one's consciousness beyond the realm of the physical state. It takes a lifetime of devotion. While Edgar Cayce's lifetime was drawing to a close, other individuals were expanding their understanding of spiritual reality.

Dr. Franklin Loehr, a Congregational minister and son of a Presbyterian minister, served as chaplain in a heavy bomber group in the Air Corps of the U.S. Army during World War II. Dr. Loehr's religious prejudices were inherited and strictly orthodox; he considered all mediums to be fakes and weirdos. True, at every funeral service he conducted he assured everybody present that their loved ones 'live after death,' and that they were all 'immortal souls,' but he never got specific, nor offered proof. During burial services for young servicemen he relied upon the same Biblical phrases that had been used since the dawn of Christianity. The Bible was his authority for revealing to the world that human beings were, in truth, spiritual beings, heirs to a kingdom of everlasting life:

"And I give unto them eternal life; and they shall never perish, neither shall any man pluck them out of my hand."

"For the wages of sin is death; but the gift of God is eternal life through Jesus Christ our Lord."

"Verily, verily, I say unto you; he that believeth on me hath everlasting life."

For a man whose mind was as scientific as it was spiritual, promises of life in the hereafter eventually wore thin when faced time after time with the end of a young man's life in the here and now. Anguish deepened within him every time he looked down upon the many flag-draped coffins of young men killed in action—men whom he eulogized, repeating the oft-used phrase, "Ashes to ashes; dust to dust."

Men who had been vibrant and alive now lay lifeless and still. Serious questions about the deaths of those young men began to form in his mind. What happens at death, he wondered? Does consciousness die? If there is life after death, as promised in the Bible, why can't it be proven? If a human being is immortal, can his mind remember his immortality? If life exists after death, then life must surely exist before birth. Can immortality be proven in a laboratory?

As a student of Divinity young Franklin received his education from books and in classrooms. The war provided a different method of education in the brutal classroom of reality. Death stared him in the face almost daily. Death was a fact, the understanding of which he was required to accept on faith. But Franklin Loehr had a dual nature. He was inspired by religion and he was inspired by science. He chose religion as his vocation, but his scientific need for facts awakened within him a definite mission: to seek proof of the Biblical promise of old - the existence of life after death.

When the war ended, Reverend Loehr became a minister in a parish in Northampton, Massachusetts. Memories of the war remained in the forefront of his mind, and in 1948 he and a small group of like-minded ministers formed the Hadley workshop, an independent study group under no constraint of organized religion, to research as scientifically as possible the teachings in the Bible they had preached all during the war: life after death and the effectiveness of prayer. A soldier could pray for his safe return and still is killed in action. Catholics prayed over water and the water became holy. Christ cursed the fig tree and it died. What, he wondered, was the dichotomy behind prayer? How does prayer work?

The Hadley workshop freely investigated such interesting subjects as group dynamics, Dianetics, even spiritualism. To do this they had to start with a new state of mind, an open mind. Prejudices had to be abandoned.

One Sunday afternoon a member of the Hadley workshop heard a fine Boston medium, the late Mrs. Ruth Mathias, and invited her to the next group meeting. Two of the Hadley members had been chaplains – a fact unknown to Mrs. Mathias – and in trance she brought through men from their commands that had been lost in combat - men whom they had eulogized.

"His boys" from the Air Corps, as well as other dead people, came back to Dr. Loehr. They spoke to him and in dozens of ways proved to him not only that we live after death but that there are ways of sending messages back to us from the otherside. It had been a startling research session and had produced facts. Dr. Loehr learned what had happened to a plane that had been lost off Montauk Point on Good Friday, 1944. A midair explosion had taken place, throwing the plane into a wild spin from which no one could escape.

He had found the evidence he had been seeking, proof of the Bible's most profound promise: life after death does exist.

Dr. Loehr worked with Mrs. Mathias personally and extensively. In addition, Ralph Harlow, a professor for fifty years at famed Smith College in Northampton—and a long time psychic researcher with the American Society for Psychical Research—became his mentor.

While writing his sermons, Dr. Loehr developed "inspiration writing." In September of 1948 he started a series of twenty-six sermons, which came through on the Tuesday morning before the Sunday service. His pen raced across the paper. The church attendance, which had climbed steadily for the three years of his preaching, now went off the charts. He used many of those sermons again in the great cathedral in Los Angeles.

The next step on Dr. Loehr's investigative agenda was ready to be taken.

In 1949 Dr. Loehr moved to Los Angeles and formed The Religious Research Foundation of America, Inc. Their major project was to investigate the power of prayer. He had learned through his research with the Hadley workshop that life after death does exist. Now, as an agent of the Lord, he wanted scientific evidence that "ask and ye shall receive" was not just talk but was a fact.

Tangible objects had to be used to receive prayer in which results could immediately be measured. Jesus used a grain of mustard seed in a parable; seeds and plants were a logical choice. A laboratory was set up. For three years, 156 church members prayed to plants: first to the seeds prior to planting, then to the soil, then to the water. An equal amount of plants were planted with no prayer given to them.

Dr. Glenn Clark of Camps Farthest Out and Dr. J.B. Rhine of Duke University directed their own prayer research with plants in the early 1950s, but Religious Research did the most definitive work in the field with some nine hundred experiments, twenty-seven thousand seeds and seedlings, and more than eighty thousand measurements. A double planting of seeds had been made, with one planting getting prayer and the other seed being denied prayer.

The results were startling. Statistics showed that prayer can make a difference; but they also learned some fundamental facts about prayer. They discovered at least four kinds of power exist in prayer: mental, emotional, psychical, and spiritual.

They also learned something about how to use each power.

Mental power (clear visualization) and emotional power (strong feeling) in prayer comes from within the person doing the praying, while psychical power (help from saints or departed loved ones) and spiritual power (God) comes from outside of the person doing the praying.....but comes through that person.

It was learned that the greatest prayer was not to supplicate, not to ask for a specific request, but to allow God to express His will through you, as in the Lord's Prayer, *Thy will be done!* To pray to be a channel for God's will is the supreme prayer. We do not use the spiritual power in prayer; the spiritual power uses us.

Prayer, it was determined, is not the best tool for every purpose. To oversell prayer is to lead to later disillusionment with prayer. God gave us intelligence and talent—and He expects us to use them. It might be said that intelligence and talent are God's will to us and for us, and to use them is another form of prayer. We also pray by "doing." Prayer should not be used for purposes contrary to God's plan. The profitable use of prayer is to supplement the forces of nature, not to supplant them, wrote Dr. Loehr.

After three years of researching the power of prayer on plants, Dr. Loehr concluded:

Prayer is a powerful tool given by God to man, but it is not the only tool he gives us. We need to learn more about prayer and develop ever greater skill and power in using it all the days of our lives. And, also, we need to discover and develop the other tools he gives us: knowledge, faith, skill, humility, discrimination, determination, courage, indwelling and outgoing love, etc., etc., etc. Man is to know not only how to use prayer, but also what to use instead of prayer, and when and how.

The late Aldous Huxley, social researcher and author of *Brave New World,* one of the most popular science-fiction books of all time, and Maria, his wife, were early supporters of Dr. Loehr's prayer/plant research. They brought the project to the attention of Doubleday, who published the research and its results in 1959 as *The Power of Prayer on Plants.* Reviews of the book appeared in Time and other major magazines.

Twenty-five years later the British Broadcasting Company sent a team to film Dr. Loehr in a special sealed prayer/plant experiment they set up to duplicate his research. The project was the closing segment of the NOVA program *The Green Machine*, which has aired on American PBS stations at least four times.

Dr. Loehr had come a long way since his days as a young chaplain in the U.S. Army Air Corps, when he hoped to one day prove that his Christian faith could be supported by scientific facts. He had proven to his satisfaction that human life did continue after death, that positive prayer had a positive effect, that negative prayer had a negative effect and that these effects could be measured. A prayer researcher lost her patience toward a plant that wasn't doing well and cursed it, calling it a communist. The plant died.

Unbeknownst to Dr. Loehr, the next step in his search for facts to support his faith was about to appear.

In 1951 a member of the Hadley workshop, Reverend Paul Mc-Clurkin, PhD. visited Los Angeles and informed Dr. Loehr about his independent discovery of past life recall and regression therapy. He was truly one of the earliest pioneers in the field. As a result of this visit, Dr. Loehr underwent six months of intensive recall sessions in which he recalled several dozen of his past lives and found the answers—the missing links—to his present life. He had tapped into his immortal self.

But the best was yet to come.

Dr. Loehr's college degree was in science, earned at the justly famous chemistry department of Monmouth College, Illinois. While there he worked briefly on some chemical research for Dow Chemical Company before going on to McCormack Presbyterian Seminary in Chicago.

During his four years of college and three years at seminary the subject of reincarnation never once came up. He didn't know the difference between reincarnation and transmigration.

Reincarnation is the simple discovery that we, as souls, take more than one Earth life to learn what this Earth has to teach us but always as human beings. Transmigration is the much looser theory that the soul 'migrates' across the various life streams (you may be a human this time, a cow the next time, a tree the time after that.).

While working as an administrative assistant to Dr. James Fifield of the First Congregational Church of Los Angeles in 1951, Dr. Loehr counseled Mrs. Grace Wittenberger about her inability to conceive due to the closure of her fallopian tubes.

Dr. Loehr had taken all the psychological and pastoral psychiatry training available while in seminary at the army Chaplain School at Harvard, and later at the special Army Air Corp Chaplain School in San Antonio. His ministry in several pastorates, as well as his chaplaincy, developed his confidence to handle problems like Mrs. Wittenberger's.

She and her husband had been married for more than two years. Both wanted children, but none came. Various medical treatments had proved useless. Knowing that her condition could be psychosomatic—tensions in the mind sealing the tubes—her gynecologist sent her to a psychologist. Nothing was found in the present life and personality of this healthy, normal American girl that would produce this effect.

Dr. Loehr called in a psychiatrist for assurance - who only corroborated the findings of the psychologist.

By September of 1951, Dr. Loehr knew something he had not known before: that in our subconscious minds we carry the memories of our past lives; and these past lives often have tremendous effect upon our present lives.

Realizing he could do for Mrs. Wittenberger what Dr. McClurkin had done for him—but not realizing Mrs. Wittenberger didn't know anything about reincarnation—Dr. Loehr blurted out, "It still could be psychosomatic, but with the cause in a previous life."

He knew his recall of a dozen or more of his own past lives had allowed him to become more enlightened. He didn't suppose there was one chance in a hundred, one in a thousand, that she would accept his proposal.

"That's all right," replied Mrs. Wittenberger, whose maternal instinct was strong, "If there is any chance at all."

Late in the month of September she recalled a former life that held the key to her sterility. Four or five months of intensive, hard psychotherapy continued. The diagnosis proved true. The work was accomplished and her healing came.

In December 1952 her first child was born; and the second summer after that - as if to underscore the reality of her healing - a second child was born.

Dr. Loehr was far too engrossed in the tasks of his great church to give any thought to finding and developing a medium, but something about the deep, relaxed reverie into which Mrs. Wittenberger entered reminded him, during her fifth session, of how Mrs. Mathias had looked while in a trance. After the session ended, curiosity prodded Dr. Loehr to ask - what turned out to be a fateful question - "Are you a medium?"

"A medium? What is that?" Mrs. Wittenberger asked.

Dr. Loehr explained that as a telephone is a medium for carrying vocal communication, so a psychic, or sensitive, or medium, is simply a person through whom persons in the discarnate realm (dead, no physical body) can make contact with persons in the incarnate realm (in the body). During man's long centuries of ignorance he has been inclined either to worship these mediums as prophets, saints, and seeresses, or to condemn them as warlocks and witches. In reality their special quality is that they have developed the faculty of seeing, hearing, or perceiving in some other way a dimension of life that is beyond our physical senses.

Mrs. Wittenberger didn't even know what a trance was.

Dr. Loehr patiently explained that whereas our usual state of consciousness keeps our ego-mind always in the forefront, there are those who can put aside their own personality-consciousness and let other consciousnesses, other intelligences, make contact through them. Dr. Loehr then asked Mrs. Wittenberger if he could try dropping her into a trance. She had sufficient confidence and agreed. Mrs. Wittenberger dropped not only into the reverie state but further into the subconscious as well. Dr. Loehr asked if there was another entity present who wished to speak. The guardian of Mrs. Wittenberger, who chose to be known as Dr. John Christopher Daniels, spoke through her. This first contact with Dr. John was the beginning of Mrs. Wittenberger's mediumship. Her psychic ability had been developed in previous life-times, under other teachers. Dr. Loehr was her discoverer much more than her developer.

Mrs. Wittenberger came with singular qualifications: she had God's plan working for her; she was brought up in a ministerial home; she spent ten years with Glenn Clark in this life, and had the benefit of her previous psychic lives in Egypt, India, and Greece; and she had experience as an American Indian life, which she recalled herself through a past-life recall session.

Despite all this, she was still far from being a life-reading medium.

Dr. Loehr worked with Mrs. Wittenberger for four years and four months before any public announcement was made of the Life Readings. Their early work was of a general exploratory nature. Her own reverie program took precedence over the psychic exploration. It was in the exploring, cleansing, and aligning of the subconscious areas that her personalities became integrated and the channel cleared for psychical and mystical super-conscious work. In between Mrs. Wittenberger's past life recall sessions and the long hours of integrating them into her present life, teaching sessions were sandwiched with Dr. John, who had come to be regarded as a fellow member of their team – and a personal companion and friend.

While a staff member of the First Congregation Church of Los Angeles, Dr. Loehr was often called for funerals at Forest Lawn, Utter-McKinley, Pierce Brothers, or any of the city's mortuaries. He had been accustomed to parishes of his own where he knew the people he buried; but all too often the only contact he could make with the family was "Phone the widow after eleven tonight," or "Come ten minutes before the funeral and meet the family."

When such requests came in, Dr. Loehr took to calling Mrs. Wittenberger. He would stop at her home; she would get into the car and he would say, "Get quiet and tell me what you feel about so and so."

Then he would give her the deceased's name and date of birth, along with any other information he had been given about the person whom he was to bury. Mrs. Wittenberger would quiet herself into a state of consciousness where Dr. John could reach her, and then she would say, "I feel this . . . I feel that . . ."

She often told things about surviving family members as well as the deceased, and the material always 'fit.' Of course the information she gave could not be shared with the family within the framework of reincarnation. There are more orthodox ways of saying things, and by using acceptable modes of expression Dr. Loehr was able to incorporate into the services the material that had come through Mrs. Wittenberger. The prayers now included a personal emphasis and a spiritual effectiveness, thanks to insights gleaned from seeing the background of past lives and the place of the present life in the ongoing pattern.

After a funeral for someone whom he had never heard of until, perhaps, the afternoon before, members of the family would say, "I don't know how you did it, but you said exactly the right thing."

Friends would say, "You must have known him for years; you described so accurately what he felt and did and was."

Dr. Loehr once made the mistake of saying to such a friend, "No, I never met the man."

After seeing the friend's startled reaction he learned never to say that again!

The giving of Life Readings began in October 1951. In August of 1952 the book *Many Mansions* by Gina Cerminara introduced Dr. Loehr to the Life Readings of Edgar Cayce.

After four years and four months of researching and testing the validity of Dr. John's Life Readings, a modest announcement was made in the monthly report of *The Religious Research Journal* in 1956.

In general those asking for a Life Reading were divided into two classes: those seeking self-understanding, and those with definite, difficult problems. The second group was the larger: a difficult or handicapped child, marital frictions beyond the usual, a long – perhaps lifetime – run of seemingly bad luck, emotional relationships that baffled and perplexed.

Every imaginable sort of human situation – and a lot they had never imagined – came up in the readings. Dr. Loehr used to read "whodunits," murder-mystery stories, for general relaxation, but he began to find them dull. The real life stories of those who came for readings were so much stronger, more suspenseful and real!

One middle-aged couple had a particular problem with their high-strung, slightly deaf teenage son. They were told in their life-reading that the son had been a passenger on the ill-fated Hindenburg zeppelin and had lost his life when it caught fire and crashed.

Normally such a person would have been kept on the other side long enough for the keenest edges of the traumatic experience to be dulled, but their son insisted on coming back very quickly because he wanted to be in on the early age of flying.

After the reading the parents phoned Dr. Loehr to say they had just remembered how the boy had loved the little planes his father would bring him but had gone into a crying spell of great fright when he had been brought a toy zeppelin.

Many marriages were held together by the Life Readings. Those marriages were not simply patched up but the underlying causes of the friction were ultimately revealed and reasons for maintaining the marriage given, as well as suggestions on how to handle difficulties. Occasionally it was suggested that a marriage on the rocks be terminated. This occurred when there was no hope of the two personalities reestablishing a good relationship, the constructive stage of the marriage was past and there was no productive reason for continuing, or because that particular marriage should never have been entered into. Although physical-readings were not given, physical health questions were often asked; if there was a cause in a past life for the present physical condition, it was traced back and suggestions made for resolving it.

Psychological situations which society calls abnormal: transvestism, hermitism, unusual interest in some particular place or problem, homosexuality and so on, were often found to have a perfectly normal cause in a past life or in the purposeful experience scheduled for a soul in this particular lifetime.

The Readings showed that each of us must incarnate many times in both masculine and feminine lives; until an individual understands and accepts this reality, and gains experience by doing it a number of times, the transition lives may be difficult. For example, a masculine soul coming into a feminine life might become frightened as puberty approached and with it the most intimate details of a woman's life and love. This woman might turn to overeating to assuage this anxiety and to produce an obesity that will make her unattractive to men.

A feminine soul, coming into an early masculine experience, might put on all the swagger of a leather-coated, wild-riding motorcyclist, a surface show of supposed ultra masculinity designed to hide the femininity underneath.

Dr. Loehr considered the homosexual and transvestite groups organized during the 1970s to have much reincarnational carry-over.

Much of the tension that marked the 1960s counter-culture, according to the Readings, was carry-over from the frightening conditions under which many met their deaths in World War II.

Others who received Life Readings did so out of their deep quest for self-understanding. Who am I? Why was I born to my particular parents? Why did I have these brothers and sisters, or no brothers or sisters? Why this marriage, or these marriages, or no marriage? Why these children, or no children? Why these life situations? Why my interests, my problems, my life pathway, and why my particular personality traits, abilities, difficulties? Who am I and why? The seekers posed these questions and their seeking was rewarded with knowledge and spiritual growth. I know. I was one of those seekers.

In one reading a man with a high I.Q. was so obsessed with the need to be right and in control that he simply could not understand why he had lost friends and alienated people all throughout his life. His Life Reading said his soul had incarnated in the pre-Civil War American South and had become a capable and strong-minded woman. This man had been the mistress of a large plantation with many slaves who, of course, had to obey her without question. The men folk around were almost equally vulnerable to her control due to their code of chivalry. Although slavery was abolished more than a century ago, the old pattern of conduct held over within the subconscious of the new person to the point where certain paranoid traits began to show. The new personality had not made the transition from living under that former set of circumstances – which she thoroughly enjoyed – to another set of circumstances where the old ways didn't work. The personality would probably never learn in this lifetime; and it won't be until the personality, after death, assesses the failures of this life that the learning will come.

A daughter who thought she didn't want college - and whom her family thought was not college material - was advised to go to college; reasons were given and a particular line of study and life's work was suggested. The suggested subject caught her interest and even though she was in her final year of high school she applied to three colleges for admission. She was accepted by her first choice, enrolled in the suggested line of study and changed her entire life.

The Life Readings have not gone along with the idea that we have thousands or millions of Earth lives, nor that there is some arbitrary period of time, such as a thousand years, between them. If we don't learn what Earth has to teach us in a hundred lifetimes, we're simply not going to learn it here! Moreover, our lifetimes are fitted in as the proper settings of domestic, social, scientific, and historical developments come about.

Not everything is cut and dried. Many lifetimes find a person quite free to make a lot of choices; these choices then establish the karma for future lifetimes. Karma is simply the natural consequence of our choices, the reactions that follow our actions. It may be good as well as bad. The central requirement is growth, not punishment. Free will is not only present, it is decisive. It is not what happens to us that counts but how we react to what happens to us. This reaction sets our development and also reveals how far we have come.

Not everyone who received a Life Reading was happy with the result. Religious Research's first assistant, Dorothy Hillman, had a talented young friend who had hoped to make his living as an artist, but no one ever bought his paintings. He was also an electronics wizard, having made his own color organ (an instrument that converts sound waves into electrical current). It was asked in his Reading why he couldn't sell his paintings.

"Ego," was the answer.

The young man was so infuriated with the answer he tried to get

Hugh Lynn Cayce (son of Edgar Cayce) to publicly condemn the Life Readings of Religious Research, which was not done of course. The young man's reaction was evidence that the answer was correct. His response was that of an egotist.

Gina Cerminara, researcher of the Edgar Cayce Life Readings and author of *Many Mansions,* and *Many Mansions-II*, was one of the earliest recipients of a Life Reading from Dr. John. Evidently Miss Cerminara did not feel her past incarnations reflected favorably upon a researcher of reincarnation for she requested her reading be removed from the files. It is my strong suspicion that Miss Cerminara was black in her past incarnation, which, because of ignorance and prejudice, she might have felt it prudent to keep secret. She always denied knowing of her past lives. Dorothy Hillman was a friend of Miss Cerminara's and read her Life Reading. Dorothy refused to divulge any of the contents of Miss Cerminara's past lives because, Dorothy said, "She's Gina."

Dr. Loehr considered it an honor to have given readings for members of the Cayce family. He also gave a reading for a woman who had received a Life Reading from Edgar Cayce. The past lives and the karma of this woman were the same as read by both men. The woman was told she had leukemia due to a lifetime in ancient Rome when she had witnessed Christians being torn apart by lions in the arena; and because she laughed at the shedding of blood, her blood was being shed in this lifetime in the form of cancer of the blood. This is one of the many splendid examples of karma presented by Miss Cerminara in *Many Mansions* that left a lasting impression on me.

The Readings often involved specific questions. For instance: Will California be destroyed in 1958 or 1961 or 1964?

Dr. John's answer was, "We still consider Los Angeles real estate a good investment."

Another question often asked was: "How may I prepare for a favorable reincarnation?"

"To live this lifetime well," was the response.

The question: "What is my major purpose in this incarnation?" was always asked.

The person who was truly concerned with doing the best job he or she could in this life, finding their purpose, discovering their abilities, achieving the learning, fulfilling the relationships, performing the service for their incarnation – that person was welcomed, honored, and assisted by the information brought in the Life Readings.

"This present lifetime," wrote Dr. Loehr, "has an important place in the ongoing of our soul, the spiritual evolution of our individuality. In general, the best way to prepare for a favorable incarnation is to find, and do, and be, that which we are to do and be and become, in this lifetime, so that our spiritual development can then move to its next chapter and not have to do this chapter, or parts of it, over again."

Dr. Loehr came to realize that the Life Readings of Dr. John had changed more lives for more good than he himself had reached and changed in all his years as a parish minister and chaplain.

"The picture of human life presented by the readings," wrote Dr. Loehr, "made absolute sense, held high challenge and fulfillment, made no impossible demands but a more insistent general demand for goodness and growth, and showed man most clearly in the relationship that religion has preached, as a spiritual being, verily akin unto the Creator, a child of God, growing into a greater fullness of godliness as we increasingly learn about experiences, life, and ourselves."

The meeting of Mrs. Wittenberger and Dr. Loehr may have been the result of a young lady seeking counsel, or it might have been the result of Divine guidance, as indicated in the following poem Mrs. Wittenberger wrote eleven years before she met Dr. Loehr and Dr. John:

RECOLLECTION

Sometimes in quiet places
I often think that I
Might rub a thin spot in the air
And watch the past come by.

I might see knights and ladies
In a now centuried home
As they are often pictured

In ancient lay and tome;

I might watch kings and presidents
Decide affairs of state
In vaulted halls of government,
On some historic date;

Or – I might stand in a stable
Among the oxen mild
And see a Mary-mother
And her new born child.

Grace Wittenberger –

SAINTS AND MYSTICS

Edgar Cayce was the most famous psychic-mystic, or clairvoyant, of the twentieth century. Many people consider Edgar Cayce to be the greatest psychic of our age. There is a spot in time that belongs exclusively to Edgar Cayce; but Cayce was not the first person to possess clairvoyant medical and Life Reading ability - and he will not be the last.

In 1784 the Marquis de Puysegur discovered a shepherd boy named Victor, who, while in a hypnotic trance, diagnosed illness in the manner of Edgar Cayce. A hundred years later, in the 1840s, a young man with limited education, by the name of Andrew Jackson Davis, became clairvoyant when hypnotized and became known as the Poughkeepsie Seer and Clairvoyant. He wrote of his readings in a massive book *"The Principles of Nature, Her Divine Revelations, and A Voice To Mankind."* Psychic ability goes back to the beginning of human life on Earth. It reveals itself at different times and in various ways. There is not a civilization in history that did not possess individuals with psychic power, or psychic ability. The mind, itself, is a psychic instrument.

It is difficult to go against the "establishment," especially the religious establishment; and Edgar Cayce had the misfortune of being pitted against both the religious establishment and the medical establishment, just as Jesus was pitted against the religious establishment and the medical establishments in his time – and we know what happened to Jesus.

Edgar Cayce paved the way for revealing the Immortal Truth in the twentieth century by his amazing medical diagnoses for hopelessly sick individuals. Edgar Cayce had used the scientific method to prove that his Life Readings were correct. Jesus had used the scientific method to prove his mission was blessed of God when he healed the sick, cast out devils, cleansed lepers, allowed the blind to see, and he even raised the dead.

In earlier times individuals with psychic powers were hanged or burned alive at the stake. Individuals with psychic power in the mid-dle-ages, a time known as the Dark Ages, were burned alive; hang-ings, and being crushed to death, continued in Salem, Massachusetts, by the fearful religious and political controllers in society, otherwise known as "the establishment." More women were burned alive at the stake in the middle-ages than men. In order to maintain their control over the populace, the Church controllers expanded their burning tactics from being burned alive at the stake to being burned alive in ovens. Women and two- and three-year old children were thrown into ovens to be consumed by fire. Hundreds and thousands a week were put to death in that horrible manner. Thus, in the twentieth century, those same Christian controllers returned to Earth to receive the same treatment they had inflicted upon Christians in the middle-ages, and ended up in SS concentration camps to be burned in ovens, to be cleansed of their evil, evil they had committed against innocent Christians - in the darkest of ages. .

In France death threats of being burned alive were directed to-ward Bernadette Soubirous after she told of her visions of the Blessed Virgin Mary in the grotto at Lourdes. Death threats of being burned alive were viciously directed to a brother and his two sisters - who saw a vision of the Virgin Mary at Fatima, Portugal.

Dr. Franklin Loehr used the method of science when he used prayer on plants to prove that a spiritual contact exists between na-ture and the human being – thus paving the way for the acceptance of Life Readings channeled by counselor-guide Dr. John Christo-pher Daniels through Reverend Grace Wittenberger, and later by Dr. Loehr, himself. Thirty years of Life Readings under the auspices of The Religious Research Foundation of America, Inc., added to the accuracy of the Immortal Truth revealed in the Akashic Records of the Life Readings.

It is a gift from our Creator that a cosmic contact exists within the consciousness of human-beings. Religions have known of this fact and they have done their best to control the revelations within this power, so that they, themselves, can be the determining factor. Saints and mystics of old had the ability to read the Immortal Truth in the Akashic Records but they were not allowed to reveal what had been cosmically revealed to them in their visions without the approval and censorship of their church hierarchy. The visions of Venerable Anne Catherine Emmerich, from the book *The Dolorous Passion of Our Lord Jesus Christ* is an exception to this rule.

Anne Catherine Emmerich was born on September 8, 1774, at Flamske, near Koesfeld, Westphalia, Germany, and on November 13, 1803, she became a nun of the Augustinian Order at the Convent of Agnetenberg. She died on February 9, 1824. She was told in mystic vision that her gift of seeing past, present, and future was greater than that possessed by anyone else in history. From the year 1812 until her death she bore the stigmata of Jesus, including a cross over her heart and wounds from the crown of thorns.

During the years 1821 and 1822, Ann's visions became more and more concentrated on the life of Jesus and the holy persons about him. The records of these visions, which still exist in their original form, were made by the late Clements Brentano with almost documentary precision. He extracted from them everything relating to the Life of Christ, and was thus able to present to the reader the public life of Jesus, day by day, according to Catherine Emmerich's vision. The last portion of these records has been printed under the title of *The Dolorous Passion of Our Lord* - a book that inspired Mel Gibson to film *The Passion of the Christ*. (Dolorous, pertaining to grief, pain, sorrow.)

Ann Catherine's visions did not always coincide with scripture. For instance, she saw the real historical date of the birth of Christ a whole month earlier, on November 25th.

During the Incarnation of Christ, or the birth of Jesus, the Virgin Mary was a little over fourteen years old, according to the vision of Ann Catherine. It is my understanding that "visions" is the lifting up of consciousness from within to allow for the reading of the Akashic Records, or the Immortal Truth.

Akashic Records, according to Cayce, are events written upon the skein of time and space. Everything we have ever done, thought, or said is written upon the skein of time and space. This record becomes our Immortal Truth, referred to in the Bible as the Book of Judgment, or the Book of God's Remembrance. We read this record after we die.

During Ann Catherine's visions she could read these records, only the records are referred to by the Catholic Faith as "visions of ecstasy." Ann Catherine saw the life of the Blessed Virgin Mary in her ecstatic visions.

Christianity teaches that Jesus was conceived without sin. Being conceived without sin can be interpreted to mean human conception is sinful. I don't believe human conception is sinful or that it is the reason for the virgin birth. I believe the virgin birth had a higher purpose. I believe the purpose of the Immaculate Conception was to inform the world that the birth of Jesus was a very special event, blessed by God, Himself, as evidence that Jesus, the Christ, is "The Way," or "The Right Way" to follow, which puts Jesus at the "top of the list" of human beings, one might say. Cayce said the Immaculate Conception was "a projection of mind into matter." No one apparently asked Cayce just how the projection of mind into matter worked.

According to the visions of Anne Catherine Emmerich Jesus was not the only member of the Holy Family to have an Immaculate Conception. The Virgin Mary, the mother of Jesus, was also conceived immaculately. On page 73 Catherine Emmerich stated:

"I had a vision of Mary's most holy soul and of its being united to the most pure body. In the glory by which the Most Holy Trinity is usually represented in my visions I saw a movement like a great shining mountain, and yet also like a human figure; and I saw something rise out of the midst of this figure towards its mouth and go forth from it like a shining brightness. Then I saw the brightness standing separate before the Face of God, turning and shaping itself—or rather being shaped--for I saw that while this brightness took human form, yet it was by the Will of God that it received a form so unspeakably beautiful. I saw, too, that God showed the beauty of this soul to the angels, and that they had unspeakable joy in its beauty."

Anne Catherine was unable to describe in words all that she saw and understood.

Anne Catherine Emmerich:

"When seventeen weeks and five days after the conception of the

Blessed Virgin had gone by (that is to say, five days before Anna's pregnancy was half accomplished), I saw Our Lady's holy mother lying asleep in her bed in her house near Nazareth. Then there came a shining light above her, and a ray from this light fell upon the middle of her side, and the light passed into her in the shape of a little shining human figure. In the same instant I saw Our Lady's holy mother raise herself on her couch surrounded by light. She was in ecstasy, and had a vision of her womb opening like a tabernacle to enclose a shining little virgin from whom man's whole salvation was to spring. I saw that this was the instant in which for the first time the child moved within her. Anna then rose from her couch, dressed herself, and announced her joy to the holy Joachim. They both thanked God, and I saw them praying under the tree in the garden where the angel had comforted Anna. It was made known to me that the Blessed Virgin's soul was united to her body five days earlier than with other children, and that her birth was twelve days earlier."

Page 77:

"In the moment when the new-born child lay in the arms of her holy mother Anna, I saw that at the same time the child was presented in heaven in the sight of the Most Holy Trinity, and greeted with unspeakable joy by all the heavenly hosts. Then I understood that there was made known to her in a supernatural manner her whole future with all her joys and sorrows. Mary was taught infinite mysteries, and yet was and remained a child. This knowledge of her we cannot understand, because our knowledge grows on the tree of good and evil. She knew everything in the same way as a child knows its mother's breast and that it is to drink from it. As the vision faded in which I saw the child Mary being thus taught in heaven through grace, I heard her weep for the first time."

Ann Catherine Emmerich continues: (page 158)

"In order to state as clearly as I can how the approach of the Incarnation, and with it the approach of the most Holy Sacrament of the Altar, was explained to me, I can only repeat how everything was set before my eyes in a great series of pictures; although it is impossible, owning to my present condition and to many interruptions from without, to bring what I saw into a detailed and comprehensible whole. I can only say in general: First I saw the Blessing of the Promise which God gave to the First Man in Paradise, and from that Blessing I saw a ray of light proceed to the Blessed Virgin as she stood there opposite St. Elisabeth, reciting the *Magnificat* in prayer. Then I saw Abraham, who had received this blessing from God, and I again saw a ray of light proceeding from him to the Blessed Virgin. Then came the other Patriarchs who were the holders and bearers of that holy treasure, and from each of them a ray of light fell upon Mary. Then I saw the passage of this Blessing down the ages until it reached Joachim. He was endowed with the highest Blessing from the inmost sanctuary of the Temple so that he might become the father of the most holy Virgin Mary conceived without original sin. In her the Word became Flesh by the operation of the Holy Ghost and dwelt amongst us hidden for nine months in her, as the Ark of the Covenant of the New Testament, until in the fullness of time we saw His glory, born of the Virgin Mary, a glory as it were of the only begotten of the Father, full of grace and truth."

There were times when I unexpectedly found *The Life of the Blessed Virgin Mary--From the Visions of Venerable Anne Catherine Emmerich*--to be a tedious read, and I am disappointed considering the book is from visions of the Akashic Records, or the Immortal Truth. The book seems overly expressed with Catholic terminology that heavily colors the revelations, i.e. the Most Holy this and the Blessed that. But neither Edgar Cayce of The Association of Spiritual Enlightenment, or spirit counselor-guide Dr. John Christopher Daniels of the Religious Research Foundation ever gave a more inspirational description of the birth of Jesus, the Christ. On page 193 of *The Life of the Blessed Virgin Mary*, Ann Catherine Emmerich describes the scene of the birth of Jesus as revealed in her ecstatic vision of the Akashic Records:

"I saw the radiance round the Blessed Virgin ever growing greater. The light of the lamps which Joseph had lit was no longer visible.

Our Lady knelt on her rug in an ample ungirt robe spread out round her, her face turned toward the east. At midnight she was wrapped in an ecstasy of prayer. I saw her lifted from the earth, so that I saw the ground beneath her. Her hands were crossed on her breast. The radiance about her increased; everything, even things without life, were in a joyful inner motion, the stones of the roof, of the walls, and of the floor of the cave became as it were alive in the light. Then I no longer saw the roof of the cave; a pathway of light opened above Mary, rising with ever-increasing glory towards the height of heaven. In this pathway of light there was a wonderful movement of glories interpenetrating each other, and, as they approached, appearing more clearly in the form of choirs of heavenly spirits. Meanwhile the Blessed Virgin, borne up in ecstasy, was now gazing downwards, adoring her God, whose Mother she had become and who lay on the earth before her in the form of a helpless new-born child. I saw our Redeemer as a tiny child, shining with a light that overpowered all the surrounding radiance, and lying on the carpet at the Blessed Virgin's knees. It seemed to me as if He were at first quite small and then grew before my eyes. But the movement of the intense radiance was such that I cannot say for certain how I saw it.

"The Blessed Virgin remained for some time rapt in ecstasy. I saw her laying a cloth over the Child, but at first she did not touch Him or take Him up. After some time I saw the Child Jesus move and heard Him cry. Then Mary seemed to come to herself, and she took the Child up from the carpet, wrapping Him in the cloth which covered Him, and held Him in her arms to her breast. She sat there enveloping herself and the Child completely in her veil, and I think Mary suckled the Redeemer. I saw angels round her in human forms, lying on their faces and adoring the Child. It might have been an hour after His birth when Mary called St. Joseph, who was still lying in prayer. When he came near, he threw himself down on his face in devout joy and humility. It was only when Mary begged him to take to his heart, in joy and thankfulness, the holy present of the Most High God that he stood up, took the Child Jesus in his arms, and praised God with tears of joy.

"The Blessed Virgin then wrapped the Child Jesus in swaddling-bands. I cannot now remember how these bands were wound round;

I only know that the Child was wrapped to His armpits first in red and then white bands, and that His head and shoulders were wrapped in another little cloth. Mary had only four sets of swaddling bands with her. Then I saw Mary and Joseph sitting side by side on the bare earth with their feet under them. They did not speak, and seemed both to be sunk in meditation. On the carpet before Mary lay the new-born Jesus in swaddling-clothes, a little child, beautiful and radiant as lightning. Ah, I thought, this place enshrines the salvation of the whole world, and no one guesses it. Then they had the Child in the manger, which was filled with rushes and delicate plants and covered with a cloth hanging over the sides. It stood above the stone trough lying on the ground, to the right of the entrance, where the cave makes a big curve towards the south. This part of the cave was at a lower level than the place where our Lord was born: the floor slanted downwards in a step-like formation. After laying the Child in the crib, they both stood beside Him giving praise to God with tears of joy. Joseph then arranged the Blessed Virgin's resting place and her seat beside the crib. Both before and after the birth of Jesus, I saw her dressed in white and veiled. I saw her there in the first days after the Nativity, sitting, kneeling, standing, and sleeping on her side, wrapped up in no way ill, or exhausted. When people came to see her, she wrapped herself up more closely and sat upright on her lying-in coverlet."

On page 144 Ann Catherine Emmerich states:

"That night, as I contemplated the Mystery of the Incarnation, I was taught many things. Anna was given the grace of interior knowledge. The Blessed Virgin knew that she had conceived the Messiah, the Son of the Most High. All that was within her was open to the eyes of her spirit. But she did not then know that the Throne of David His father, which was to be given Him by the Lord God, was a supernatural one; nor did she then know that the House of Jacob, over which He was, as Gabriel declared, to rule for eternity, was the Church, the congregation of regenerated mankind. She thought that the Redeemer would be a holy king, who would purify His people and give them victory over Hell. She did not then

know that this King, in order to redeem mankind, must suffer a
bitter death."

It was Ann Catherine's above vision of the birth of Jesus that
made me want to read in greater detail the death and resurrection of
Jesus, as Catherine saw it in her vision. I wanted to see the spirit of Jesus ascend into Heaven after his death, then descend from Heaven to
spiritualize his lifeless body with his Christ energy, to make it whole
and take it with him.

I had seen Mel Gibson's *The Passion of the Christ*, which, while
realistic in its presentation, left me distressed. The story was too painful. It wasn't spiritual enough. I felt the motion picture was too brutal
and had over-done the flagellation of Jesus to the point of excess.
How could anyone have lived through that, I wondered? I was surprised Jesus hadn't been killed from the sadistic beatings alone.

I wanted to see in my mind, or enter into as much as was possible, the glory of Jesus' resurrection. So I read *The Dolorous Passion of
Our Lord Jesus Christ,* from the visions of Anne Catherine Emmerich,
from which this chapter is based.

To my surprise the story of Jesus, as told by Anne Catherine,
was more brutal than depicted in Mel Gibson's motion picture. How
could any human-being, I wondered, be so sadistic in their brutality
to almost beat the life force out of a person, to beat him again and
again and again?

It is not my intention to take credit where credit is not due. With
the exception of a modest amount of creative license, the following
story of Jesus' Passion is virtually word for word as described by Anne
Catherine in *The Dolorous Passion of Our Lord Jesus Christ.*

Jesus had not only been savagely beaten, he was vilified, denied
by his friends, covered with spittle and other filth which had been
thrown over him while his hands were kept tightly bound together.
His feet were swollen and torn. When one group tired of their assaults
another group took over. Jesus was stripped of all save his undergarment, which was stained and soiled by the filth which had been flung
upon it; a long chain was hanging around his neck, which struck his
knees as he walked. He tottered rather than walked, and was almost
unrecognizable from the effects of his sufferings during the night; he

was colorless, haggard, his face swollen and bleeding. He was mocked with derisive gestures by the dregs of society, whom the High Priests had gathered together to call him King, and toss in his path stones, bits of wood and filthy rags; during this pretended triumphal entry.

The executioners of Jesus were malefactors from the frontiers of Egypt, who had been condemned for their crimes to hard labor and were employed principally in making canals and in erecting public buildings, the most criminal being selected to act as executioners in the Praetorium.

The executioners had many times scourged criminals to death. They resembled wild beasts or demons, and appeared to be half drunk. They struck out at Jesus with their fists, and dragged him by the cords with which he was pinioned and, finally, they barbarously knocked him down against the pillar.

Jesus trembled and shuttered as he stood before the pillar and took off his garments as quickly as he could, but his hands were bloody and swollen. The only return he made when his executioners struck and abused him was to pray for them. Two ruffians, thirsting for blood, began in the most barbarous manner to scourge Jesus' sacred body from head to foot. Jesus writhed as a worm under the blows of those barbarians. Jesus' groans resembled a touching cry of prayer and supplication, more than moans of anguish.

The clamor of the Pharisees and the people formed another species of accompaniment, which, among deafening thunder storms, smothered Jesus' mournful cries. In their place could be heard, *'Put him to death!' 'Crucify him!'*

Several servants of the High Priests went up to the brutal executioners and gave them money; as also a large jug filled with a strong bright red liquid, which quite inebriated them, and increased their cruelty tenfold toward their innocent victim. The two ruffians continued to strike Jesus with unremitting violence for a quarter of an hour, and were then succeeded by two others. His body was entirely covered with black, blue, and red marks; the blood was trickling down on the ground, and yet the furious cries which issued from among the assembled crowd showed that their cruelty was far from being satiated.

Two executioners commenced scourging Jesus with the greatest possible fury; they made use of a different kind of rod—a species of thorny sticks, covered with knots and splinters. The blows from these sticks tore his flesh to pieces; his blood spouted out so as to stain their arms, and he groaned, prayed, and shuddered.

Two fresh executioners took over the flagging; their scourges were composed of small chains, or straps covered with iron hooks, which penetrated to the bone, and torn off large pieces of flesh at every blow.

The barbarians were not yet satisfied. They untied Jesus, and again fastened him up with his back turned towards the pillar. As he was totally unable to support himself in an upright position, they passed cords round his waist, under his arms, and above his knees, and having bound his hands tightly into the rings which were placed at the upper part of the pillar, they re commenced scourging him with even greater fury than before; and one among them struck him constantly on the face with a new rod. The body of Jesus was perfectly torn to shreds—it was but one wound. He looked at his torturers with eyes filled with blood, as if entreating mercy; but their brutality increased, and his moans became more feeble.

The scourging continued without intermission for three quarters of an hour, when a stranger of lowly birth, a relation to Ctesiphon, the blind man whom Jesus had cured, rushed from amidst the crowd, and approached the pillar with a knife shaped like a cutlass in his hand. 'Cease!' he exclaimed. 'Cease! Scourge not this innocent man unto death!'

The drunken miscreants, taken by surprise, stopped short, while the man quickly severed the cords which bound Jesus to the pillar; then he disappeared among the crowd. Jesus fell almost without consciousness on the ground, which was bathed with his blood. The executioners left him there, and rejoined their companions who were amusing themselves in the guardhouse with drinking - and plaiting the crown of thorns.

During the scourging of Jesus, Anne Catherine Emmerick saw weeping angels approach Jesus many times; she likewise heard the prayers Jesus constantly addressed to his Father for the pardon of our sins—prayers which never ceased during the whole time of the infliction of the cruel punishment. While Jesus lay bathed in his blood Ann Catherine saw an angel present to him a vase containing a bright-looking beverage which appeared to reinvigorate him to a certain degree.

The archers soon returned, and after giving Jesus blows with their sticks, bade him rise and follow them. He raised himself with the greatest difficulty, as his trembling limbs could scarcely support the weight of his body; they did not give him sufficient time to put on his clothes, but threw his upper garment over his naked shoulders and led him to the guard house where he wiped the blood, which trickled down his face, with a corner of his garment. When he passed before the benches on which the High Priests were seated, they cried out, 'Put him to death! Crucify him! Crucify him!' and then turned away disdainfully.

The executioners led him into the interior of the guard-house, which was filled with slaves, archers, hodmen, and the very dregs of the people. A gallery encircled the inner court of the guard-house where Jesus was crowned with thorns, and the doors were open.

About fifty of the rabble-rousers, the greatest part were slaves or servants of the jailers and soldiers, gathered round the building but were soon displaced by a thousand Roman soldiers. Although forbidden to leave their ranks, these soldiers nevertheless did their utmost by laughter and applause to incite the cruel executioners to redouble their insults, and increase tenfold their cruelty. Then they tore off the garments of Jesus, thereby reopening all his wounds; threw over his shoulders an old scarlet mantle which barely reached his knees, dragged him to the seat prepared, and pushed him roughly down upon it, having first placed the crown of thorns upon his head.

The crown of thorns was made of three branches plaited together; the greatest part of the thorns being purposely turned inwards so as to pierce Jesus' head; tied the twisted branches onto Jesus' forehead; then they put a large reed into his hand, doing so with derisive gravity as if they were really crowning him king. They then seized the reed and struck his head so violently his eyes were filled with blood; they knelt before him, denied him, spat in his face, and buffeted him, saying '*Hail, King of the Jews!*' Then they threw down his stool, pulled him up again from the ground on which he had fallen, and reseated him with great brutality.

Anne Catherine said it was quite impossible to describe the cruel outrages which were thought of and perpetrated by the monsters in human form. The sufferings of Jesus from thirst, caused by the fever which his wounds and sufferings had brought on, were intense. He trembled all over, his flesh was torn piecemeal, his tongue contracted, and the only refreshment he received was the blood which trickled from his head on to his parched lips. The shameful scene was protracted a full half-hour, and the Roman soldiers continued during the whole time to applaud and encourage the perpetration of still greater outrages.

When Jesus was conducted by the executioners to Pilate's palace, the scarlet cloak was still thrown over his shoulders, the crown of thorns on his head, and the reed in his fettered hands. He was unrecognizable, his eyes, mouth, and beard were covered with blood; his body was one wound, and his back bowed down as that of an aged man, while every limb trembled as he walked. When Pilate saw him standing at the entrance of his tribunal, even he was startled, and shuddered with horror and compassion, while the barbarous priests and the populace continued their insults and mockery.

Jesus ascended the stairs. Pilot came forward; the trumpet was sounded. Pilot announced to the Chief Priests and the bystanders: *'Behold, I bring him forth to you, that you may know that I find no cause in him.'*

The archers then led Jesus up to Pilate, in the state of degradation to which he was reduced. Terrible and heartrending, indeed, was the spectacle he presented, and an exclamation of horror burst from the multitude, followed by a dead silence, when he with difficulty raised his wounded head crowned with thorns, and cast his exhausted glance on the excited throng. Pilate exclaimed, as he pointed him out to the people: *'Ecce homo! Behold the man!'*

The hatred from the High Priests and their rabble-rousing followers, increased at the sight of Jesus, and they cried out, 'Put him to death; crucify him.'

'Are you not content?' replied Pilate. 'The punishment he has received is beyond question sufficient to deprive him of all desire of making himself king.'

But they cried out the more, and the multitude joined in the cry, 'Crucify him; crucify him!'

Pilot then sounded the trumpet to demand silence, and said, *'Take you him and crucify him, for I find no cause in him.'*

The priests replied, 'We have a law, and according to that law he ought to die because he made himself the Son of God.'

The words, 'he made himself the Son of God,' revived fears within Pilate; he took Jesus into another room and asked him: *'Whence art thou?'*

Jesus made no answer.

'Speakest thou not to me?' said Pilate; *'Knowest thou not that I have power to crucify thee, and power to release thee?'*

'Thou shouldst not have any power against me,' replied Jesus, 'unless it were given thee from above; therefore he that hath delivered me to thee hath the greater sin.'

The undecided, weak conduct of Pilate filled his wife, Claudia Procles, with anxiety; she again sent him the pledge, to remind him of his promise, but he only returned a vague, superstitious answer, importing that he should leave the decision of the case to the gods.

The enemies of Jesus, the High Priests and the Pharisees, having heard of the efforts which were being made by Claudia to save him, caused a report to be spread among the people that the partisans of Jesus had seduced her, that he would be released, and then join the Romans and bring about the destruction of Jerusalem and the extermination of the populace.

Pilot was beside himself; and he again addressed the enemies of Jesus, declaring that *'he found no crime in him,'* but they demanded Jesus' death more clamorously. In order to obtain some information which might enlighten him as to the course he ought to pursue, he therefore returned to the Praetorium, went alone into a room, and sent for Jesus. Pilate glanced at the mangled and bleeding Jesus and exclaimed inwardly: 'Is it possible that he can be God?'

Then he turned to Jesus and adjured him to tell him if he was God, if he was the king who had been promised to the Jews, where his kingdom was, and to what class of gods he belonged.

Jesus' reply was solemn and severe: 'his kingdom was not of this world,' and he spoke strongly of the many hidden crimes with which the conscience of Pilate was defiled; warned him of the dreadful fate which would be his if he did not repent; and finally declared that he himself, the Son of Man, would come at the last day to pronounce a just judgment upon him.

Pilate was frightened and angry at the words of Jesus; he returned to the balcony and again declared that he would release Jesus; but they cried out: *'If thou release this man, thou are not Caesar's friend. For whosoever maketh him-self a king speaketh against Caesar.'*

Others threatened to accuse Pilot to the Emperor of having disturbed their festival; that he must make up his mind at once, because they were obliged to be in the temple by ten o'clock that night. Their cry, *'Crucify him! Crucify him!'* resounded on all sides; it re-echoed even from the flat roofs of the houses near the forum where many persons were assembled

Pilot saw that all his efforts were in vain, that he could make no impression on the infuriated mob; their yells and imprecations were deafening, and he began to fear an insurrection. Therefore he took water, and washed his hands before the people, saying, *'I am innocent of the blood of this just man; look you to it.'*

A frightful and unanimous cry then came from the dense multitude who were assembled from all parts of Palestine: 'His blood be upon us and upon our children.'

Pilot was solely anxious to get out of the difficulty without harm to himself; he became more undecided than ever; his conscience whispered—'Jesus is innocent;' his wife said, 'He is holy;' his superstitious feelings made him fear that Jesus was the enemy of his gods; and his cowardice filled him with dread lest Jesus, if he was a god, wreak vengeance upon his judge. He was irritated and alarmed at the last words of Jesus, and he made another attempt for his release; but the rabble-rousers and High Priests instantly threatened to lay an accusation against him before the Emperor. This terrified him and he determined to accede to their wishes, although firmly convinced in his own mind of the innocence of Jesus, and perfectly conscious that by pronouncing sentence of death upon him he should violate every law of justice, besides breaking the promise he had made to his wife in the morning. Thus he sacrificed Jesus to the enmity of the masses crying for Jesus' death; and washed his hands before the people, saying, *'I am innocent of the blood of this just man; look you to it.'*

Pilot commenced his preparations for passing sentence. He called for the dress which he wore on state occasions, put a species of diadem, set in precious stones, on his head, changed his mangle, and caused a staff to be carried before him. He was surrounded with soldiers, preceded by officers belonging to the tribunal, and followed by Scribes, who carried rolls of parchments and books used for inscribing names and dates. One man walked in front, who carried the trumpet. The procession marched in this order from Pilate's palace to the forum, where an elevated seat, used on these particular occasions, was placed opposite to the pillar where Jesus was scourged. This tribunal was called Cabbatha.

Jesus was still clothed in his purpose garment, his crown of thorns upon his head, and his hands manacled, when the archers brought him up to the tribunal, and placed him between the two thieves.

As soon as Pilot was seated, he again addressed the enemies of Jesus, *'Behold your king!'*

But the cries of 'Crucify him! Crucify him!' resounded on all sides.

'Shall I crucify your king?' Pilot asked.

The High Priests responded, 'We have no king but Caesar!'

Pilot found it was utterly hopeless to say anything more, and commenced his preparations for passing sentence. The two thieves had received their sentence of crucifixion some time before; but the High Priests had obtained a respite for them in order that Jesus might suffer the additional indignity of being executed with two infamous criminals.

The ferocious joy of the executioners—the triumphant countenance of the High Priests, added to the deplorable condition to which Jesus was reduced; and the agonizing grief of his beloved Mother.

After a long preamble, which was composed of the most pompous and exaggerated eulogy of the Emperor Tiberius, Pilate spoke of the accusations which had been brought against Jesus by the High Priests. They had condemned Jesus to death for having disturbed the public peace, and broken their laws by calling himself the Son of

God and King of the Jews; and that the people had unanimously demanded that their decree should be carried out.

Notwithstanding his oft repeated conviction of the innocence of Jesus, Pilot was not ashamed of saying that he likewise considered their decision a just one, and that he should therefore pronounce sentence—which he did with the words: 'I condemn Jesus of Nazareth, the King of the Jews, to be crucified;' and he ordered the executioners to bring the cross.

Pilot then wrote down the sentence, and those who stood behind him copied it out three times. The words which he wrote were quite different from those he had pronounced: 'I have been compelled, for fear of an insurrection, to yield to the wishes of the High Priests, the Sanhedrim, and the people, who tumultuously demanded the death of Jesus of Nazareth, whom they accused of having disturbed the public peace, and also of having blasphemed and broken their laws. I have given him up to them to be crucified, although their accusations appeared to be groundless. I have done so for fear of their alleging to the Emperor that I encourage insurrections, and cause dissatisfactions among the Jews by denying them the rights of justice.'

The High Priests were extremely dissatisfied at the words of the sentence, which they said were not true; and they clamorously surrounded the tribunal to persuade Pilot to alter the inscription, and not to put *King of the Jews*, but that he said, *I am the King of the Jews.*

Pilot was vexed and answered impatiently, '*What I have written I have written!*'

During the time that Pilate was pronouncing sentence, Claudia Procles, his wife, sent back the pledge which he had given her, and in the evening she left his palace and joined the friends of Jesus, who concealed her in a subterraneous vault in the house of Lazarus at Jerusalem. Claudia Procles became a Christian, followed St. Paul, and became his particular friend.

Jesus was given up to the hands of the archers, and the clothes which he had taken off in the court of Caiphas were brought for him to put on again. Some charitable persons had washed them. The ruffians who surrounded Jesus untied his hands for his dress to be changed, and roughly dragged off the scarlet mantle with which they had clothed him in mockery, thereby reopening all his wounds; he put on his own linen under-garment with trembling hands, and they threw his scapular over his shoulders. As the crown of thorns was too large and prevented the seamless robe, which his mother had made for him, from going over his head, they pulled it off violently, heedless of the pain inflicted upon him. His white woolen dress was next thrown over his shoulders, and then his wide belt and cloak. They again tied round his waist a ring covered with sharp iron points, and to it they fastened the cords by which he was led, all with their usual cruelty.

The High Priests, Annas and Caiphas, left off disputing with Pilate, and angrily retired, taking with them the sheets of parchment on which the sentence was written; they went away in haste, fearing that they should get to the temple too late for the Paschal sacrifice. Thus did the High Priests, unknowingly to themselves, leave the true Paschal Lamb. They went to a temple made of stone, to immolate and to sacrifice that lamb which was but a symbol, and they left the true Paschal Lamb, who was being led to the Altar of the Cross by the cruel executioners; they were most careful not to contract exterior defilement, while their souls were completely defiled by anger, hatred, and envy. They had said, *'His blood be upon us and upon our children!'*

And by these words they had performed the ceremony, and had placed the hand of the sacrificer upon the head of the Victim. Thus were the two paths formed—the one leading to the altar belonging to the Jewish law, the other leading to the Altar of Grace; Pilot, who trembled in the presence of the true God, and yet adored his false gods, took a middle path and returned to his palace. The iniquitous sentence was given at about ten in the morning.

The journey with the cross, from
The Dolorous Passion of Our Lord Jesus Christ:

It was the custom among pagans for the priest to embrace a new altar, and Jesus in like manner embraced his cross, that august altar on which the bloody and expiatory sacrifice was about to be offered. The archers soon made him rise, and then kneel down again, and almost without any assistance, place the heavy cross on his right shoulder, supporting its great weight with his right hand. Anne Catherine said she saw angels come to Jesus' assistance, otherwise, she said, he would have been unable even to raise it from the ground.

While Jesus was still on his knees and praying, the executioners put the arms of the crosses, which were a little curved and not as yet fastened to the center pieces, on the backs of the two thieves, and tied their hands tightly to them. The middle parts of the crosses were carried by slaves, as the transverse pieces were not to be fastened to them until just before the time of execution.

The trumpet sounded to announce the departure of Pilate's horsemen, and one of the Pharisees belonging to the escort came up to the kneeling Jesus, and said, 'Rise, we have had a sufficiency of thy fine speeches; rise and set off.'

They roughly pulled him up, and he then felt upon his shoulders the weight of that cross which symbolized the cross everyone must carry after him, according to his true and holy command to follow him.

Thus began, wrote Ann Catherine, that triumphant march of the King of Kings - a march so ignominious on earth – and so glorious in heaven.

The sight of Jesus trembling beneath his burden, reminded Ann Catherine Emmerich of Isaac, when he carried the wood destined for his own sacrifice up the mountain.

Pilot intended to go to Calvary at the head of a detachment of soldiers, to prevent the possibility of an insurrection. He was on horseback, in armor, surrounded by officers and a body of cavalry, and followed by about three hundred of the infantry, who came from the frontiers of Italy and Switzerland.

The procession was headed by a trumpeter, who sounded his trumpet at every corner and proclaimed the sentence. A number of women and children walked behind the procession with ropes, nails, wedges, and baskets filled with different articles in their hands; others, who were stronger, carried poles, ladders, and the center pieces of the crosses of the two thieves, and some of the Pharisees followed on horseback.

A boy, who had charge of the inscription which Pilate had written for the cross, likewise carried the crown of thorns, which had been temporarily removed from the head of Jesus, on a long stick; but he did not appear to be hard-hearted like the others.

Ann Catherine next beheld Jesus, his bare feet swollen and bleeding, his back bent as though he were about to sink under the heavy weight of the cross, and his whole body covered with wounds and blood. He appeared to be half fainting from exhaustion, weak from loss of blood, and parched with thirst produced by fever and pain. He supported the cross on his right shoulder with his right hand, the left arm hung almost powerless at his side, but he endeavored to hold up his long garment to prevent his bleeding feet from getting entangled in it.

Four archers who held the cords which were fastened round his waist, walked at some distance from Jesus; the two archers in front pulled Jesus forward, and the two behind dragged him back, so that he could not get on at all without great difficulty. His hands were cut by the cords with which they had been bound; his face bloody and disfigured; his hair and beard saturated with blood; the weight of the cross and of his chains combined to press and make the woolen dress cleave to his wounds, and reopen them: derisive and heartless words alone were addressed to him, but he continued to pray for his persecutors, and his countenance bore an expression of combined love and resignation.

Many soldiers under arms walked by the side of the procession, and after Jesus, came the two thieves, who were likewise led, the arms of their crosses, separate from the middle, being placed upon their backs, and their hands tied tightly to the two ends. They were clothed in large aprons, with a sort of sleeveless scapular which covered the upper part of their bodies, and they had straw caps upon their heads. The good thief was calm, but the other was furious and never ceased cursing and swearing. The rear of the procession was brought up by the remainder of the Pharisees on horseback, who rode to and fro to keep order.

Pilot and his courtiers were at a certain distance behind; he was in the midst of his officers clad in armor, preceded by a squadron of cavalry, followed by three hundred foot soldiers; he crossed the forum and then entered one of the principal streets, for he was marching through the town in order to prevent any insurrection among the people.

Jesus was conducted by a narrow back street so that the procession would not inconvenience persons going to the Temple, and likewise in order that Pilate and his band might have the whole principal street entirely to themselves.

The crowd had dispersed and started in different directions almost immediately after the reading of the sentence, and the greatest part of the Jews either returned to their own houses, or to the Temple, to hasten their preparations for sacrificing the Paschal Lamb. A certain number were still hurrying on in disorder to see the melancholy procession pass; the Roman soldiers prevented all persons from joining the procession, therefore the most curious were obliged to go round by back streets, or to quicken their steps so as to reach Calvary before Jesus.

The street through which they led Jesus was both narrow and dirty; he suffered much in passing through it, because the archers were close and harassed him. Persons stood on the roofs of the houses and at the windows, and insulted him with opprobrious language; the slaves who were working in the streets threw filth and mud at him: even the children, incited by his enemies, had filled their pinafores with sharp stones, which they threw down before their doors as he passed, that he might be obliged to walk over them.

A subterranean aqueduct proceeding from Mount Zion passed under the street where Jesus' procession was taking place. In the vicinity was a hollow area which was often filled with water and mud after rain, and a large stone was placed in its center to enable persons to pass over more easily. When Jesus reached this spot, his strength was perfectly exhausted; the archers dragged and pushed him without showing the slightest compassion. Jesus fell down against this stone and the cross fell by his side. The executioners were obliged to stop; they abused and struck him unmercifully. The procession came to a standstill, which caused a degree of confusion. Jesus held out his hand for someone to assist him: 'Ah,' he exclaimed 'all will soon be over;' and he prayed for his enemies.

'Lift him up,' said the Pharisees, 'otherwise he will die in our hands.'

There were many women and children following the procession; the former wept, and the latter were frightened. Jesus, however, received support from above and raised his head; but the cruel men put the crown of thorns again on his head before they pulled him out of the mud, and no sooner was he once more on his feet than they replaced the cross on his back. The crown of thorns which encircled his head increased his pain inexpressibly, and obliged him to bend on one side to give room for the cross, which lay heavily on his shoulders.

John and Mary remained near a doorway with their eyes fixed on the procession, which was advancing by slow degrees. When those who were carrying the instruments for the execution approached, the Mother of Jesus saw their insolent and triumphant looks; she could not control her feelings, but joined her hands as if to implore the help of heaven, upon which one executioner then said to his companions: 'What woman is that who is uttering such lamentations?'

'She is the Mother of the Galilaean,' one man replied.

When the men heard this, they began to make game of the grief of this afflicted Mother; they pointed at her, and one of them took the nails which were to be used for fastening Jesus to the cross, and presented them to her in an insulting manner; but she turned away, fixed her eyes upon Jesus, who was drawing near, and leant against the pillar for support lest she should again faint from grief. Her cheeks were pale as death, and her lips almost blue.

The Pharisees, on horseback, passed by first; followed by the boy who carried the inscription. Then Jesus followed. He was almost sinking under the heavy weight of his cross, and his head, still crowned with thorns, was drooping in agony. He cast a look of compassion and sorrow upon his Mother, staggered, and fell for the second time upon his hands and knees. Mary was agonized at this sight; she forgot all else; she saw neither soldiers nor executioners; nothing but her dearly-loved Son; and, springing from the doorway into the midst of the group who were insulting and abusing him, she threw herself on her knees by his side and embraced him.

The only words Ann Catherine heard were, 'Beloved Son!' and 'Mother!' but she did not know whether these words were really uttered, or whether they were in her mind.

A momentary confusion ensued. John and the holy women endeavored to raise Mary from the ground, and the archers reproached her, one of them saying, 'What has thou to do here, woman? He would not have been in our hands if he had been better brought up.'

A few of the soldiers looked touched, and, although they obliged the Blessed Virgin to retire to the doorway, not one laid a hand upon her. John and the women surrounded her as she fell half fainting against a stone, which was near the doorway, and upon which the impression of her hands remained. This stone was very hard, and was afterwards removed to the first Catholic Church built in Jerusalem, near the Pool of Bethsaida, during the time that St. James the Less was Bishop of that city.

The two disciples carried the Mother of Jesus into the house, and the door was shut. In the meantime the archers had raised Jesus, and obliged him to carry the cross in a different manner.

The procession had reached an arch formed in an old wall belonging to the town, opposite to a square, in which three streets terminated, when Jesus stumbled against a large stone which was placed in the middle of the archway; the cross slipped from his shoulder, he fell upon the stone and was totally unable to rise. Many respectable looking persons who were on their way to the Temple stopped, and exclaimed compassionately: 'Look at that poor man; he is certainly dying!' but his enemies showed no compassion. This fall caused a fresh delay, as Jesus could not stand up again, and the Pharisees said to the soldiers: 'We shall never get him to the place of execution alive if you do not find some one to carry his cross.'

At this moment Simon of Cyrene, happened to pass by, accompanied by his three children. He was a gardener, just returning home after working in a garden near the eastern wall of the city, and carrying a bundle of lopped branches. The soldiers perceiving by his dress that he was a pagan seized him and ordered him to assist Jesus in carrying his cross. He refused at first, but was soon compelled to obey, although his children, being frightened, cried and made a great noise, upon which some women quieted and took charge of them.

Simon was much annoyed, and expressed the greatest vexation at being obliged to walk with a man in so deplorable a condition of dirt and misery; but Jesus wept, and cast such a mild and heavenly look upon him that he was touched, and instead of continuing to show reluctance, helped him to rise, while the executioners fastened one arm of the cross on his shoulders, and he walked behind Jesus, thus relieving him in a great measure from its weight; and when all was arranged, the procession moved forward.

Simon was a stout-looking man, apparently about forty years of age. His children were dressed in tunics made of a variegated material; the two eldest children joined the disciples; the third was much younger, but a few years later went to live with St. Stephen. Simon had not carried the cross behind Jesus any length of time before he felt his heart deeply touched by grace.

While the procession was passing through a long street, an in incident took place which made a strong impression upon Simon. Numbers of respectable persons were hurrying towards the temple, of whom many got out of the way when they saw Jesus, from a Pharisaical fear of defilement, while others, on the contrary, stopped and expressed pity for his sufferings. But when the procession had advanced about two hundred steps from the spot where Simon began to assist our Lord in carrying his cross, the door of a beautiful house on the left opened, and a woman of majestic appearance, holding a young girl by the hand, came out, and walked up to the very head of the possession. Seraphia was the name of the brave woman who thus dared to confront the enraged multitude; she was the wife of Sirach, one of the councilors belonging to the Temple, and was afterwards known by the name of Veronica, which name was given from the words *vera icon* (true portrait), to commemorate her brave conduct on this day.

Seraphia had prepared some excellent aromatic wine, which she intended to present to Jesus to refresh him on his dolorous way to Calvary. She had been standing in the street for some time, and at last went back into the house to wait. She was, when Ann Catherine saw her, enveloped in a long veil, and holding a little girl of nine years of age whom she had adopted, by the hand; a large veil was likewise hanging on her arm, and the little girl endeavored to hide the jar of wine when the procession approached. Those who were marching at the head of the procession tried to push her back; but she made her way through the mob, the soldiers, and the archers, reached Jesus, fell on her knees before him, and presented the veil, saying at the same time, 'Permit me to wipe the face of my Lord.' Jesus took the veil in his left hand, wiped his bleeding face, and returned it with thanks. Seraphia kissed it, and put it under her cloak. The girl then timidly offered the wine, but the brutal soldiers would not allow Jesus to drink it. The suddenness of this courageous act of Seraphia had surprised the guards, and caused a momentary although unintentional halt, of which she had taken advantage to present the veil to her Divine Master. The Pharisees and the guards were greatly exasperated, not only by the sudden halt, but much more by the public testimony of veneration which was thus paid to Jesus, and they revenged themselves by striking and abusing him, while Seraphia returned in haste to her house.

No sooner did she reach her room than she placed the woolen veil on a table, and fell almost senseless on her knees. A friend who entered the room a short time after, found her thus kneeling, with the child weeping by her side, and saw, to his astonishment the bloody countenance of Jesus imprinted upon the veil, a perfect likeness, although heartrending and painful to look upon. He roused Seraphia, and pointed to the veil. She again knelt down before it, and exclaimed through her tears, 'Now I shall indeed leave all with a happy heart, for my Lord has given me a remembrance of himself.'

The texture of this veil was a species of very fine wool; it was three times the length of its width, and was generally worn on the shoulders. It was customary to present these veils to persons who were in affliction, or over-fatigued, or ill, that they might wipe their faces with them, and it was done in order to express sympathy or compassion.

Veronica kept this veil until her death, and hung it at the head of her bed; it was then given to the Blessed Virgin, who left it to the Apostles, and they afterwards passed it on to the Church.

Seraphia and John the Baptist were cousins, her father and Zacharias being brothers. When Joachim and Anna brought the Blessed Virgin, who was then only four years old, up to Jerusalem, to place her among the virgins in the temple, they lodged in the house of Zacharias, which was situated near the fish market. Seraphia was at least five years older than the Blessed Virgin, was present at her marriage with St. Joseph, and was likewise related to the aged Simeon, who prophesied when the Child Jesus was put into his arms. She was brought up with his sons, both of whom, as well as Seraphia, he imbued with his ardent desire of seeing our Lord. When Jesus was twelve years old, and remained teaching in the Temple, Seraphia, who was not then married, sent food for him every day to a little inn, a quarter of a mile from Jerusalem, where he dwelt when he was not in the Temple.

Mary went there for two days, when on her way from Bethlehem to Jerusalem to offer her Child in the Temple. The two old men who kept this inn were Essenians, and well acquainted with the Holy Family; it contained a kind of foundation for the poor, and Jesus and his disciples often went there for a night's lodging.

Seraphia married rather late in life; her husband Sirach, was descended from the chaste Susannah, and was a member of the Sanhedrim. He was at first greatly opposed to Jesus, and his wife suffered much on account of her attachment to Jesus, and to the holy women, but Joseph of Arimathea and Nicodemus brought him to a better state of feeling, and he allowed Seraphia to follow Jesus.

When Jesus was unjustly accused in the court of Caiphas, the husband of Seraphia joined with Joseph and Nicodemus in attempts to obtain the liberation of Jesus, and all three resigned their seats in the Council.

Serephia was about fifty at the time of the triumphant procession of Jesus into Jerusalem on Palm Sunday. Anne Catherine saw Seraphia take off her veil and spread it on the ground for him to walk upon. It was this same veil, which she presented to Jesus, at his second procession, a procession which outwardly appeared to be far less glorious, but was in fact much more so. This veil, obtained for her the name of Veronica, and it is still shown for the veneration of the faithful.

Jesus fell seven times on the way to his crucifixion. The number seven appears often in Biblical and esoteric literature. There are the seven days of creation. The seven churches, which Cayce said, are the seven spiritual centers of the Endocrine system where God dwells within our body. This Endocrine system is referred to in The Revelation as the seven golden candlesticks, the seven spiritual centers; seven stars are the seven angels of the seven churches, the messengers of the seven spiritual centers. More information concerning Edgar Cayce's interpretation of Revelation is as follows:

The Tree of Life: the Endocrine system, the seven spiritual centers of the body.

Paradise of God: where peace may be found.

The Synagogue of Satan: falseness in self.

Second Death: the falling away after having passed into the understanding.

The place where Satan dwells: where there is jealousy, greed, hate, etc..

The Morning Star represents an "awakening," "light," "spiritual awareness."

Power over the nations represents power over the whole of the physical body, the un- spiritual cells of the physical body.

The Open Door – is the awakening, which takes place in Lyden – Pineal centers.

Throne: within the head of the physical body - where we meet our Father.

Four and twenty elders: the twenty-four cranial nerves that control the five senses of the body.

Book of Life: the Christ's Records, those written in are those who have not climbed up some other way.

Seven Lamps: seven spirits of God; helpful influences without.

Four beasts: physical desires of the four lower centers:

1) Self-preservation,
2) Sustenance
3) Propagation of species
4) Self-gratification.

Book with seven seals: The physical body with the seven spiritual centers.

A New Song: A new understanding.

The Seven Churches: The seven psychic centers, the Pineal, Pituitary, Thyroid, Thymus, Adrenal, Lyden, Female Gonads, Male Gonads.

Tree of Life: Endoctrine system – the seven spiritual centers of the body.

Paradise of God: Where peace may be found.

Where Satan dwells: Where there is jealousy, greed, hate, etc.

Doctrine of Balaam: Blind to higher morality; the reward sought through popularity, applause, worldliness, etc.

Jezebel: Those who are false to the cause they espouse, and those who would lead others astray.

Four horses: Emotions

The morning star: An awakening, light, spiritual awareness.

Power over the nations: Power over the whole of the physical body, the un-spiritualized cells of the physical body.

144,000 sealed: Spiritualized cellular structures of the twelve major divisions of the body.

Angel with golden censer: Influence of good that goes out from each soul.

(The above information given through Edgar Cayce should be enough to declare anyone a saint -- saith I.)

The Endocrine System

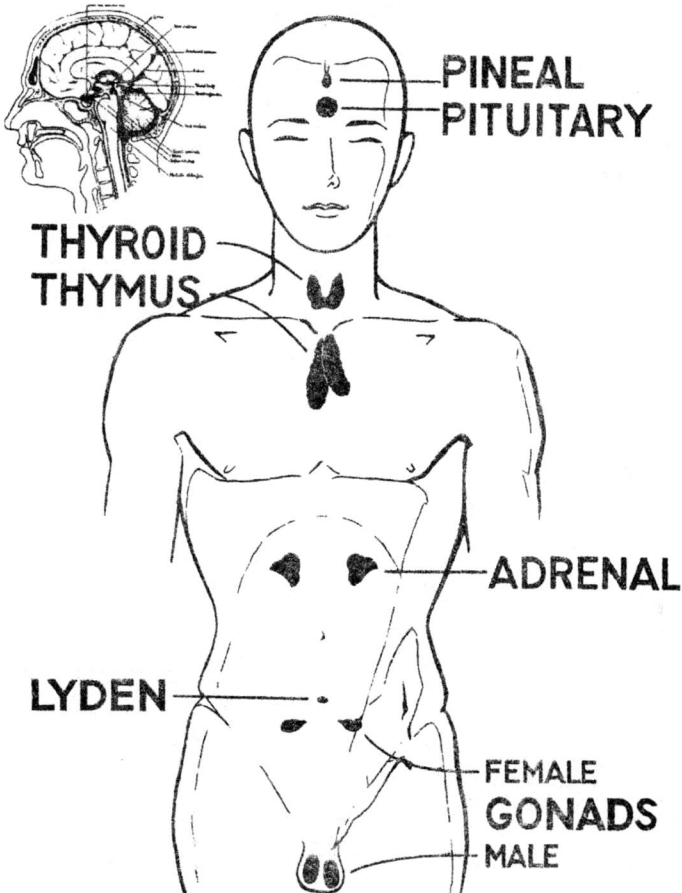

TO THE READER

Venerable Anne Catherine had been a seamstress; and this is why some of her observations come across as perhaps too detailed. Ann Catherine was seeing events in Jesus' Passion from the eyes of a seamstress, one who would notice every little detail.

It was not my intention, at the beginning of this book, to use as much material as I have from the visions of Ann Catherine Emmerich to describe the crucifixion of Jesus – but the more I studied her visions, the more I was drawn to the passion of Jesus. I was being provided a first hand account of the suffering of Jesus, the Christ, and, emotionally, I felt his pain. Anne Catherine's visions took me from here and put me to there.

I have seen black and white Hollywood movies of Jesus and I have seen Technicolor movies of Jesus, but movies never took me out of my seat and put me into the picture. I saw; I observed, but I might say, I never actually felt his pain.

Anne Catherine's visions did that for me; they put me into the picture. It no longer was enough to just write about the sacrifice of Jesus; I wanted to share this intimate experience with others, to pass the experience along to those who might read this book. I want to do for others what the visions of Anne Catherine did for me.

More than two thousand years have passed since the crucifixion of Jesus, but as I read from the Visions of Ann Catherine, the Jesus story is happening right now. It will happen to you as you read it. We deserve to experience the pain of this event because it is the greatest part of the greatest story ever told – the greatest sacrifice ever made - the greatest spiritual contribution to our lives.

Read and experience the passion of Jesus on the cross and you will be transformed into a higher spiritual dimension. You will never be the same again. That is what reading about the sacrifice of Jesus will do for each of us.

We Begin With Preparations for the Paschal Lamb
Holly Thursday, the 29th of March

Yesterday evening it was that the last great public repast of our Lord and his friends took place in the house of Simon the Leper, at

Bethania, and Mary Magdalen for the last time anointed the feet of Jesus with precious ointment. Judas was scandalized upon this occasion, and hastened forthwith to Jerusalem again to conspire with the High Priests for the betrayal of Jesus into their hands.

After the repast, Jesus returned to the house of Lazarus, and some of the Apostles went to the inn situated beyond Bethania. During the night Nicodemus again came to Lazarus' house, had a long conversation with Jesus, and returned before daylight to Jerusalem, being accompanied part of the way by Lazarus.

The disciples had already asked Jesus where he would eat the Pash. Before dawn, Jesus sent for Peter, James, and John, spoke to them at some length concerning all they had to prepare and order at Jerusalem, and told them that when ascending Mount Zion, they would meet the man carrying a pitcher of water. They were already well acquainted with this man, for at the last Pasch, at Bethania, it had been him who prepared the meal for Jesus, and this is why St. Matthew says: *a certain man.*

They were to follow him home, and say to him: *The Master saith, My time is near at hand, with thee. I make the pasch with my disciples* (Matt. xxvi. 18). They were then to be shown the supper-room, and make all necessary preparations.

Anne Catherine saw the two Apostles ascending towards Jerusalem, along a ravine, to the south at the Temple, and in the directions of the north side of Zion. On the southern side of the mountain on which the Temple stood, there were some rows of houses; and they walked opposite these houses, following the stream of an intervening torrent. When they had reached the summit of Mount Zion, which is higher than the mountain of the Temple, they turned their steps toward the south, and, just at the beginning of a small ascent, met the man who had been named to them; they followed and spoke to him as Jesus had commanded.

He was much gratified by their words, and answered, that a supper had already been ordered to be prepared at his house (probably by Nicodemus), but that he had not been aware for whom, and was delighted to learn that it was for Jesus.

This man's name was Heli, and he was the brother-in-law of Zachary of Hebron, in whose house Jesus had in the preceding year

announced the death of John the Baptist. He had only one son, who
was a Levite, and a friend of St. Luke, before the latter was called by
Jesus, and five daughters, all of whom were unmarried. He went up
every year with his servants for the festival of the Pasch, hired a room
and prepared the Pasch for persons who had no friend in the town to
lodge with. This year he had hired a supper-room which belonged to
Nicodemus and Joseph of Arimathea. He showed the two Apostles its
position and interior arrangement.

The Supper Room

On the southern side of Mount Zion, not far from the ruined castle of David, and the market held on the ascent leading to that Castle,
there stood, towards the east, an ancient and solid building, between
rows of thick trees, in the midst of a spacious court surrounded by
strong walls. To the right and left of the entrance, other buildings
were to be seen adjoining the wall, particularly to the right, where
stood the dwelling of the major-domo, and close to it the house in
which the Blessed Virgin and the holy women spent most of their
time after the death of Jesus. The supper-room, which was originally
larger, had formerly been inhabited by David's brave captains, who
had there learned the use of arms.

Previous to the building of the Temple, the Ark of the Covenant
had been deposited there for a considerable length of time, and traces
of its presence were still to be found in an underground room. Ann
Catherine had also seen the Prophet Malachy hidden beneath this
same roof: he there wrote his prophecies concerning the Blessed Sacrament and the Sacrifice of the New Law. Solomon held this house in
honor, and performed within its walls some figurative and symbolical
action, which Anne Catherine has forgotten. When a great part of
Jerusalem was destroyed by the Babylonians, this house was spared.
Anne Catherine had seen many other things concerning this same
house, but she only remembers what she has now told.

This building was in a very dilapidated state when it became the
property of Nicodemus and Joseph of Arimathea, who arranged the
principal building in a very suitable manner, and let it as a supper-
room to strangers coming to Jerusalem for the purpose of celebrating
the festival of the Pasch. Thus it was that Jesus had made use of it the

previous year. Moreover, the house and surrounding buildings served as warehouses for monuments and other stones, and as workshops for the laborers; for Joseph of Arimathea possessed valuable quarries in his own country, from which he had large blocks of stone brought, that his workmen might fashion them, under his own eyes, into tombs, architectural ornaments, and columns, for sale. Nicodemus had a share in this business, and used to spend many leisure hours himself in sculpturing. He worked in the room, or in a subterraneous apartment which was beneath it, excepting at the times of the festivals; and this occupation brought him into connection with Joseph of Arimathea, they had become friends, and often joined together in various transactions.

On a morning when Peter and John were conversing with the man who had hired the supper-room, Ann Catherine saw Nicodemus in the buildings to the left of the court, where a great many stones which filled up the passages leading to the supper-room had been placed. A week before she had seen several persons engaged in putting the stones on one side, cleaning the court, and preparing the supper-room for the celebration of the Pasch; it even appears to her that there were among them some disciples of Jesus, perhaps Aram and Themein, the cousins of Joseph of Arimathea.

The supper-room, properly so called, was nearly in the center of the court; its length was greater than its width; it was surrounded by a row of low pillars, and if the spaces between the pillars had been cleared, would have formed a part of the large inner room, for the whole edifice was, as it were, transparent; only it was usual, except on special occasions, for the passages to be closed up. The room was lighted by apertures at the top of the walls. In front, there was first a vestibule, into which three lamps hung from the platform; the walls were ornamented for the festival, half way up, with beautiful matting or tapestry, and an aperture had been made in the roof, and covered over with transparent blue gauze.

The back part of this room was separated from the rest by a curtain, also of blue transparent gauze. This division of the supper-room into three parts gave a resemblance to the Temple—thus forming the outer Court, the Holy, and the Holy of Holies. In the last of these divisions, on both sides, the dresses and other things necessary for

the celebration of the feast were placed. In the center there was a species of altar. A stone bench raised on three steps, and of a rectangular
triangular shape, came out of the wall it must have constituted the
upper part of the oven used for roasting the Paschal Lamb, for to-day
the steps were quite heated during the repast. Ann Catherine cannot
describe in detail all that there was in this part of the room, but all
kinds of arrangements were being made there for preparing the Paschal Supper.

Above this hearth, or altar, there was a species of niche in the
wall, in front of which she saw an image of the Paschal Lamb, with a
knife in its throat, and the blood spearing to flow drop by drop upon
the altar; but she does not remember distinctly how that was done.
In a niche in the wall there were three cupboards of various colors,
which turned like tabernacles, for opening or closing. A number of
vessels used in the celebration of the Pasch were kept in them; later,
the Blessed Sacrament was placed there.

In the rooms at the sides of the supper-room, there were some
couches, on which thick coverlids rolled up were placed, and which
could be used as beds. There were spacious cellars beneath the whole
of this building. The Ark of the Covenant was formerly deposited under the very spot where the hearth was afterwards built. Five gutters,
under the house, served to convey the refuse to the slope of the hill,
on the upper part of which the house was built. Anne Catherine had
previously seen Jesus preach and perform miraculous cures there, and
the disciples frequently passed the night in the side rooms.

Arrangements for eating the Paschal Lamb

When the disciples had spoken to Heli of Hebron, the latter went
back into the house by the court, but they turned to the right, and hastened down the north side of the hill, through Zion. They passed over
a bridge, and walking along a road covered with brambles, reached
the other side of the ravine, which was in front of the Temple, and
of the row of houses which were to the south of that building. There
stood the house of the aged Simeon, who died in the Temple after
the presentation of Jesus; and his sons, some of whom were disciples
of Jesus in secret, were actually living there. The Apostles spoke to
one of them, a tall dark-complexioned man, who held some office in

the Temple. They went with him to the eastern side of the Temple, through that part of Ophel by which Jesus made his entry into Jerusalem on Palm Sunday, and thence to the cattle-market, which stood in the town, to the north of the Temple. In the southern part of this market she saw little enclosures in which some beautiful lambs were gambling about. Here it was that lambs for the Pasch were bought. She saw the son of Simeon enter one of these enclosures; and the lambs gamboled round him as if they knew him. He chose out four which were carried to the supper-room. In the afternoon she saw him in the supper-room, engaged in preparing the Paschal Lamb.

. Ann Catherine Emmerich saw Peter and John go to several different parts of the town, and order various things. She saw them also standing opposite the door of a house situated to the north of Mount Calvary, where the disciples of Jesus lodged the greatest part of the time, and which belonged to Seraphia (afterwards called Veronica). Peter and John sent some disciples from thence to the supper-room, giving them several commissions, which she has forgotten.

They also went into Seraphia's house, where they had several arrangements to make. Her husband, who was a member of the council, was usually absent and engaged in business; but even when he was at home she saw little of him. She was a woman of about the age of the Mother of Jesus, and had long been connected with the Holy Family; for when the Child Jesus remained the three days in Jerusalem after the feast, it was she who supplied him with food.

The two Apostles took from there, among other things, the chalice of which Jesus made use in the institution of the Holy Eucharist.

The chalice used at the Last Supper

The chalice which the Apostles brought from Veronica's house was wonderful and mysterious in its appearance. It had been kept a long time in the temple among other previous objects of great antiquity, the use and origin of which had been forgotten. The same has been in some degree the case in the Christian Church, where many consecrated jewels have been forgotten and fallen into disuse with time. Ancient vases and jewels, buried beneath the Temple, had often been dug up, sold, or reset. Thus it was that, by God's permission, this holy vessel, which none had ever been able to melt down on account of its being made of some unknown material, and which had been found by the priests in the treasury of the Temple among other objects no longer made use of, had been sold to some antiquaries. It was bought by Seraphia, was several times made use of by Jesus in the celebration of festivals, and, from the day of the Last Supper became the exclusive property of the Christian community. This vessel was not always the same as when used by Jesus at his Last Supper, and perhaps it was upon that occasion that the various pieces which composed it were first put together.

The great chalice stood upon a plate, out of which a species of tablet could be drawn, and around it were six little glasses. The great chalice contained another smaller vase; above it there was a small plate, and then came a round cover. A spoon was inserted in the foot of the chalice, and could be easily drawn out for use. All these different vessels were covered with fine linen, and, if Ann Catherine is not mistaken, they were wrapped up in a case made of leather.

The cup was pear-shaped, massive, dark-colored, and highly polished, with gold ornaments and two small handles by which it could be lifted. The foot was of virgin gold, elaborately worked, ornamented with a serpent and a small bunch of grapes, and enriched with previous stones.

The chalice was left in the Church of Jerusalem, in the hands of St. James the Less; and she could see that it was still preserved in that town— it will reappear some day, in the same manner as before. Other Churches took the little cups which surrounded it; one was taken to Antioch, and another to Ephesus. They belonged to the patriarchs, who drank some mysterious beverage out of them when they received or gave a Benediction - as Ann Catherine has seen many times.

The great chalice had formerly been in the possession of Abraham; Melchisedech brought it with him from the land of Semiramis to the land of Canaan, when he was beginning to found some settlements on the spot where Jerusalem was afterwards built; he made use of then for offering sacrifice, when he offered bread and wine in the presence of Abraham, and he left it in the possession of that holy patriarch. This same chalice had also been preserved in Noah's Ark.

Jesus goes up to Jerusalem

In the morning, while the Apostles were engaged at Jerusalem in preparing for the Pasch, Jesus, who had remained at Bethania, took an affecting leave of the holy woman, of Lazarus, and of his Blessed Mother, and gave them some final instructions. Ann Catherine saw Jesus conversing apart with his Mother, and he told her among other things, that he had sent Peter, the apostle of faith, and John, the apostle of love, to prepare for the Pasch at Jerusalem. He said, in speaking of Magdalen, whose grief was excessive, that her love was great, but still somewhat human, and that on this account her sorrow made her beside herself. He spoke also of the schemes of the traitor Judas, and the Blessed Virgin prayed for him. Judas had again left Bethania to go to Jerusalem, under pretence of paying some debts that were due. He spent his whole day in hurrying backwards and forwards from one Pharisee to another, and making his final agreements with them. He was shown the soldiers who had been engaged to seize the person of Jesus, and he so arranged his journeys to and fro as to be able to account for his absence. Ann Catherine beheld all his wicked schemes and all his thoughts. He was naturally active and obliging, but these good qualities were choked by avarice, ambition, and envy, which passions he made no effort to control. In our Lord's absence he had even performed miracles and healed the sick.

When Jesus announced to his Blessed Mother what was going to take place, she besought him, in the most touching terms, to let her die with him. But he exhorted her to show more calmness in her sorrow than the other women, told her that he should rise again, and named the very spot where he should appear to her. She did not weep much, but her grief was indescribable, and there was something almost awful in her look of deep recollection.

Jesus returned thanks, as a loving Son, for all the love she had borne him, and pressed her to his heart. He also told her that he would make the Last Supper with her, spiritually, and named the hour at which she would receive his precious Body and Blood. Then once more he, in touching language, bade farewell to all, and gave them different instructions.

About twelve o'clock in the day, Jesus and the nine Apostles went from Bethania up to Jerusalem, followed by seven disciples, who, with the exception of Nathaniel and Silas, came from Jerusalem and the neighborhood. Among these were John, Mark, and the son of the poor widow who, the Thursday previous, had offered her mite in the Temple, whilst Jesus was preaching there. Jesus had taken him into his company a few days before. The holy women set off later.

Jesus and his companions walked around Mount Olivet, about the valley of Josaphat, and even as far as Mount Calvary. During the whole of this walk, he continued giving them instructions. He told the Apostles, among other things, that until then he had given them his bread and his wine, but that this day he was going to give them his Body and Blood, his whole self—all that he had and all that he was. The countenance of Jesus bore so touching an expression while he was speaking, that his whole soul seemed to breathe forth from his lips, and he appeared to be languishing with love and desire for the moment when he should give himself to man. His disciples did not understand him, but thought that he was speaking of the Paschal Lamb. No words can give an adequate idea of the love and resignation which were expressed in these last discourses of Jesus at Bethania, and on his way to Jerusalem.

The seven disciples who had followed Jesus to Jerusalem did not go there in his company, but carried the ceremonial habits for the Pasch to the supper-room, and then returned to the house of Mary, the mother of Mark. When Peter and John arrived at the supper-room with the chalice, all the ceremonial habits were already in the vestibule, whither they had been brought by his disciples and some companions. They had also hung the walls with drapery, cleared the higher openings in the sides, and put up three lamps. Peter and John then went to the Valley of Josaphat, and summoned Jesus and the twelve Apostles. The disciples and friends, who were also to make their Pasch in the supper-room, came later.

The Last Pasch

Jesus and his disciples divided into three groups. Jesus ate the Paschal Lamb with the twelve Apostles in the supper-room, properly so called; Nathaniel with twelve other disciples in one of the lateral rooms, and Eliacim (the son of Cleophas and Mary, the daughter of

Heli), who had been a disciple of John the Baptist, with twelve more, in another side-room.

Three lambs were immolated for them in the temple, but there was a fourth lamb which was immolated in the supper-room, and was the one eaten by Jesus with his Apostles. Judas was not aware of this circumstance, because being engaged in plotting his betrayal of Jesus, he only returned a few moments before the repast, and after the immolation of the lamb had taken place. Most touching was the scene of the immolation of the lamb to be eaten by Jesus and his Apostles; it took place in the vestibule of the supper-room. The Apostles and disciples were present, singing the 118th Psalm. Jesus spoke of a new period then beginning, and said that the sacrifice of Moses and the figure of the Paschal Lamb were about to receive their accomplishment, but that on this very account, the lamb was to be immolated in the same manner as formerly in Egypt, and that they were really about to go forth from the house of bondage.

The vessels and necessary instruments were prepared, and then the attendants brought a beautiful little lamb, decorated with a crown, which was sent to the Blessed Virgin in the room where she had remained with the other holy women. The lamb was fastened with its back against a board by a cord around its body, and reminded Ann Catherine of Jesus tied to the pillar and scourged. The son of Simeon held the lamb's head; Jesus made a slight incision in its neck with the point of a knife, which he then gave to the son of Simeon, that he might complete killing it. Jesus appeared to inflict the wound with a feeling of repugnance, and he was quick in his movements, although his countenance was grave and his manner such as to inspire respect.

The blood flowed into a basin, and the attendants brought a branch of hyssop, which Jesus dipped in it. Then he went to the door of the room, stained the side-posts and the lock with blood, and placed the branch which had been dipped in blood above the door. He then spoke to the disciples, and told them, among other things, that the exterminating angel would pass by, that they would adore in that room without fear or anxiety, when he, the true Paschal Lamb, should have been immolated—that a new epoch and a new sacrifice were about to begin, which would last to the end of the world.

They then went to the other side of the room, near the hearth where the Ark of the Covenant had formerly stood. Fire had already been lighted there, and Jesus poured some blood upon the hearth, consecrating it as an altar; and the remainder of the blood and the fat were thrown on the fire beneath the altar after which Jesus, followed by his Apostles, walked round the supper-room, singing some psalms, and consecrating it as a new Temple. The doors were all closed during this time. Meanwhile the son of Simeon had completed the preparation of the lamb. He passed a stake through its body, fastening the front legs on a cross piece of weed, and stretching the hind ones along the stake. It bore a strong resemblance to Jesus on the cross, and was placed in the oven, to be there roasted with the three other lambs brought from the Temple.

The Paschal Lambs of the Jews were all immolated in the vestibule of the Temple, but in different parts, according as the persons who were to eat them were rich or poor strangers. The Paschal Lamb belonging to Jesus was not immolated in the Temple, but everything else was done strictly according to the law. Jesus again addressed his disciples, saying that the lamb was but a figure, that he himself would next day be the true Paschal Lamb, together with other things which Ann Catherine has forgotten.

When Jesus had finished his instructions concerning the Paschal Lamb and its signification, the time being come, and Judas also returned, the tables were set out. The disciples put on traveling clothes which were in the vestibule, different shoes, a white robe resembling a shirt, and a cloak, which was short in front and longer behind, their sleeves were large and turned back, and they girded up their clothes around the waist. Each party went to their own table; and two sets of disciples in the side rooms, and Jesus and his Apostles in the supper-room. They held staves in their hands, and went two and two to the table, where they remained standing, each in his own place, with the stave resting on his arms, and his hands upraised.

The table was narrow and about half a foot higher than the knees of a man; in shape it resembled a horseshoe, and opposite Jesus, in the inner part of the half-circle, there was a space left vacant, that the attendants might be able to set down the dishes.

As far as Ann Catherine can remember, John, James the Greater, and James the Less, sat on the right-hand of Jesus; after them Bartholomew, and then, (round the corner) Thomas and Judas Iscariot. Peter, Andrew, and Thaddeus sat on the left of Jesus; next came Simon, and then (round the corner) Matthew and Philip.

The Paschal Lamb was placed on a dish in the center of the table. Its head rested on its front legs, which were fastened to a cross-stick, its hind legs being stretched out, and the dish was garnished with garlic. By the side there was a dish with the Paschal roast meat, then came a plate with green vegetables balanced against each other, and another plate with small bundles of bitter herbs, which had the appearance of aromatic herbs. Opposite Jesus there was also one dish with different herbs, and a second containing a brown-colored sauce or beverage. The guests had before them some round loaves instead of plates, and they used ivory knives.

After the prayer, the major-domo laid the knife for cutting the lamb on the table before Jesus, who placed a cup of wine before him, and filled six other cups, each one of which stood between two Apostles. Jesus blessed the wine and drank, and the Apostles drank two together out of one cup. Then Jesus proceeded to cut up the lamb; his Apostles presented their pieces of bread in turn, and each received his share. They ate it in haste, separating the flesh from the bone, by means of their ivory knives, and the bones were afterwards burnt. They also ate the garlic and green herbs in haste, dipping them in the sauce. All this time they remained standing, only leaning slightly on the backs of their seats. Jesus broke one of the loaves of unleavened bread, covered up a part of it, and divided the remainder among his Apostles. Another cup of wine was brought, but Jesus drank not of it: '*Take this,*' he said, '*and divide it among you for I will not drink from henceforth of the fruit of the vine, until that day when I shall drink it with you new in the kingdom of my Father*') Matt. xxvi. 29).

When they had drunk the wine they sang a hymn; then Jesus prayed or taught, and they again washed their hands. After this they sat down.

Jesus cut up another lamb, which was carried to the holy women in one of the buildings of the court, where they were seated at table. The Apostles ate some more vegetables and lettuce. The countenance of Jesus bore an indescribable expression of serenity and recollection, greater than Ann Catherine had ever before seen. He bade the Apostles forget all their cares. The Blessed Virgin also, as she sat at table with the other women, looked most placid and calm. When the other women came up, and took hold of her veil to make her turn round and speak to them, her every movement expressed the sweetest self-control and placidity of spirit.

At first Jesus conversed lovingly and calmly with his disciples, but after a while he became grave and said: *'Amen, amen, I say to you, that one of you is about to betray me'*; he said, *He that dippeth his hand with me in the dish'* (Matt. xxvi. 21, 23).

Jesus was then distributing the lettuce, of which there was only one dish, to those Apostles who were by his side, and he had given Judas, who was nearly opposite to him, the office of distributing it to the others. When Jesus spoke of a traitor, an expression which filled all the Apostles with fear, he said: *'He that dippeth his hand with me in the dish,'* which means: 'one of the twelve who are eating and drinking with me—one of those with whom I am eating bread.'

He did not plainly point out Judas to the others by these words; for *to dip the hand in the same dish* was an expression used to signify the friendliest and most intimate intercourse. He was desirous, however, to give a warning to Judas, who was then really dipping his hand in the dish with Jesus, to distribute the lettuce. Jesus continued to speak: *'The Son of man indeed goeth,'* he said, *'as it is written of him: but woe to that man by whom the Son of man shall be betrayed: It were better for him if that man had not been born.'*

The Apostles were very much troubled, and each one of them exclaimed: *'Lord, is it I?'* for they were all perfectly aware that they did not entirely understand his words.

Peter leaned towards John, behind Jesus, and made him a sign to ask Jesus who the traitor was to be, for, having so often been reproved by Jesus, he trembled lest it should be himself who was referred to. John was seated at the right hand of Jesus, and as all were leaning on their left arms, using the right to eat; his head was close to the bosom of Jesus. He leaned then on his breast and said: *'Lord, who is it?"*

Anne Catherine did not see Jesus say to him with his lips: *'He it is to whom I shall reach bread dipped.'* Ann Catherine did not know whether Jesus whispered it to him, but John knew it, when Jesus having dipped the bread, which was covered with lettuce, gave it tenderly to Judas, who also asked: *'Is it I, Lord?'*

Jesus looked at him with love, and answered him in general terms.

Among the Jews, to give bread dipped was a mark of friendship and confidence; Jesus on this occasion gave Judas the morsel, in order thus to warn him, without making known his guilt to the others. But the heart of Judas burned with anger, and during the whole time of the repast, Ann Catherine saw a frightful little figure seated at Jesus' feet, and sometimes ascending to his heart. She did not see John repeat to Peter what he had learned from Jesus, but he set his fears at rest by a look.

The Washing of the Feet

They rose from the table, and while they were arranging their clothes, as they usually did before making their solemn prayer, the major-domo (head of the household) came in with two servants to take away the table. Jesus, standing in the midst of his Apostles, spoke to them long, in a most solemn manner. Ann Catherine could not repeat exactly his whole discourse, but she remembered he spoke of his kingdom, of his going to his Father, of what he would leave them now that he was about to be taken away, etc. He also gave them some instructions concerning penance, the confession of sin, repentance, and justification.

Anne Catherine felt that these instructions referred to the washing of the feet, and she saw that all the Apostles acknowledged their sins and repented of them, with the exception of Judas. This discourse was long and solemn. When it was concluded, Jesus sent John and James the Less to fetch water from the vestibule, and he told the Apostles to arrange the seats in a half circle. He went himself into the vestibule, where he girded himself with a towel. During this time, the Apostles spoke among themselves, and began speculating as to which of them would be the greatest, for Jesus having expressly announced that he was about to leave them and that his kingdom was near at hand, they felt strengthened anew in their idea that he had secret plans, and that he was referring to some earthly triumph which would be theirs at the last moment.

Meanwhile Jesus, in the vestibule, told John to take a basin, and James a pitcher filled with water, with which they followed him into the room, where the major-domo had placed another empty basin.

Jesus, on returning to his disciples in so humble a manner, addressed them a few words of reproach on the subject of the dispute which had arisen between them, and said among other things, that he himself was their servant, and that they were to sit down, for him to wash their feet. They sat down, therefore, in the same order as they had sat at table. Jesus went from one to the other, poured water from the basin which John carried, onto the feet of each, and then, taking the end of the towel where-with he was girded, wiped them.

Most loving and tender was the manner of Jesus while thus humbling himself at the feet of his Apostles.

Peter, when his turn came, endeavored through humility to prevent Jesus from washing his feet: *'Lord,'* he exclaimed, *'dost thou wash my feet?'*

Jesus answered: *'What I do, thou knowest not now, but thou shalt know hereafter.'*

It appeared to Anne Catherine that Jesus said privately: 'Simon, thou hast merited for my Father to reveal to thee who I am, whence I come, and whither I am going, thou alone hast expressly confessed it, therefore upon thee will I build my Church, and the gates of hell shall not prevail against it. My power will remain with thy successors to the end of the world.'

Jesus showed him to the other Apostles, and said that when he should be no more present among them, Peter was to fill his place in their regard.

Peter said: *'Thou shalt never wash my feet!'*

Jesus replied: *'If I wash theee not, thou shalt have no part with me.'*

Then Peter exclaimed: *'Lord, not only my feet, but also my hands and my head.'*

Jesus replied: *'He that is washed, needeth not but to wash his feet, but is clean wholly, And you are clean, but not all.'*

By Jesus last words he referred to Judas. He had spoken of the washing of the feet as signifying purification from daily faults, because the feet, which are continually in contact with the earth, are also continually liable to be soiled, unless great care is taken.

The washing of the feet was spiritual, and served as a species of absolution. Peter, in his zeal, saw nothing in it but too great an act of abasement on the part of Jesus; he knew not that to save him Jesus would the very next day humble himself even to his ignominious death on the cross.

When Jesus washed the feet of Judas, it was in the most loving and affecting manner; he bent his sacred face even on to the feet of the traitor; and in a low voice bade him now at least enter into himself, for that he had been a faithless traitor for the last year. Judas appeared to be anxious to pay no heed whatever to his words, and spoke to John, upon which Peter became angry, and exclaimed: 'Judas, the Master speaks to thee!'

Then Judas gave Jesus some vague, evasive reply, such as, 'Heaven forbid, Lord!'

The others had not remarked that Jesus was speaking to Judas, for his words were uttered in a low voice, in order not to be heard by them, and besides, they were all engaged in putting on their shoes. Nothing in the whole course of the Passion grieved Jesus so deeply as the treason of Judas.

Jesus finally washed the feet of John and James.

He then spoke again on the subject of humility, telling them that he that was the greatest among them was to be as their servant and that henceforth they were to wash one another's feet. Then he put on his garments, and the Apostles let down their clothes which they had girded up before eating the Paschal Lamb.

Institution of the Holy Eucharist

By command of Jesus, the major-domo had again laid out the table, which he had raised a little; then, having placed it once more in the middle of the room, he stood one urn filled with wine, and another with water underneath it. Peter and John went into the part of the room near the hearth, to get the chalice which they had brought from Seraphia's house, and which was still wrapped up in its covering. They carried it between them as if they had been carrying a tabernacle, and placed it on the table before Jesus. An oval plate stood there, with three fine white azymous loaves, placed on a piece of linen, by the side of the half loaf which Jesus had set aside during the Paschal meal, also, a jar containing wine and water, and three boxes, one filled with thick oil, a second with liquid oil, and the third empty.

In earlier times it had been the practice for all at table to eat of the same loaf and drink of the same cup at the end of the meal, thereby to express their friendship and brotherly love, and to welcome and bid farewell to each other. Ann Catherine believed Scripture must contain something upon this subject.

On the day of the Last Supper, Jesus raised this custom (which had hitherto been no more than a symbolical and figurative rite) to the dignity of the holiest of sacraments. One of the charges brought before Caiphas, on occasion of the treason of Judas, was, that Jesus had introduced a novelty into the Paschal ceremonies, but Nicodemus proved from Scripture that it was an ancient practice.

Jesus was seated between Peter and John, the doors were closed, and everything was done in the most mysterious and imposing manner. When the chalice was taken out of its covering, Jesus prayed, and spoke to his Apostles with the utmost solemnity. Ann Catherine saw him giving them an explanation of the Supper, and of the entire ceremony, and she was forcibly reminded of a priest teaching others to say Mass.

He then drew a species of shelf with grooves from the board on which the jars stood, and taking a piece of white linen with which the chalice was covered, spread it over the board and shelf. She then saw him lift a round plate, which he placed on this same shelf, off the top of the chalice. He next took the azymous loaves from beneath the linen with which they were covered, and placed them before him on the board; then he took out of the chalice a smaller vase, and ranged the six little glasses on each side of it. Then he blessed the bread and also the oil, to the best of her belief, after which he lifted up the paten with the loaves upon it, in his two hands, raised his eyes, prayed, offered, and replaced the paten on the table, covering it up again. He then took the chalice, had some wine poured into it by Peter, and some water, which he first blessed, by John, adding to it a little more water, which he poured into a small spoon, and after this he blessed the chalice, raised it up with a prayer, made the oblation, and replaced it on the table.

John and Peter poured some water on his hands, which he held over the plate on which the azymous loaves had been placed; then he took a little of the water which had been poured on his hands, in the spoon that he had taken out of the lower part of the chalice, and poured it on theirs. After this, the vase was passed round the table, and all the Apostles washed their hands in it. Ann Catherine did not remember whether this was the precise order in which these ceremonies were performed; all she knew was that they reminded her in a striking manner of the holy sacrifice of the Mass.

Meanwhile, Jesus became more and more tender and loving in his demeanor; he told his Apostles that he was about to give them all that he had, namely, his entire self, and he looked as though perfectly transformed by love. Anne Catherine saw Jesus becoming transparent, until he resembled a luminous shadow. He broke the bread into several pieces, which he laid together on the paten, and then took a corner of the first piece and dropped it into the chalice. At the moment he was doing this, Anne Catherine seemed to see the Blessed Virgin receiving the Holy Sacrament in a spiritual manner, although she was not present in the supper-room. Ann Catherine does not know how it was done, but she thought she saw Mother Mary enter without touching the ground, and appear before Jesus to receive the Holy Eucharist; after which Ann Catherine saw Mary no more. Jesus had told her in the morning, at Bethania, that he would keep the Pasch with her spiritually, and he had named the hour at which she was to betake herself to prayer, in order to receive it in spirit.

Again he prayed and taught; his words came forth from his lips like fire and light, and entered into each of the Apostles with the exception of Judas. He took the paten with the pieces of bread (Ann Catherine does not know whether he had placed it on the chalice) and said: '*Take and eat; this is my Body which is given for you.*'

Jesus stretched forth his right hand as if to bless, and, while he did so, a brilliant light came from him' his words were luminous; the bread entered the mouths of the Apostles as a brilliant substance, and light seemed to penetrate and surround them all; Judas alone remaining dark.

Jesus presented the bread first to Peter, next to John and then he made a sign to Judas to approach. Judas was thus the third who received the Adorable Sacrament, but the words of Jesus appeared to turn aside from the mouth of Judas and come back to their Divine Author. So perturbed was Ann Catherine in spirit at this sight, that her feelings can not be described. Jesus said to Judas: *'That which thou dost, do quickly.'*

Jesus then administered the Blessed Sacrament to the other Apostles, who approached two and two.

Jesus raised the chalice by its two handles to a level with his face, and pronounced the words of consecration. While doing so, he appeared wholly transfigured, as if it were transparent, and as though entirely passing into what he was going to give his Apostles. He made Peter and John drink from the chalice which he held in his hand, and then placed it again on the table. John poured the Divine Blood from the chalice into the smaller glasses, and Peter presented them to the Apostles, two of whom drank together out of the same cup. Ann Catherine thinks, but is not quite certain, that Judas also partook of the chalice; he did not return to his place, but immediately left the supper-room, and the other Apostles thought that Jesus had given him some commission to do. He left without praying or making any thanksgiving, and hence you may perceive how sinful it is to neglect returning thanks either after receiving our daily food, or after partaking of the Life-Giving Bread of Angels.

During the entire meal, Ann Catherine had seen a frightful little figure, with one foot like a dried bone, remaining close to Judas, but when he had reached the door, she beheld three devils pressing around him; one entered into his mouth, the second urged him on, and the third preceded him. It was night and they seemed to be lighting him, whilst he hurried onward like a madman.

Jesus poured a few drops of the Precious Blood remaining in the chalice into the little vase of which she has already spoken, and then placed his fingers over the chalice, while Peter and John poured water and wine upon them.

This done, he caused them to drink again from the chalice; and what remained of its contents was poured into the smaller glasses and distributed to the other Apostles. Then Jesus wiped the chalice, put into it the little vase containing the remainder of the Divine Blood, and placed over it the paten with the fragments of the consecrated bread, after which he again put on the cover, wrapped up the chalice, and stood it in the midst of the six small cups. The Apostles received in communion those remains of the Sacrament, after the Resurrection.

Anne Catherine does not remember seeing Jesus eat and drink of the consecrated elements; neither did she see Melchizedech, when offering the bread and wine, taste of them himself. It was made known to her why priests partake of them, although Jesus did not.

Sister Emmerich suddenly looked up, and appeared to be listening. Some explanation was given her on this subject but the following words were all that she could repeat: 'If the office of distributing it had been given to angels, they would not have partaken, but if priests did not partake, the Blessed Eucharist would be lost—it is through their participation that it is preserved.

There was an indescribable solemnity and order in all the actions of Jesus during the institution of the Holy Eucharist, and his every movement was most majestic. Anne Catherine saw the Apostles noting things down in the little rolls of parchment which they carried on their persons. Several times during the ceremonies she remarked that they bowed to each other, in the same way that priests do.

Private Instructions and Consecrations

Jesus gave his Apostles some private instructions; he told them how they were to preserve the Blessed Sacrament in memory of him, even to the end of the world; he taught them the necessary forms for making use of and communicating it, and in what manner they were, by degrees, to teach and publish this mystery; finally he told them when they were to receive what remained of the consecrated Elements, when to give some to the Blessed Virgin, and how to consecrate themselves after he should have sent them the Divine Comforter. He then spoke concerning the priesthood, the sacred unction, and the preparation of the Chrism and Holy Oils. He had there three boxes, two of which contained a mixture of oil and balm. He taught them how to make this mixture, what parts of the body were to be anointed with them, and upon what occasions. She remembered among other things, that he mentioned a case in which the Holy Eucharist could not be administered; perhaps what he said had reference to Extreme Unction, for her recollections on this point are not very clear. Jesus spoke of different kinds of anointing, and in particular of that of kings, and he said that even wicked kings who were anointed, derived from it especial powers. He put ointment and oil in the empty box, and mixed them together, but she could not say for certain whether it was at this moment, or at the time of the consecration of the bread, that Jesus blessed the oil.

Anne Catherine then saw Jesus anoint Peter and John, on whose hands he had already poured the water which had flowed on his own, and to whom he had given to drink out of the chalice. Then he laid his hands on their shoulders and heads, while they, on their part, joined their hands and crossed their thumbs, bowing down profoundly before him. He anointed the thumb and fore-finger of each of their hands, and marked a cross on their heads with Chrism. He said also that this would remain with them until the end of the world.

James the Less, Andrew, James the Greater, and Bartholomew, were also consecrated. She saw likewise that on Peter's bosom he crossed a sort of stole worn round the neck, whilst on the others he simply placed it crosswise, from the right shoulder to the left side. She does not know whether this was done at the time of the institution of the Blessed Sacrament, or only for the anointing.

Anne Catherine understood that Jesus communicated to them by this unction something essential and supernatural, beyond her power to describe. Jesus told them that when they should have received the Holy Spirit they were to consecrate the bread and wine, and anoint the other Apostles. It was made known to Ann Catherine that on the day of Pentecost, Peter and John imposed their hands upon the other Apostles, and a week later upon several of the disciples.

After the Resurrection, John gave the Adorable Sacrament for the first time to the Blessed Virgin. This event was solemnized as a festival among the Apostles. It is a festival no longer kept in the Church on earth, but Anne Catherine saw it celebrated in the Church triumphant. For the first few days after Pentecost, Anne Catherine saw only Peter and John consecrate the Blessed Eucharist, but after that the others also consecrated.

Jesus next proceeded to bless fire in a brass vessel, and care was taken that it should not go out, but it was kept near the spot where the Blessed Sacrament had been deposited, in one division of the ancient Paschal hearth, and fire was always taken from it when needed for spiritual purposes.

All that Jesus did upon this occasion was done in private, and taught equally in private. The Church has retained all that was essential of these secret instructions and, under the inspiration of the Holy Ghost, developed and adapted them to all her requirements.

Whether Peter and John were both consecrated bishops, or Peter alone as bishop and John as priest, or to what dignity the other four Apostles were raised, Ann Catherine cannot pretend to say. But the different ways in which Jesus arranged the Apostles' stoles appear to indicate different degrees of consecration.

When the holy ceremonies were concluded, the chalice (near which the blessed Chrism also stood) was re-covered, and the Adorable Sacrament carried by Peter and John into the back part of the room, which was divided off by a curtain, and from thenceforth became the Sanctuary. The spot where the Blessed Sacrament was deposited was not very far above the Paschal stove. Joseph of Arimathea and Nicodemus took care of the Sanctuary and of the supper-room during the absence of the Apostles.

Jesus again instructed his Apostles for a considerable length of time, and also prayed several times. He frequently appeared to be conversing with his Heavenly Father, and to be overflowing with enthusiasm and love. The Apostles also were full of joy and zeal, and asked him various questions which he forthwith answered. The Scriptures must contain much of this last discourse and conversation. He told Peter and John different things to be made known later to the other Apostles, who in their turn were to communicate them to the disciples and holy women according to the capacity of each for such knowledge. He had a private conversation with John, whom he told that his life would be longer than the lives of the others. He spoke to him also concerning seven Churches, some crowns and angels, and instructed him in the meaning of certain mysterious figures, which signified, to the best of Anne Catherine's knowledge, different epochs. The other Apostles were slightly jealous of this confidential communication being made to John.

Jesus spoke also of the traitor. 'Now he is doing this or that,' he said, and Anne Catherine saw Judas doing exactly as Jesus said of him. As Peter was vehemently protesting that he would always remain faithful, Jesus said to him: *'Simon, behold Satan hath desired to have you that he may sift you as wheat. But I have prayed for thee that thy faith fail not; and thou being once converted, confirm thy brethren.'*

Again, Jesus said, that whither he was going they could not follow him, when Peter exclaimed: *'Lord, I am ready to go with thee both into prison and to death.'*

And Jesus replied: *'Amen, amen, I say to thee, before the cock crow twice, thou shalt deny me thrice.'*

Jesus, while making known to his Apostles that trying times were at hand for them, said: *'When I sent you without purse, or scrip, or shoes, did you want anything?'*

They answered: *'Nothing.'*

'But now,' he continued, *'he that hath a purse let him take it, and likewise a scrip, and he that hath not, let him sell his coat and buy a sword. For I say to you, that this that is written must yet be fulfilled in me: And with the wicked was he reckoned. For the things concerning me have an end.'*

The Apostles only understood his words in a carnal sense, and Peter showed him two swords, which were short and thick, like cleavers. Jesus said: *'It is enough; let us go hence.'*

Then they sang the thanksgiving hymn, put the table on one side, and went into the vestibule.

There Jesus found his Mother, Mary of Cleophas, and Magdalen, who earnestly besought him not to go to Mount Olivet, for a report had spread that his enemies were seeking to lay hands on him. But Jesus comforted them with a few words, and hastened onward—it being then about nine o'clock.

They went down the road by which Peter and John had come to the supper-room, and directed their steps towards Mount Olivet.

Anne Catherine has always seen the Pasch and the institution of the Blessed Sacrament take place in the order related above. But her feelings were each time so strongly excited and her emotions so great that she could not give much attention to all the details, but now she saw them more distinctly. No words can describe how painful and exhausting such a sight as beholding the hidden recesses of hearts, is; the love and constancy of Jesus, and to know at the same time all that was going to befall him. She wondered how it would be possible to observe all that is merely external; the heart overflowing with admiration, gratitude, and love—the blindness of men seems perfectly incomprehensible—and the soul overwhelmed with sorrow at the thought of the ingratitude of the whole world, and of her own sins.

The eating of the Paschal Lamb was performed by Jesus rapidly, and in entire conformity with all the legal ordinances. The Pharisees were in the habit of adding some minute and superstitious ceremonies.

THE PASSION

If thou knowest not how to meditate on high and heavenly things, rest on the Passion of Christ, and willingly dwell in his sacred wounds. For if thou fly devoutly to the wounds and previous stigmas of Jesus, thou shalt feel great comfort in tribulation.'
(Imitation of Christ, book ii. Chap. i.)

Introduction

On the evening of the 18th of February, 1823, a friend of Sister Emmerich went up to the bed where she was lying apparently asleep; and being much struck by the beautiful and mournful expression of her countenance, felt himself inwardly inspired to raise his heart fervently to God, and offer the Passion of Christ to the Eternal Father, in union with the sufferings of all those who have carried their cross after him.

While making this short prayer, he chanced to fix his eyes for a moment upon the stigmatized hands of Sister Emmerich. She immediately hid them under the counterpane, starting as if someone had given her a blow. He felt surprised at this, and asked her, 'What has happened to you?'

'Many things,' she answered, in an expressive tone.

While he was considering what her meaning could be, she appeared to be asleep. At the end of about a quarter of an hour she suddenly started up with all the eagerness of a person having a violent struggle with another, stretched out both her arms, clenching her hand, as if to repel an enemy standing on the left side of her bed, and exclaimed in an indignant voice: 'What do you mean by this contract of Magdalum?'

Then she continued to speak with the warmth of a person who is being questioned during a quarrel—'Yes, it is that accursed spirit—the liar from the beginning—Satan, who is reproaching him about the Magdalum contract, and other things of the same nature, and says that he spent all that money upon himself.'

When asked, 'Who has spent money? Who is being spoken to in that way?' she replied, 'Jesus, my adorable Spouse, on Mount Olivet.'

Then she again turned to the left, with menacing gestures, and exclaimed, 'What meanest thou, O father of lies, with thy Magdalum contract? Did he not deliver twenty-seven poor prisoners at Thirza, with the money derived from the sale of Magdalum? I saw him, and thou darest to say that he has brought confusion into the whole estate, driven out its inhabitants, and squandered the money for which it was sold? But thy time is come, accursed spirit! Thou wilt be chained, and his heel will crush thy head.'

Here she was interrupted by the entrance of another person; her friends thought that she was in delirium, and pitied her. The following morning she owned that the previous night she had imagined herself to be following Jesus to the Garden of Olives, after the institution of the Blessed Eucharist, but that just at that moment someone having looked at the stigmas on her hands with a degree of veneration, she felt so horrified at this being done in the presence of Jesus, that she hastily hid them with a feeling of pain.

She then related her vision of what took place in the Garden of Olives, and as she continued her narrations the following days, the friend who was listening to her was enabled to connect the different scenes of the Passion together. But as, during Lent, she was also celebrating the combats of Lord Jesus with Satan in the desert, she had to endure in her own person many sufferings and temptations. Hence there were a few pauses in the history of the Passion, which were, however, easily filled up by means of some later communications.

Anne Catherine usually spoke in common German, but when in a state of ecstasy, her language became much purer, and her narrations partook at once of child-like simplicity and dignified inspiration. Her friend wrote down all that she had said, directly he returned to his own apartments; for it was seldom that he could so much as even take notes in her presence. The Giver of all good gifts bestowed upon him memory, zeal and strength to bear much trouble and fatigue, so that he has been enabled to bring this work to a conclusion. His conscience tells him that he has done his best, and he humbly begs the reader, if satisfied with the result of his labors, to bestow upon him the alms of an occasional prayer.

Jesus in the Garden of Olives

When Jesus left the supper-room with the eleven Apostles, after the institution of the Adorable Sacrament of the Altar, his soul was deeply oppressed and his sorrow on the increase.

He led the eleven, by an unfrequented path, to the Valley of Josaphat. As they left the house, Ann Catherine saw the moon, which was not yet quite at the full, rising in front of the mountain.

As Jesus waited with his Apostles about the valley, he told them that here he should one day return to judge the world, but not in a state of poverty and humiliation, as he then was, and that men would tremble with fear and cry: *'Mountains, fall upon us!'*

His disciples did not understand him, and thought by no means for the first time that night, that weakness and exhaustion had affected his brain. He said to them again:

'All you shall be scandalized in me this night. For it is written: I will strike the shepherd, and the sheep of the flock shall be dispersed. But after I shall be risen again, I will go before you to Galilee.'

The Apostles were still in some degree animated by the spirit of enthusiasm and devotion with which their reception of the Blessed Sacrament and the solemn and affecting words of Jesus had inspired them. They eagerly crowded round him, and expressed their love in a thousand different ways, earnestly protesting that they would never abandon him. But as Jesus continued to talk in the same strain, Peter exclaimed: *'Although all shall be scandalized in thee, I will never be scandalized!'*

And Jesus answered him: *'Amen, I say to thee, that in this night, before the cock crow, thou wilt deny me thrice.'*

But Peter still insisted, saying: *'Yea, though I should die with thee, I will not deny thee.'*

And the others all said the same. They walked onward and stopped, by turns, for the sadness of Jesus continued to increase. The Apostles tried to comfort him by human arguments, assuring him that what he foresaw would not come to pass. They tired themselves in these vain efforts, began to doubt, and were assailed by temptation.

They crossed the brook Cedron, not by the bridge where, a few hours later, Jesus was taken prisoner, but by another, for they had left the direct road. Gethsemani, whither they were going, was about a mile and a half distant from the supper-hall, for it was three quarters of a mile from the supper-hall to the Valley of Josaphat, and about as far from thence to Gethsemani.

The place called Gethsemani (where latterly Jesus had several times passed the night with his disciples) was a large garden, surrounded by a hedge, and containing only some fruit trees and flowers, while outside there stood a few deserted unclosed buildings.

The Apostles and several other persons had keys of this garden, which was used sometimes as a pleasure ground, and sometimes as a place of retirement for prayer. Some arbors made of leaves and branches had been raised there, and eight of the Apostles remained in them, and were later joined by others of the disciples. The Garden of Olives was separated by a road from that of Gethsemani, and was open, surrounded only by an earthen wall, and smaller than the Garden of Gethsemani. There were caverns, terraces, and many olive-trees to be seen in this garden, and it was easy to find there a suitable spot for prayer and meditation. It was to the wildest part that Jesus went to pray.

It was about nine o'clock when Jesus reached Gethsemani with his disciples. The moon had risen, and already gave light in the sky, although the earth was still dark. Jesus was most sorrowful, and told his apostles that danger was at hand. The disciples felt uneasy, and he told eight of those who were following him to remain in the Garden of Gethsemani while he went on to pray. He took with him Peter, James, and John, and going on a little further, entered into the Garden of Olives. No words can describe the sorrow which then oppressed his soul for the time of trial was near. John asked him how it was that he, who had hitherto always consoled them, could now be so dejected?

'My soul is sorrowful even unto death,' was Jesus' reply. And he beheld sufferings and temptations surrounding him on all sides, and drawing nearer and nearer, under the forms of frightful figures borne on clouds. Then it was that he said to the three Apostles: *'Stay you here and watch with me. Pray, lest ye enter into temptation.'*

Jesus went a few steps to the left, down a hill, and concealed himself beneath a rock, in a grotto about six feet deep, while the Apostles remained in a species of hollow above. The earth sank gradually the further you entered this grotto, and the plants which were hanging from the rock screened its interior like a curtain from persons outside.

When Jesus left his disciples, Ann Catherine saw a number of frightful figures surrounding him in an ever-narrowing circle. His sorrow and anguish of soul continued to increase, and he was trembling all over when he entered the grotto to pray, like a wayworn traveler hurriedly seeking shelter from a sudden storm, but the awful visions pursued him even there, and became more and more clear and distinct. Alas! This small cavern appeared to contain the awful picture of all the sins which had been or were to be committed from the fall of Adam to the end of the world, and of the punishment which they deserved. It was here, on Mount Olivet, that Adam and Eve took refuse when driven out of Paradise to wander homeless on earth, and they had wept and bewailed themselves in this very grotto.

Anne Catherine felt that Jesus, in delivering himself up to Divine Justice in satisfaction for the sins of the world, caused his divinity to return, in some sort, into the bosom of the Holy trinity, concentrated himself, so to speak, in his pure, loving and innocent humanity, and strong only in his ineffable love, gave it up to anguish and suffering.

Jesus fell on his face, overwhelmed with unspeakable sorrow, and all the sins of the world displayed themselves before him, under countless forms and in all their real deformity. He took them all upon himself, and in his prayer offered his own adorable Person to the justice of his Heavenly Father, in payment for so awful a debt. But Satan, who was enthroned amid all these horrors, and even filled with diabolical joy at the sight of them, let loose his fury against Jesus, and displayed before the eyes of his soul increasingly awful visions, at the same time addressing his adorable humanity in words such as these:

'Takest thou even this sin upon thyself? Art thou willing to bear its penalty? Art thou prepared to satisfy for all these sins?'

And now a long ray of light, like a luminous path in the air, descended from Heaven; it was a procession of angels who came up to Jesus and strengthened and reinvigorated him. The remainder of the grotto was filled with frightful visions of our crimes; Jesus took them all upon himself, but that adorable Heart, which was so filled with the most perfect love for God and man, was flooded with anguish, and overwhelmed beneath the weight of so many abominable crimes. When this huge mass of iniquities, like the waves of a fathomless ocean, had passed over his soul, Satan brought forward innumerable temptations, as he had formerly done in the desert, even daring to adduce various accusations against him.

'And takest thou all these things upon thyself,' he exclaimed, 'thou who art not unspotted thyself?' Then he laid to the charge of our Lord, with infernal impudence, a host of imaginary crimes. He reproached him with the faults of his disciples, the scandals which they had caused, and the disturbances which he had occasioned in the world by giving up ancient customs.

No Pharisee, however wily and severe, could have surpassed Satan on this occasion; he reproached Jesus with having been the cause of the massacre of the Innocents, as well as of the sufferings of his parents in Egypt, with not having saved John the Baptist from death, with having brought disunion into families, protected men of despicable character, refused to cure various sick persons, injured the inhabitants of Gergesa by permitting men possessed by the devil to overturn their vats, and demons to make swine case themselves into the sea; with having deserted his family, and squandered the property of others; in one word Satan, in the hopes of causing Jesus to waver, suggested to him every thought by which he would have tempted at the hour of death an ordinary mortal who might have performed all these actions without a superhuman intention; for it was hidden from him that Jesus was the Son of God, and he tempted him only as the most just of men.

Our Divine Savior permitted his humanity thus to preponderate over his divinity, for he was pleased to endure even those temptations with which holy souls are assailed at the hour of death concerning the merit of their good works. That he might drink the chalice of suffering even to the dregs, he permitted the evil spirit to tempt his sacred humanity, as he would have tempted a man who should wish to attribute to his good works some special value in themselves, over and above what they might have by their union with the merits of Jesus.

There was not an action out of which he did not contrive to frame some accusation, and he reproached Jesus, among other things, with having spent the price of the property of Mary Magdalen at Magdalum, which he had received from Lazarus.

Among the sins of the world which Jesus took upon himself, Ann Catherine saw also her own; and a stream, in which she distinctly beheld each of her faults, appeared to flow towards her from out of the temptations with which Jesus was encircled. During this time her eyes were fixed upon Jesus; with him she wept and prayed, and with him she turned towards the consoling angels. Truly did Jesus writhe like a worm beneath the weight of his anguish and sufferings.

Whilst Satan was pouring forth his accusations against Jesus, it was with difficulty that Ann Catherine could restrain her indignation, but when Jesus spoke of the sale of Magdalen's property, she could no longer keep silence, and exclaimed: 'How canst thou reproach him with the sale of this property as with a crime? Did I not myself see Jesus spend the sum which was given him by Lazarus in works of mercy, and deliver twenty-eight debtors imprisoned at Thirza?'

At first Jesus looked calm, as he kneeled down and prayed, but after a time his soul became terrified at the sight of the innumerable crimes of men, and of their ingratitude towards God, and his anguish was so great that he trembled and shuddered as he exclaimed: *Father, if it is possible, let this chalice pass from me! Father, all things are possible to thee; remove this chalice from me!'*

But the next moment Jesus added: *'Nevertheless, not my will but thine be done.'*

His will and that of his Father were one, but now that his love had ordained that he should be left to all the weakness of his human nature, he trembled at the prospect of death.

Anne Catherine saw the cavern in which Jesus was kneeling, filled with frightful figures; she saw all the sins, wickedness, vices, and ingratitude of mankind torturing and crushing him to the earth; the horror of death and terror which he felt as man at the sight of the expiratory sufferings about to come upon him, surrounded and assailed his Divine Person under the forms of hideous specters. He fell from side to side, clasping his hands; his body was covered with a cold sweat, and he trembled and shuddered. He then arose, but his knees were shaking and apparently scarcely able to support him; his countenance was pale, and quite altered in appearance, his lips white, and his hair standing on end.

It was about half-past ten o'clock when he arose from his knees, and, bathed in a cold sweat, directed his trembling, weak foot-steps towards his three Apostles. With difficulty did he ascend the left side of the cavern, and reach a spot where the ground was level, and where they were sleeping, exhausted with fatigue, sorrow and anxiety. He came to them like a man overwhelmed with bitter sorrow, who terror urges to seek his friends, but like also to a good shepherd, who, when warned of the approach of danger, hastens to visit his flock, the safety of which is threatened; for he well knew that they also were being tried by suffering and temptation.

The terrible visions never left him, even while he was thus seeking his disciples. When he found that they were asleep, he clasped his hands and fell down on his knees beside them, overcome with sorrow and anxiety, and said: *'Simon sleepest thou?'*

They awoke, and raised him up, and he, in his desolation of spirit, said to them: *'What? Could you not watch one hour with me?'*

When they looked at him, and saw him pale and exhausted, scarcely able to support him-self, bathed in sweat, trembling and shuddering, -- when they heard how changed and almost inaudible his voice had become, they did not know what to think, and had he not been still surrounded by a well-known halo of light, they would never have recognized him as Jesus.

John said to him: 'Master, what has befallen thee? Must I call the other disciples? Ought we to take to flight?'

Jesus answered: *'Were I to live, teach, and perform miracles for thirty-three years longer, that would not suffice for the accomplishment of what must be fulfilled before this time tomorrow. Call not the eight; I did not bring them hither, because they could not see me thus agonizing without being scandalized; they would yield to temptation, forget much of the past, and lose their confidence in me. But you, who have seen the Son of Man transfigured, may also see him under a cloud, and in dereliction of spirit; nevertheless, watch and pray, lest ye fall into temptation, for the spirit indeed is willing, but the flesh is weak.'*

By these words Jesus sought at once to encourage them to persevere, and to make known to them the combat which his human nature was sustaining against death, together with the cause of his weakness. In his overwhelming sorrow, he remained with them nearly a quarter of an hour, and spoke to them again. He then returned to the grotto, his mental sufferings being still on the increase, while his disciples, on their part, stretched forth their hands towards him, wept, and embraced each other, asking, 'What can it be? What is happening to him? He appears to be in a state of complete desolation.'

After this, they covered their heads, and began to pray, sorrowfully and anxiously.

About an hour and a half had passed since Jesus entered the Garden of Olives. It is true that Scripture tells us he said, *'Could you not watch one hour with me?'* but his words should not be taken literally, nor according to our way of counting time. The three Apostles who were with Jesus had prayed at first, but then they had fallen asleep, but temptation had come upon them by reason of their want of trust in God. The other eight, who had remained outside the garden, did not sleep, for our Lord's last words, so expressive of suffering and sadness, had filled their hearts with sinister forebodings, and they wandered about Mount Olivet, trying to find some place of refuge in case of danger.

The town of Jerusalem was very quiet; the people were in their houses, engaged in preparing for the feast, but Anne Catherine saw, here and there, some of the friends and disciples of Jesus walking to and fro, with anxious countenances, conversing earnestly together, and evidently expecting some great event.

The Mother of Jesus, Magdalen, Martha, Mary of Cleophas, Mary Salome, and Salome had gone from the supper-hall to the house of Mary, the mother of Mark.

Mary was alarmed at the reports which were spreading, and wished to return to the town with her friends, in order to hear something of Jesus. Lazarus, Nicodemus, Joseph of Arimathea, and some relations from Hebron, came to see and endeavor to tranquillize her, for, as they were aware, either from their own knowledge or from what the disciples had told them, of the mournful predictions which Jesus had made in the supper-room, they had made inquiries of some

Pharisees of their acquaintance, and had not been able to hear that any conspiracy was on foot for the time against Jesus.

Being utterly ignorant of the treason of Judas, they assured Mary that the danger could not yet be very great, and that the enemies of Jesus would not make any attempts upon his person, at least until the festival was over. Mary told them how restless and disturbed in mind Judas had latterly appeared, and how abruptly he had left the supper-room. She felt no doubt of his having gone to betray Jesus, for she had often warned him that he was a son of perdition. The holy women then returned to the house of Mary, the mother of Mark.

When Jesus, unrelieved of all the weight of his sufferings, returned to the grotto, he fell prostrate, with his face on the ground and his arms extended, and prayed to his Eternal Father; but his soul had to sustain a second interior combat, which lasted three quarters of an hour.

Angels came and showed him, in a series of visions, all the sufferings that he was to endure in order to expiate sin; how great was the beauty of man, the image of God, before the fall, and how that beauty was changed and obliterated when sin entered the world. He beheld how all sins originated in that of Adam, the signification and essence of concupiscence, its terrible effects on the powers of the soul, and likewise, the signification and essence of all the sufferings entailed by concupiscence. They showed him the satisfaction which he would have to offer to Divine Justice, and how it would consist of a degree of suffering in his soul and body which would comprehend all the sufferings due to the concupiscence of all mankind, since the debt of the whole human race had to be paid by that humanity which alone was sinless—the humanity of the Son of God.

The angels showed Jesus all these things under different forms, and Ann Catherine felt what the angels were saying, although she heard no voice. No tongue can describe what anguish and what horror overwhelmed the soul of Jesus at the sight of so terrible an expiation—his sufferings were so great, indeed, that a bloody sweat issued forth from all the pores of his body.

Whilst the adorable humanity of Christ was thus crushed to the earth beneath this awful weight of suffering, the angels appeared filled with compassion; there was a pause, and Anne Catherine perceived that they were earnestly desiring to console Jesus, and praying to that effect before the throne of God. For one instant there appeared to be, as it were, a struggle between the mercy and justice of God and that love which was sacrificing itself. She was permitted to see an image of God, not as before, seated on a throne, but under a luminous form. Ann Catherine beheld the divine nature of the Son in the Person of the Father and, as it were with-drawn into his bosom; the Person of the Holy Ghost proceeded from the Father and the Son, it was, so to speak, between them, and yet the whole formed only one God—but these things are indescribable.

All this was more an inward perception than a vision under distinct forms, and it appeared to Ann Catherine that the Divine Will of Jesus withdrew in some sort into the Eternal Father, in order to permit all those sufferings which his human will besought his Father to spare him, to weigh upon his humanity alone. She saw this at the time when the angels, filled with compassion, desired to console Jesus, who, in fact, was slightly relieved at that moment. Then all disappeared, and the angels retired from Jesus, whose soul was about to sustain fresh assaults.

When Jesus, on Mount Olivet, was pleased to experience and overcome that violent repugnance of human nature to suffering and death which constitutes a portion of all sufferings, the tempter was permitted to do to him what he does to all men who desire to sacrifice themselves in a holy cause.

In the first portion of the agony, Satan displayed before the eyes of Jesus the enormity of that debt of sin which he was going to pay, and was even bold and malicious enough to seek fault in the very works of our Savior himself. In the second agony, Jesus beheld, to its fullest extent and in all its bitterness, the expiatory suffering which would be required to satisfy Divine Justice. This was displayed to him by angels; for it belongs not to Satan to show that expiation is possible, and the father of lies and despair never exhibits the works of Divine Mercy before men.

Jesus having victoriously resisted all these assaults by his entire and absolute submission to the will of his Heavenly Father, a succession of new and terrifying visions were presented before his eyes, and that feeling of doubt and anxiety which a man on the point of making some great sacrifice always experiences, arose in the soul of Jesus, as he asked himself the tremendous question:

'And what good will result from this sacrifice?'

Then a most awful picture of the future was displayed before his eyes and overwhelmed his tender heart with anguish.

When God had created the first Adam, he cast a deep sleep upon him, opened his side, and took one of his ribs, of which he made Eve, his wife and the mother of all the living. Then he brought her to Adam, who exclaimed: *'This now is bone of my bones, and flesh of my flesh.... Wherefore a man shall leave father and other, and shall cleave to his wife, and they shall be two in one flesh.'*

That was the marriage of which it is written: *'This is a great Sacrament. I speak in Christ and in the Church.'*

Jesus Christ, the second Adam, was pleased also to let sleep come upon him—the sleep of death on the cross, and he was also pleased to let his side be opened, in order that the second Eve, his Virgin Spouse, the Church, the mother of all the living might be formed from it. It was his will to give her the blood of redemption, the water of purification, and his spirit—the three which render testimony on earth—and to bestow upon her also the holy Sacraments, in order that she might be pure, holy and undefiled; he was to be her head, and we were to be her members, under submission to the head, the bones of his bones, and the flesh of his flesh.

In taking human nature, that he might suffer death for us, he had also left his Eternal Father, to cleave to his Spouse, the Church, and he became one flesh with her, by feeding her with the Adorable Sacrament of the Altar, in which he unites himself unceasingly with us. He has been pleased to remain on earth with his Church, until we shall all be united together by him within her fold, and he has said: *'The gates of hell shall never prevail against her.'*

To satisfy his unspeakable love for sinners, our Lord had become man and a brother of these same sinners, that so he might take upon himself the punishment due to all their crimes. He had contemplated with deep sorrow the greatness of this debt and the unspeakable sufferings by which it was to be acquitted. Yet he had most joyfully given himself up to the will of his Heavenly Father as a victim of expiation. Now, however, he beheld all the future sufferings, combats, and wounds of his heavenly Spouse; in one word, he beheld the ingratitude of men.

The soul of Jesus beheld all the future sufferings of his Apostles, disciples, and friends; after which he saw the primitive Church, numbering but a few souls in her fold at first, and then in proportion as her numbers increased, disturbed by heresies and schisms breaking out among her children, who repeated the sin of Adam by price and disobedience. He saw the tepidity, malice, and corruption of an infinite number of Christians, the lies and deceptions of proud teachers, all the sacrileges of wicked priests, the fatal consequences of each sin, and the abomination of desolation in the kingdom of God, in the sanctuary of those ungrateful human beings whom he was about to redeem with his blood at the cost of unspeakable sufferings.

The scandals of all ages, down to the present day and even to the end of the world—every species of error, deception, mad fanaticism, obstinacy, and malice—were displayed before his eyes, and he held, as it were floating before him, all the apostates, heresiarchs, and pretended reformers, who deceive men by an appearance of sanctity. The corrupters and the corrupted of all ages outraged and tormented him for not having been crucified after their fashion, or for not having suffered precisely as they settled or imagined he should have done. They vied with each other in tearing the seamless robe of his Church; many ill-treated, insulted, and denied him, and many turned contemptuously away, shaking their heads at him, avoiding his compassionate embrace, and hurrying on to the abyss where they were finally swallowed up. He saw countless numbers of other men who did not dare openly to deny him, but who passed on in disgust at the sight of the wounds of his Church, as the Levite passed by the poor man who had fallen among robbers. Like unto cowardly and faithless children, who desert their mother in the middle of the night, at the sight of the thieves and robbers to whom their negligence or their malice has opened the door, they fled from his wounded Spouse.

He beheld all these men, some-times separated from the true Vine, and taking their rest amid the wild fruit trees, sometimes like lost sheep, left to the mercy of the wolves, led by base hirelings into bad pasturages, and refusing to enter the fold of the Good Shepherd who gave his life for his sheep. They were wandering homeless in the desert in the midst of the sand blown about by the wind, and were obstinately determined not to see his City placed upon a hill, which could not be hidden, the house of his Spouse, his Church built upon a rock, and with which he had promised to remain to the end of ages.

They built upon the sand wretched tenements, which they were continually pulling down and rebuilding, but in which there was neither altar nor sacrifice; they had weathercocks on their roofs, and their doctrines changed with the wind, consequently they were forever in opposition one with the other. They never could come to a mutual understanding, and were forever unsettled, often destroying their own dwellings and hurling the fragments against the Corner-Stone of the Church, which always remained unshaken.

As there was nothing but darkness in the dwellings of these men, many among them, instead of directing their steps towards the Candle placed on the Candlestick in the House of the Spouse of Christ, wandered with closed eyes around the gardens of the Church, sustaining life only by inhaling the sweet odors which were diffused from them far and near, stretching forth their hands towards shadowy idols, and following wandering stars which led them to wells where there was no water. Even when on the very brink of the precipice, they refused to listen to the voice of the Spouse calling them, and, though dying with hunger, derided, insulted, and mocked at those servants and messengers who were sent to invite them to the Nuptial Feast.

They obstinately refused to enter the garden, because they feared the thorns of the hedge, although they had neither wheat with which to satisfy their hunger nor wine to quench their thirst, but were simply intoxicated with pride and self-esteem, and being blinded by their own false lights, persisted in asserting that the Church of the Word made flesh was invisible.

Jesus beheld them all; he wept over them, and was pleased to suffer for all those who do not see him and who will not carry their crosses after him in his City built upon a hill—his Church founded upon a rock, to which he has given himself in the Holy Eucharist, and against which the gates of Hell will never prevail.

Bearing a prominent place in these mournful visions which were beheld by the soul of Jesus, Ann Catherine saw Satan, who dragged away and strangled a multitude of men redeemed by the blood of Christ and sanctified buy the unction of his Sacrament.

Jesus beheld with bitterest anguish the ingratitude and corruption of the Christians of the first and of all succeeding ages, even to the end of the world, and during the whole of this time the voice of the tempter was incessantly repeating: 'Canst thou resolve to suffer for such ungrateful reprobates?' while the various apparitions succeeded each other with intense rapidity, and so violently weighted down and crushed the soul of Jesus, that his sacred humanity was overwhelmed with unspeakable anguish. Jesus—the Anointed of the Lord—the Son of Man—struggled and writhed as he fell on his knees, with clasped hands, as it were annihilated beneath the weight of his suffering.

So violent was the struggle which then took place between his human will and his repugnance to suffer so much for such an ungrateful race that, from every pore of his sacred body there burst forth large drops of blood, which fell trickling on to the ground. In his bitter agony, he looked around, as though seeking help, and appeared to take Heaven, earth, and the stars of the firmament to witness of his sufferings.

Anne Catherine saw Jesus still praying in the grotto, struggling against the repugnance to suffering which belonged to human nature, and abandoning himself wholly to the will of his Eternal Father. Here the abyss opened before him, and he had a vision of the first part of Limbo. He saw Adam and Eve, the patriarchs, prophets, and just men, the parents of his Mother, and John the Baptist, awaiting his arrival in the lower world with such intense longing, that the sight strengthened and gave fresh courage to his loving heart.

His death was to open Heaven to these captives—his death was to deliver them out of that prison in which they were languishing in eager hope! When Jesus had, with deep emotion, looked upon these saints of antiquity, angels presented to him all the bands of saints of future ages, who, joining their labors to the merits of his Passion, were, through him, to be united to his Heavenly Father.

Most beautiful and consoling was this vision, in which he beheld salvation and sanctification flowing forth in ceaseless streams from the fountain of redemption opened by his death.

The apostles, disciples, virgins, and holy women, the martyrs, confessors, hermits, popes, and bishops, and large bands of religious of both sexes—in one word, the entire army of the blessed—appeared before him. All bore on their heads triumphal crowns, and the flowers of their crowns differed in form, in color, in odor, and in perfection, according to the difference of the sufferings, labors and victories which had procured them eternal glory. Their whole life, and all their actions, merits, and power, as well as all the glory of their triumph, came solely from their union with the merits of Jesus Christ.

The reciprocal influence exercised by these saints upon each other, and the manner in which they all drank from one sole Fountain—the Adorable Sacrament and the Passion of our Lord—formed a most touching and wonderful spectacle. Nothing about them was devoid of deep meaning—their works, martyrdom, victories, appearance, and dress—all, though indescribably varied was confused together in infinite harmony and unity; and this unity in diversity was produced by the rays of one single Sun, by the Passion of the Lord, of the Word made flesh, in whom was life, the light of men, which shined in darkness, and the darkness did not comprehend it.

The army of future saints passed before the soul of Jesus, which was thus placed between the desiring patriarchs, and the triumphant band of the future blessed, and these two armies joining together, and completing one another, so to speak, surrounded the loving Heart of Jesus as with a crown of victory.

This most affecting and consoling spectacle bestowed a degree of strength and comfort upon the soul of Jesus. He so loved his brethren and creatures that, to accomplish the redemption of one single soul, he would have accepted with joy all the sufferings to which he was now devoting himself. As these visions referred to the future, they were diffused to a certain height in the air. But these consoling visions faded away, and the angels displayed before him the scenes of his Passion quite close to the earth, because it was near at hand.

Ann Catherine beheld every scene distinctly portrayed, from the kiss of Judas to the last words of Jesus on the cross, and she saw in this single vision all that she saw in her meditations on the Passion. The treason of Judas, the flight of the disciples, the insults which were offered Jesus before Annas and Caiphas, Peter's denial, the tribunal of Pilate, Herod's mockery, the scourging and crowning with thorns, the condemnation to death, the carrying of the cross, the linen cloth presented by Veronica, the crucifixion, the insults of the Pharisees, the sorrows of Mary, of Magdalen, and of John, the wound of the lancc in his side, after death; -- in one word, every part of the Passion was shown to him in the minutest detail. He accepted all voluntarily, submitting to everything for the love of man. He saw also and felt the sufferings endured at that moment by his Mother, whose interior union with his agony was so entire that she had fainted in the arms of her two friends.

When the visions of the Passion were concluded, Jesus fell on his face like one at the point of death; the angels disappeared, and the bloody sweat became more copious, so that Anne Catherine saw it had soaked his garment. Entire darkness reigned in the cavern when she beheld an angel descend to Jesus. This angel was of higher stature than any whom Ann Catherine had before beheld, and his form was also more distinct and more resembling that of a man. He was clothed like a priest in a long floating garment, and bore before him, in his hands, a small vase, in shape resembling the chalice used at the Last Supper. At the top of this chalice, there was a small oval body, about the size of a bean, and which diffused a reddish light. The angel, without touching the earth with his feet, stretched forth his right hand to Jesus, who arose, when he placed the mysterious food in his mouth, and gave him to drink from the luminous chalice. Then he disappeared.

Jesus having freely accepted the chalice of his sufferings, and received new strength, remained some minutes longer in the grotto, absorbed in calm meditation, and returning thanks to his Heavenly Father. He was still in deep affliction of spirit, but supernaturally comforted to such a degree as to be able to go to his disciples without tottering as he walked, or bending beneath the weight of his sufferings. His countenance was still pale and altered, but his step was firm and determined. He had wiped his face with a linen cloth, and rearranged his hair, which hung about his shoulders, matted together and damp with blood.

When Jesus came to his disciples, they were lying, as before, against the wall of the terrace, asleep, and with their heads covered.

Our Lord told them that then was not the time for sleep but that they should arise and pray:

'Behold the hour is at hand, and the Son of Man shall be betrayed into the hands of sinners.'

He said: *'Arise, let us go, behold he is at hand that will betray me. It were better for him, if that man had not been born.'*

The Apostles arose in much alarm, and looked round with anxiety. When they had somewhat recovered them-selves, Peter said warmly: 'Lord, I will call the others, that so we may defend thee.'

But Jesus pointed out to them at some distance in the valley, on the other side of the Brook of Cedron, a band of armed men who were advancing with torches, and he said that one of their number had betrayed him. He spoke calmly, exhorted them to console his Mother, and said: *'Let us go and meet them—I shall deliver myself up without resistance into the hands of my enemies.'*

Jesus then left the Garden of Olives with the three Apostles, and went to meet the archers on the road which led from that garden to Gethsemani.

When the Blessed Virgin, under the care of Magdalen and Salome, recovered her senses, some disciples, who had seen the soldiers approaching, conducted her back to the house of Mary, the mother of Mark. The archers took a shorter road than that which Jesus followed when he left the supper-room.

The grotto in which Jesus had this day prayed was not the one where he usually prayed on Mount Olivet. He commonly went to a cabin at a greater distance off, where, one day, after having cursed the barren fig-tree, he had prayed in great affliction of spirit, with his arms stretched out, and leaning against a rock.

The traces of his body and hands remained impressed on the stone, and were honored later, but it was not known on what occasion the miracle had taken place. Ann Catherine had several times seen similar impressions left upon the stone, either by the Prophets of the Old Testament, or by Jesus, Mary, or some of the apostles; and she has also seen those made by the body of St. Catherine on Mount Sinai. These impressions do not seem deep, but resemble what would be made upon a thick piece of dough, if a person leaned his hand upon it.

Judas and his Band

Judas had not expected that his treason would have produced such fatal results. He had been anxious to obtain the promised reward, and to please the Pharisees by delivering up Jesus into their hands, but he had never calculated on things going so far, or thought that the enemies of his Master would actually bring him to judgment and crucify him; his mind was engrossed with the love of gain alone, and some astute Pharisees and Sadducees, with whom he had established an intercourse, had constantly urged him on to treason by flattering him. He was sick of the fatiguing, wandering, and persecuted life which the Apostles led. For several months past he had continually stolen from the alms which were consigned to his care, and his avarice, grudging the expenses incurred by Magdalen when she poured the previous ointment on the feet of Jesus, incited him to the commission of the greatest of crimes. He had always hoped that Jesus would establish a temporal kingdom, and bestow upon him some brilliant and lucrative post in it, but finding himself disappointed, he turned his thoughts to amassing a fortune. He saw that sufferings and persecutions were on the increase for Jesus and his followers, and he sought to make friends with the powerful enemies of Jesus before the time of danger, for he saw that Jesus did not become a king, whereas the actual dignity and power of the High Priest, and all who were attached to his service, made a very strong impression upon his mind.

He began to enter by degrees into a close connection with their agents, who were constantly flattering him, and assuring him in strong terms that, in any case, an end would speedily be put to the career of Jesus. He listened more and more eagerly to the criminal suggestions of his corrupt heart, and he had done nothing during the last few days but go back and forth in order to induce the chief priests to come to some agreement. But they were unwilling to act at once, and treated him with contempt. They said that sufficient time would not intervene before the festival day, and that there would be a tumult among the people. The Sanhedrin alone listened to his proposals with some degree of attention. After Judas had sacrilegiously received the Blessed Sacrament, Satan took entire possession of him, and he went off at once to complete his crime.

He in the first place sought those persons who had hitherto flattered and entered into agreements with him, and who still received him with pretended friendship. Some others joined the party, and among the number Annas and Caiphas, but the latter treated him with considerable pride and scorn. All these enemies of Christ were extremely undecided and far from feeling any confidence of success, because they mistrusted Judas.

Ann Catherine saw the empire of Hell divided against itself; Satan desired the crime of the Jews, and earnestly longed for the death of Jesus, the Converter of souls, the Holy Teacher, the Just Man, who was so abhorrent to him; but at the same time he felt an extraordinary interior fear of the death of the innocent Victim, who would not conceal himself from his persecutors. She saw Jesus then, on the one hand, stimulate the hatred and fury of the enemies of Jesus, and on the other, insinuate to some of their number that Judas was a wicked, despicable character, and that the sentence could not be pronounced before the festival, or a sufficient number of witnesses against Jesus be gathered together.

A short time before when Judas had received the price of his treason, a Pharisee had gone out, and sent seven slaves to fetch wood with which to prepare the Cross for Jesus, in case he should be judged, because the next day there would not be sufficient time on account of the commencement of the Paschal festivity. They procured this wood from a spot about three-quarters of a mile distant, near a high wall, where there was a great quantity of other wood belonging to the Temple, and dragged it to a square situated behind the tribunal of Caiphas. The principal piece of the Cross came from a tree formerly growing in the Valley of Josaphat, near the torrent of Cedron, and which, having fallen across the stream, had been used as a sort of bridge.

Judas next began to make his arrangements with those who were to accompany him. He wished to enter the garden before them, and embrace and salute Jesus as if he were returning to him as his friend and disciple, and then for the soldiers to run forward and seize the person of Jesus. He was anxious that it should be thought that they had come there by chance, that so, when they had made their appearance, he might run away like the other disciples and be no more heard of.

He likewise thought that, perhaps, a tumult would ensue, that the Apostles might defend themselves, and Jesus pass through the midst of his enemies, as he had so often done before. He dwelt upon these thoughts especially, when his pride was hurt by the disdainful manner of the people in his regard; but he did not repent, for he had wholly given himself up to Satan. It was his desire also that the soldiers following him should not carry chains and cords, and his accomplices pretended to accede to all his wishes, although in reality they acted with him as with a traitor who was not to be trusted, but to be cast off as soon as he had done what was wanted.

The soldiers received orders to keep close to Judas, watch him carefully, and not let him escape until Jesus was seized, for he had received his reward, and it was feared that he might run off with the money, and Jesus not be taken after all, or another be taken in his place.

The band of men chosen to accompany Judas was composed of twenty soldiers, selected from the temple guard and from others of the military who were under the orders of Annas and Caiphas. They were dressed very much like the Roman soldiers, had morions like them, and wore hanging straps round their thighs, but their beards were long, whereas the Roman soldiers at Jerusalem had whiskers only, and shaved their chins and upper lips. They all had swords, some of them being also armed with spears, and they carried sticks with lanterns and torches; but when they set off they only lighted one. It had at first been intended that Judas should be accompanied by a more numerous escort but he drew their attention to the fact that so large a number of men would be too easily seen, because Mount Olivet commanded a view of the whole valley. Most of the soldiers remained, therefore, at Ophel, and sentinels were stationed on all sides to put down any attempt which might be made to release Jesus.

Judas set off with the twenty soldiers, but he was followed at some distance by four archers, who were only common bailiffs, carrying cords and chains, and after them came the six agents with whom Judas had been in communication for some time. One of these was a priest and a confidant of Annas; a second was devoted to Caiphas; the third and fourth were Pharisees; and the other two Sadduceans and Herodians. These six men were courtiers of Annas and Caiphas, acting in the capacity of spies, and most bitter enemies of Jesus.

The soldiers remained on friendly terms with Judas until they reached the spot where the road divides the Garden of Olives from the Garden of Gethsemani, but there they refused to allow him to advance alone, and entirely changed their manner, treating him with much insolence and harshness.

Jesus is Arrested

Jesus was standing with his three Apostles on the road between Gethsemani, and the Garden of Olives, when Judas and the band who accompanied him made their appearance.

A warm dispute arose between Judas and the soldiers, because he wished to approach first and speak to Jesus quietly as if nothing was the matter, and then for them to come up and seize Jesus, thus letting him suppose that he had no connection with the affair. But the men answered rudely. 'Not so, friend, thou shalt not escape from our hands until we have the Galilean safely bound,' and seeing the eight Apostles who hastened to rejoin Jesus when they heard the dispute which was going on, they (not withstanding the opposition of Judas) called up four archers, whom they had left at a little distance, to assist.

When by the light of the moon Jesus and the three Apostles first saw the band of armed men, Peter wished to repel them by force of arms, and said: 'Lord, the other eight are close at hand, let us attack the archers,' but Jesus bade him hold his peace, and then turned and walked back a few steps.

At this moment four disciples came out of the garden, and asked what was taking place. Judas was about to reply, but the soldiers interrupted, and would not let him speak. These four disciples were James the Less, Philip, Thomas, and Nathaniel; the last named, who was a son of the aged Simeon, had with a few others joined the eight Apostles at Gethsemani, being perhaps sent by the friends of Jesus to know what was going on, or possibly simply incited by curiosity and anxiety. The other disciples were wandering to and fro, on the lookout, and ready to fly at a moment's notice.

Jesus walked up to the soldiers and said in a firm and clear voice, *'Whom seek ye?'*

The leaders answered, 'Jesus of Nazareth.'

Jesus said to them, *'I am he.'*

Scarcely had he pronounced these words than they all fell to the ground, as if struck with apoplexy. Judas, who stood by them, was much alarmed, and as he appeared desirous of approaching, Jesus held out his hand and said: *'Friend, whereto art thou come?'*

Judas stammered forth something about business which had brought him. Jesus answered in few words, the sense of which was: *'It were better for thee that thou hadst never been born;'* however Anne Catherine cannot remember the exact words. In the meantime the soldiers had risen, and again approached Jesus, but they waited for the sign of the kiss, which Judas had promised to salute his Master that they might recognize him. Peter and the other disciples surround Judas, and reviled him in unmeasured terms, calling him thief and traitor; he tried to mollify their wrath by all kinds of lies, but his efforts were vain, for the soldiers came up and offered to defend him, which proceeding manifested the truth at once.

Jesus again asked, *'Whom seek ye?'*

They replied: *'Jesus of Nazareth.'*

Jesus answered: *'I have told you that I am he; if therefore you seek me, let these go their way.'*

At these words the soldiers fell for the second time to the ground, in convulsions similar to those of qpilepsy, and the Apostles again surrounded Judas and expressed their indignation at his shameful treachery. Jesus said to the soldiers, *'Arise,'* and they arose, but at first quite speechless from terror. They then told Judas to give them the signal agreed upon instantly, as their orders were to seize upon no one but him whom Judas kissed. Judas therefore approached Jesus, and gave him a kiss, saying, *'Hail, Rabbi.'*

Jesus replied, *'What, Judas, dost thou betray the Son of Man with a kiss?'*

The soldiers immediately surrounded Jesus, and the archers lade hands upon him. Judas wished to fly, but the Apostles would not allow it; they rushed at the soldiers and cried out, *'Master, shall we strike with the sword?'*

Peter, who was more impetuous than the rest, seized the sword, and struck Malchus, the servant of the high priest, who wished to drive away the Apostles, and cut off his right ear; Malchus fell to the ground and a great tumult ensued.

The archers had seized upon Jesus, and wished to bind him, while Malchus and the rest of the soldiers stood around. When Peter struck the former, the rest were occupied in repulsing those among the disciples who approached too near, and in pursuing those who ran away. Four disciples made their appearance in the distance, and looked fearfully at the scene before them, but the soldiers were still too much alarmed at their late fall to trouble themselves much about them, and besides they did not wish to leave Jesus without a certain number of men to guard him.

Judas fled as soon as he had given the traitorous kiss, but was met by some of the disciples, who overwhelmed him with reproaches. Six Pharisees, however, came to his rescue, and he escaped whilst the archers were busily occupied in pinioning Jesus.

When Peter struck Malchus, Jesus said to him, *'Put up again thy sword into its place; for all that take the sword shall perish with the sword. Thinkest thou that I cannot ask my Father, and he will give me presently more than twelve legions of angels? How then shall the Scriptures be fulfilled, that so it must be done?'*

Then Jesus said, *'Let me cure this man;'* and approaching Malchus, he touched his ear, prayed, and it was healed.

The soldiers who were standing near, as well as the archers and the six Pharisees, far from being moved by this miracle, continued to insult Jesus, and said to the bystanders, 'It is a trick of the devil, the powers of witchcraft made the ear appear to be cut off, and now the same power gives it the appearance of being healed.'

Then Jesus again addressed them, *'You are come out as it were to a robber, with clubs, to apprehend me. I sat daily with you teaching in the temple, and you laid not hands upon me, but this is your hour and the power of darkness.'*

The Pharisees ordered him to be bound still more strongly, and made answer in a contemptuous tone, 'Ah! Thou couldst not overthrow us by thy witchcraft.'

Jesus made a reply but Ann Catherine did not remember Jesus' words, and all the disciples fled. The four archers and the six Pharisees did not fall to the ground at the words of Jesus, because, as was afterwards revealed to Anne Catherine, they as well as Judas, who likewise did not fall, were entirely in the power of Satan, whereas all those who fell and rose again were afterwards converted, and became Christians; they had only surrounded Jesus, and not lain hands upon him. Malchus was instantly converted by the cure wrought upon him, and during the time of the Passion his employment was to carry messages back and forth to Mary and the other friends of Jesus.

The archers, who proceeded to pinion Jesus with the greatest brutality, were pagans of the lowest extraction, short, stout, and active, with sandy complexions, resembling those of Egyptian slaves, and bare legs, arms, and neck. They tied his hands as tightly as possible with hard new cords, fastening the right-hand wrist under the left elbow, and the left-hand wrist under the right elbow. They encircled his waist with a species of belt studded with iron points, and bound his hands to it with osier bands, while on his neck they put a collar covered with iron points, and to this collar were appended two leathern straps, which were crossed over his chest like a stole and fastened to the belt. They then fastened four ropes to different parts of the belt, and by means of these ropes dragged Jesus from side to side in the cruelest manner. The ropes were new; purchased when the Pharisees first determined to arrest Jesus.

The Pharisees lighted fresh torches, and the procession started. Ten soldiers walked in front, the archers who held the ropes and dragged Jesus along, followed, and the Pharisees and ten other soldiers brought up the rear. The disciples wandered about at a distance, and wept and moaned as if beside them-selves from grief. John alone followed, and walked at no great distance from the soldiers, until the Pharisees, seeing him, ordered the guards to arrest him. They endeavored to obey, but he ran away, leaving in their hands a cloth with which he was covered, and of which they had taken hold when they endeavored to seize him. He had slipped off his coat that he might escape more easily from the hands of his enemies, and kept nothing on but a short undergarment without sleeves, and the long band which Jewish people usually wore, and which was wrapped round his neck, head, and arms.

The archers behaved in the cruelest manner to Jesus as they led him along; this they did to curry favor with the six Pharisees, who they well knew perfectly hated and detested Jesus. They led him along the roughest road they could select, over the sharpest stones, and through the thickest mire; they pulled the cords as tightly as possible; they struck him with knotted cords, as a butcher would strike a beast he is about to slaughter; and they accompanied this cruel treatment with such ignoble and indecent insults that Anne Catherine cannot recount them. The feet of Jesus were bare; he wore, besides the ordinary dress, a seamless woolen garment, and a cloak which was thrown over all. Jesus had been arrested without any order being presented or legal ceremony taking place; he was treated as a person without the pale of the law.

The procession proceeded at a good pace; when they left the road which runs between the Garden of Olives and that of Gethsemani, they turned to the right, and soon reached a bridge which was thrown over the Torrent of Cedron. When Jesus went to the Garden of Olives with the Apostles, he did not cross this bridge, but went by a private path which ran through the Valley of Josephat, and led to another bridge more to the south. The bridge over which the soldiers led Jesus was long, being thrown over not only the torrent, which was very large in this part, but likewise over the valley, which extends a considerable distance to the right and to the left, and is much lower than the bed of the river.

Anne Catherine saw Jesus fall twice before he reached the bridge, which the soldiers dragged him; but when they were half over the bridge they gave full vent to their brutal inclinations, and struck Jesus with such violence that they threw him off the bridge into the water, and scornfully recommended him to quench his thirst there.

If God had not preserved him, he must have been killed by this fall; he fell first on his knee, and then on his face, but saved himself a little by stretching out his hands, which, although so tightly bound before, were loosened; Anne Catherine knew not whether it was by a miracle, or whether the soldiers had cut the cords before they threw him into the water.

The marks of his feet, his elbows, and his fingers were miraculously impressed on the rock on which he fell and these impressions were afterwards shown for the veneration of Christians. These stones were less hard than the unbelieving hearts of the wicked men who surrounded Jesus, and bore witness at this terrible moment to the Divine Power which had touched them.

Anne Catherine had not seen Jesus take anything to quench the thirst which had consumed him ever since his agony in the garden, but he drank when he fell into the Cedron, and she heard him repeat these words from the prophetic Psalm, *'In his thirst he will drink water from the torrent'* (Psalm cviii.).

The archers still held the ends of the ropes with which Jesus was bound, but it would have been difficult to drag him out of the water on that side, on account of a wall which was built on the shore; they turned back and dragged him quite through the Cedron to the shore, and then made him cross the bridge a second time, accompanying their every action with insults, blasphemies, and blows. His long woolen garment, which was quite soaked through, adhered to his legs, impeded every movement, and rendered it almost impossible for him to walk, and when he reached the end of the bridge he fell quite down.

They pulled him up in the cruelest manner, struck him with cords, and fastened the end of his wet garment to the belt, abusing him at the same time in the most cowardly manner.

It was not quite midnight when Anne Catherine saw the four archers inhumanly dragging Jesus over a narrow path, which was choked up with stones, fragments of rock, thistles, and thorns, on the shore of the Cedron.

The six brutal Pharisees walked as close to Jesus as they could, struck him constantly with thick pointed sticks, and seeing that his bare and bleeding feet were torn by the stones and briars, exclaimed scornfully: 'His precursor, John the Baptist, has certainly not prepared a good path for him here;' or, 'The the words of Malachy, *'Behold, I send my angel before thy face, to prepare the way before thee,'* do not exactly apply now.

Every jest uttered by these men incited the archers to greater cruelty.

The enemies of Jesus remarked that several persons made their appearance in the distance; they were only disciples who had assembled when they heard that Jesus was arrested, and were anxious to discover what the end would be; but the sight of them rendered the Pharisees uneasy, lest any attempt should be made to rescue Jesus, and they therefore sent for a reinforcement of soldiers. At a very short distance from an entrance opposite to the south side of the Temple, which leads through a little village called Ophel to Mount Zion, where the residence of Annas and Caiphas were situated, Anne Catherine saw a hand of about fifty soldiers, who carried torches, and appeared ready for anything; the demeanor of these men was outrageous, and they gave loud shouts, both to announce their arrival, and to congratulate their comrades upon the success of the expedition. This caused a slight confusion among the soldiers who were leading Jesus, and Malchus and a few others took advantage of it to depart, and fly towards Mount Olivet.

When the fresh band of soldiers left Ophel, Anne Catherine saw those disciples who had gathered together disperse; some went one way, and some another. The Blessed Virgin and about nine of the holy women, being filled with anxiety, directed their steps towards the Valley of Josephat, accompanied by Lazarus, John the son of Mark, the son of Veronica, and the son of Simon. The last named was at Gethsemani with Nathaniel and the eight Apostles, and had fled when the soldiers appeared. He was giving the Blessed Virgin the account of all that had been done, when the fresh band of soldiers joined those who were leading Jesus, and she then heard their tumultuous vociferations, and saw the light of the torches they carried. This sight quite overcame her; she became insensible, and John took her into the house of Mary, the mother of Mark.

The fifty soldiers who were sent to join those who had taken Jesus, were a detachment from a company of three hundred men posted to guard the gates and environs of Ophel; for the traitor Judas had reminded the High priests that the inhabitants of Ophel (who were principally at the laboring class, and whose chief employment was to bring water and wood to the Temple) were the most attached partisans of Jesus, and might perhaps make some attempts to rescue him. The traitor was aware that Jesus had both consoled, instructed, assisted, and cured the diseases of many of these poor workmen, and that Ophel was the place where he halted during his journey from

Brethania to Hebron, when John the Baptist had just been executed. Judas also knew that Jesus had cured many of the masons who were injured by the fall of the Tower of Siloe.

The greatest part of the inhabitants of Ophel were converted after the death of Jesus, and joined the first Christian community that was formed after Pentecost, and when the Christians separated from the Jewish faith and erected new dwellings, they placed their huts and tents in the valley which is situated between Mount Olivet and Ophel, and there St. Stephen lived.

Ophel was on a hill to the south of the Temple, surrounded by walls, and its inhabitants were very poor. Ann Catherine thinks it was smaller than Dulmen.

(Dulmen is a small town in Westphalia, where Sister Emmerich had once lived.)

The slumbers of the good inhabitants of Ophel were disturbed by the noise of the soldiers; they came out of their houses and ran to the entrance of the village to ask the cause of the uproar; but the soldiers received them roughly, ordered them to return home, and in reply to their numerous questions, said, 'We have just arrested Jesus, your false prophet—he who has deceived you so grossly; the High Priests are about to judge him, and he will be crucified.'

Cries and lamentations arose on all sides; women and children ran back and forth, weeping and wringing their hands; and calling to mind all the benefits they had received from Jesus, they cast themselves on their knees to implore the protection of Heaven.

But the soldiers pushed them on one side, struck them, obliged them to return to their houses, and exclaimed, 'What further proof is required? Does not the conduct of these persons show plainly that the Galilean incites rebellion?'

They were, however, a little cautious in their expressions and demeanor for fear of causing an insurrection in Ophel, and therefore only endeavored to drive the inhabitants away from those parts of the village which Jesus was obliged to cross.

When the soldiers who led Jesus were near the gate of Ophel he again fell, and appeared unable to proceed a step further, upon which one among them, being moved to compassion, said to another, 'You see the poor man is perfectly exhausted, he cannot support himself with the weight of his chains; if we wish to get him to the High Priest alive we must loosen the cords with which his hands are bound, that he may be able to save himself a little when he falls.'

The band stopped for a moment, the fetters were loosened, and another kind-hearted soldier brought some water to Jesus from a neighboring fountain. Jesus thanked him, and spoke of the fountains of living water,' of which whose who believed in him should drink; but his words enraged the Pharisees still more, and they overwhelmed him with insults and contumelious language. Anne Catherine saw the heart of the soldier who had caused Jesus to be unbound, as also that of the one who brought him water, suddenly illuminated by grace; they were both converted before the death of Jesus, and immediately joined his disciples.

The procession started again, and reached the gate of Ophel. Here Jesus was again saluted by the cries of grief and sympathy of those who owed him so much gratitude, and the soldiers had considerable difficulty in keeping back the men and women who crowded round from all parts. They clasped their hands, fell on their knees, lamented, and exclaimed, 'Release this man unto us; release him! Who will assist, who will console us, who will cure our diseases? Release him unto us!'

It was heart-rending to look upon Jesus; his face was white, disfigured, and wounded, his hair disheveled, his dress wet and soiled, and his savage and drunken guards were dragging him about and striking him with sticks like a poor dumb animal led to the slaughter. Thus was he conducted through the midst of the afflicted inhabitants of Ophel, and the paralytic whom he had cured, the dumb to whom he had restored speech, and the blind whose eyes he had opened, united, but in vain, in offering supplications for his release.

Many persons from among the lowest and most degraded classes had been sent by Annas, Caiphas, and the other enemies of Jesus, to join the procession, and assist the soldiers both in ill-treating Jesus, and in driving away the inhabitants of Ophel.

The village of Ophel was seated upon a hill, and a great deal of timber had been placed there ready for building. The procession had to proceed down a hill, and then pass through a door made in the wall. On one side of this door stood a large building erected originally by Solomon, and on the other the pool of Bethsaida.

After passing this building, they followed a westerly direction down a steep street called Millo, at the end of which a turn to the south brought them to the house of Annas. The guards never ceased their cruel treatment of Jesus, and excused such conduct by saying that the crowds who gathered together in front of the procession compelled them to severity. Jesus fell seven times between Mount Olivet and the house of Annas.

The inhabitants of Ophel were still in a state of consternation and grief, when the sight of the Mother of Jesus, who passed through the Village accompanied by the holy women and some other friends on her way from the Valley of Cedron to the house of Mary the mother of Mark, excited them still more and they surrounded and almost carried her in their arms.

Mary was speechless from grief, and did not open her lips after she reached the house of Mary the mother of Mark, until the arrival of John, who related all he had seen since Jesus left the supper-room; and a little later she was taken to the house of Martha, which was near that of Lazarus.

Peter and John, who had followed Jesus at a distance, went in haste to some servants of the High Priest with whom the latter was acquainted, in order to endeavor by their means to obtain admittance into the tribunal where Jesus was to be tried. These servants acted as messengers, and had just been ordered to go to the houses of the ancients, and other members of the Council, to summon them to attend the meeting which was convoked. They were anxious to oblige the Apostles, but foresaw much difficulty in obtaining their admittance into the tribunal; they gave them cloaks similar to those they themselves wore, and made them assist in carrying messages to the members in order that afterwards they might enter the tribunal of Caiphas, and mingle without being recognized, among the soldiers and false witnesses, as all other persons were to be expelled.

As Nicodemus, Joseph of Arimathea, and other well-intentioned persons were members of this Council, the Apostles undertook to let them know what was going to be done in the Council, thus securing the presence of those friends of Jesus whom the Pharisees had purposely omitted to invite. In the meantime Judas wandered up and down the steep and wild precipices at the south of Jerusalem, despair marked on his every feature, and the devil pursuing him to and fro, filling his imagination with still darker visions, and not allowing him a moment's respite.

It seems that the religious hierarchy was out to destroy Jesus – the best man to have walked the face of the earth - yet those same religious authority figures represented God. I would hate to see what they would have done if they hadn't represented God.

It seems to me that God, in the religious establishment, represents Ultimate Power – then as well as now. And religious establishments tolerate no threat to their Power – the Inquisition in the middle-ages is stark testimony to that fact.

Jesus was a threat to the Power of the religious authority because Jesus placed the emphasis on good deeds performed by human-beings in their every day living, and not by worshipping in the Temple. Jesus took God out of the Temple and put God into the body of the every day person.

To Jesus, the human body is the true Temple of worship. There is no hierarchy with God. Divine Law judges according to our human deeds – good or bad. Jesus never refused to help anyone. Everyone was a brother to Jesus.

Back in Biblical days there was no medical establishment as exists today. People in Biblical times could collapse and die by the roadside if they were outsiders, or strangers. Jesus put an end to that attitude. Jesus didn't help someone because they belonged to a particular group or community. There were no barriers with Jesus. Everyone was his brother. He helped everyone in need of help; yet he was considered an enemy of the establishment. Why? Because he was breaking the controlling power of the religious establishment by demonstrating the power of God within each individual, something the religious establishment had been failing to do; and the religious establishment would tolerate no threat to their Power.

To prove he was no charlatan, Jesus healed the hopelessly sick; he allowed the blind to see, the lame to walk, and cleansed the lepers.

Every manner of illness was healed by Jesus, free, without cost to the patient. The only price the healed person was asked to pay: go and sin no more.

Because he had earned many staunch supporters, much intrigue and deception had to be used to arrest Jesus and put him to death – something the Pharisees were expert in doing.

The religious establishment - the High Priests and the Sadducees - had been teaching "one true God" for many years; they were amazed at the power over the people representing God gave to them; they liked what they had; they began to believe it was their Divine right to control the people. It was good for business, one might say. It was a good life for them – and they wanted to keep it that way.

For over two thousand years establishments have ignored the true reason for the crucifixion of Jesus: and that was to preserve the power of the religious establishment over the people. Their scapegoat tactic was to blame - the Jews.

Jesus was a Jew. He was born into the Essenes, a highly disciplined sect of Jewish believers in the One True God. Jesus' followers were Jewish as well as Samarians and anyone else from the area that had been helped by him. The followers and believers of Jesus were a diverse group. The Jews can't be blamed for the killing of Jesus anymore than Americans can be blamed for the killing of Abraham Lincoln. It was a small group of enemies within the social structure. Let us not put the blame where blame does not belong.

Means Employed by the Enemies of Jesus for Carrying out Their Designs Against Him.

No sooner was Jesus arrested than Annas and Caiphas were informed, and instantly began to arrange their plans with regard to the course to be pursued. Confusion speedily reigned everywhere—the rooms were lighted up in haste, guards placed at the entrances, and messengers dispatched to different parts of the town to convoke the members of the Council, the Scribes, and all who were to take a part in the trial. Many among them had, however, assembled at the house of Caiphas as soon as the treacherous compact with Judas was completed, and had remained there to await the course of events. The different classes of ancients were likewise assembled. And as the

Pharisees, Sadducees, and Herodians were congregated in Jerusalem from all parts of the country for the celebration of the festival, and had long been concerting measures with the Council for the arrest of Jesus, the High Priests now sent for those whom they knew to be the most bitterly opposed to Jesus, and desired them to assemble the witnesses, gather together every possible proof, and bring all before the Council.

The proud Sadducees of Nazareth, of Capharnaum, of Thirza, of Gabara, of Jotapata, and of Silo, whom Jesus had so often reproved before the people, were actually dying for revenge. They hastened to all the inns to seek out those persons whom they knew to be enemies of Jesus, and offered them bribes in order to secure their appearance. But, with the exception of a few ridiculous calumnies, which were certain to be disproved as soon as investigated, nothing tangible could be brought forward against Jesus, excepting, indeed, those foolish accusations which he had so often refuted in the synagogue.

The enemies of Jesus hastened, however, to the tribunal of Caiphas, escorted by the Scribes and Pharisees of Jerusalem,, and accompanied by many of those merchants whom Jesus drove out of the Temple when they were holding market there, as also by the proud doctors whom he had silenced before all the people, and even by some who could not forgive the humiliation of being convicted of error when he disputed with them in the Temple at the age of twelve. There was likewise a large body of impenitent sinners whom he had refused to cure, relapsed sinners whose diseases had returned, worldly young men whom he enraged by causing the money which they had been in hopes of possessing to be distributed in alms. Others there were whose friends he had cured, and who had thus been disappointed in their expectations of inheriting property; debauchees whose victims he had converted; and many despicable characters who made their fortunes by flattering and fostering the vices of the great.

All the emissaries of Satan were overflowing with rage against everything holy, and consequently with an indescribable hatred of the Holy of Holies. They were further incited by the enemies of Jesus, and therefore assembled in crowds round the palace of Caiphas, to bring forward all their false accusations and to endeavor to cover with infamy the spotless Lamb, who took upon himself the sins of the world, and accepted the burden in order to reconcile man with God.

While all the wicked beings were busily consulting as to what was best to be done, anguish and anxiety filled the hearts of the friends of Jesus, for they were ignorant of the mystery which was about to be accomplished, and they wandered about sighing, and listening to every different opinion. Each word they uttered gave rise to feelings of suspicion on the part of those whom they addressed, and if they were silent, their silence was set down as wrong. Many well-meaning but weak and undecided characters yielded to temptation, were scandalized, and lost their faith; indeed, the number of those who persevered was very small indeed. Things were the same then as they often-times are now, persons were willing to serve God if they met with no opposition from their fellow creatures, but were ashamed of the Cross if held in contempt by others. The hearts of some were, however, touched by the patience, displayed by Jesus in the midst of his sufferings, and they walked away silent and sad.

The Insults Received by Jesus in the Court of Caiphas

No sooner did Caiphas, with the other members of the Council, leave the tribunal than a crowd of miscreants—the very scum of the people--surrounded Jesus like a swarm of infuriated wasps, and began to heap every imaginable insult upon him.

Even during the trial, whilst the witnesses were speaking, the archers and some others could not restrain their cruel inclinations, but pulled out handfuls of his hair and beard, spat upon him, struck him with their fists, wounded him with sharp pointed sticks, and even ran needles into his body; but when Caiphas left the hall they set no bounds to their barbarity. They first placed a crown, made of straw and the back of trees, upon his head, and then took it off, saluting him at the same time with insulting expressions, like the following: 'Behold the Son of David wearing the crown of his father.'

A greater than Solomon is here; this is the king who is preparing a wedding feast for his son.'

Thus did they turn into ridicule those eternal truths which he had taught under the form of parables to those whom he came from heaven to save; and whilst repeating these scoffing words, they continued to strike him with their fists and sticks, and to spit in his face. Next they put a crown of reeds upon his head, took off his robe and scapular, and then threw an old torn mantle, which scarcely reached his knees, over his shoulders, around his neck they hung a long iron chain, with an iron ring at each end, studded with sharp points, which bruised and tore his knees as he walked. They again pinioned his arms, put a reed into his hand, and covered his Divine countenance with spittle. They had already thrown all sorts of filth over his hair, as well as over his chest, and upon the old mantle. They bound his eyes with a dirty rag, and struck him, crying out at the same time in loud tones, *'Prophesy unto us, O Christ, who is he that struck thee?'*

He answered not one word, but signed and prayed inwardly for them.

After many more insults, they seized the chain which was hanging on his neck, dragged him towards the room into which the Council had withdrawn, and with their sticks forced him in, vociferating at the same time, 'March forward, thou King of Straw! Show thyself to the Council with the insignia of the regal honors we have rendered unto thee.'

A large body of councillors with Caiphas at their head, were still in the room, and they looked with both delight and approbation at the shameful scene which was enacted, beholding with pleasure the most sacred ceremonies burned into derision. The pitiless guards covered him with mud and spittle, and with mock gravity exclaimed, 'Receive the prophetic unction—the regal unction.'

Then they impiously parodied the baptismal ceremonies, and the pious act of Magdalen in emptying the vase of perfume on his head. 'How canst thou presume,' they exclaimed, 'to appear before the Council in such a condition? Thou dost purify others, and thou art not pure thyself; but we will soon purify thee.'

They fetched a basin of dirty water, which they poured over his face and shoulders, whilst they bent their knees before him, and exclaimed, '

Behold thy precious unction, behold the spikenard worth three hundred pence; thou hast been baptized in the pool of Bethsaida.'

They intended by this to throw into ridicule the act of respect and veneration shown by Magdalen, when she poured the precious ointment over his head, at the house of the Pharisee.

By their derisive words concerning his baptism in the pool of Bethsaida, they pointed out, although unintentionally, the resemblance between Jesus and the Paschal lamb, for the lambs were washed in the first place in the pond near the Probatica gate, and then brought to the pool of Bethsaida, where they underwent another purification before being taken to the Temple to be sacrificed. The enemies of Jesus likewise alluded to the man who had been infirm for thirty-eight years, and who was cured by Jesus at the pool of Bethsaida; for I saw this man either washed or baptized there; I say either washed or baptized, because I do not exactly remember the circumstances.

They then dragged Jesus round the room, before all the members of the Council, who continued to address him in the reproachful and abusive language. Every countenance looked diabolical and enraged, and all around was dark, confused, and terrible. Jesus, on the contrary, was from the moment that he declared himself to be the Son of God, generally surrounded with a halo of light. Many of the assembly appeared to have a confused knowledge of this fact, and to be filled with consternation at perceiving that neither outrages nor ignominies could alter the majestic expression of his countenance.

The halo which shown around Jesus from the moment he declared himself to be the Christ, the Son of the Living God, served but to incite his enemies to greater fury, and yet it was so resplendent that they could not look at it; and Ann Catherine believes their intention in throwing the dirty rag over his head was to deaden its brightness.

Jesus Confined in the Subterranean Prison

The barbarians shut Jesus up in a little vaulted prison, the remains of which subsist to this day. Two of the archers alone remained with him, and they were soon replaced by two others. He was still clothed in the old dirty mantle, and covered with the spittle and other filth which they had thrown over him; for they had not allowed him to put on his own clothes again, but kept his hands tightly bound together.

When Jesus entered this prison, he prayed most fervently that God would accept all that he had already suffered, and all that he was about to suffer, as an expiatory sacrifice, not only for his executioners, but likewise for all who in future ages might have to suffer torments such as he was about to endure, and be tempted to impatience or anger.

The enemies of Jesus did not allow him a moment's respite, even in this dreary prison, but tied him to a pillar which stood in the center, and would not allow him to lean upon it, although he was so exhausted from ill treatment, the weight of his chains, and his numerous falls, that he could scarcely support himself on his swollen and torn feet. Never for a moment did they cease insulting him; and when the first set of guards were tired out, others replaced them.

Ann Catherine states that it is quite impossible to describe all that the Holy of Holies suffered from these heartless beings; for the sight affected her so excessively that she became really ill, and she felt as if she could not survive it. We ought, indeed, to be ashamed of that weakness and susceptibility which renders us unable to listen composedly to the descriptions, or speak without repugnance, of those sufferings which Jesus endured so calmly and patiently for our salvation. Ann Catherine states that the horror we feel is as great as that of a murderer who is forced to place his hands upon the wounds he himself has inflicted on his victim. Jesus endured all without opening his mouth; and it was man, sinful man, who perpetrated all these outrages against one who was at once their Brother, their Redeemer, and their God. Ann Catherine states that she, too, is a great sinner; and her sins caused these sufferings. At the day of judgment, when the most hidden things will be manifested, we shall see the share we have had in the torments endured by the Son of God; we shall see how far we have caused them by the sins we so frequently commit, and which are, in fact, a species of constant which we give to, and a participation in, the tortures which were inflicted on Jesus by his cruel enemies. If, alas, we reflected seriously on this, we should repeat with much greater fervor the words which we find so often in prayer books: 'Lord grant that I may die, rather than ever willfully offend thee again by sin.'

Jesus continued to pray for his enemies, and they being at last tired out left him in peace for a short time, when he leaned against the pillar to rest, and a bright light shone around him. The day was beginning to dawn—the day of his Passion, of our Redemption—and a faint ray penetrating the narrow vent-hole of the prison, fell upon the holy and immaculate Lamb, who had taken upon himself the sins of the world. Jesus turned towards the ray of light, raised his fettered hands, and, in the most touching manner, returned thanks to his Heavenly Father for the dawn of that day, which had been so long desired by the prophets, and for which he himself had so ardently sighed from the moment of his birth on earth, and concerning which he had said to his disciples, *'I have a baptism wherewith I am to be baptized, and how am I straitened until it be accomplished?'*

Anne Catherine prayed with Jesus, but she cannot give the words of his prayer, for she was completely overcome, and touched to hear Jesus return thanks to God for the terrible sufferings which he had already endured for her, and for the still greater which he was about to endure.

The archers, who were dozing, woke up for a moment, and looked at him with surprise; they said nothing, but appeared to be somewhat astonished and frightened. Jesus was confined in this prison during an hour, or thereabouts.

When Jesus was in the dungeon, Judas, who had been wandering up and down the valley of Hinnom like a madman, directed his steps towards the house of Caiphas, with the thirty pieces of silver, the reward of his treachery, still handing to his waist. All was silent around, and he addressed himself to some of the sentinels, without letting them know who he was, and asked what was going to be done to the Galilean. 'He has been condemned to death; and he will certainly be crucified,' was the reply. Judas walked to and fro, and listened to the different conversations which were held concerning Jesus. Some spoke of the cruel treatment he had received, others of his astonishing patience, while others, again, discoursed concerning the solemn trial which was to take place in the morning before the great Council. Whilst Judas was listening eagerly to the different opinions given, day dawned; the members of the tribunal commenced their preparations, and Judas slunk behind the building that he might not be seen, for like Cain he sought to hide himself from human eyes; and despair was beginning to take possession of his soul. The place in which he took refuge happened to be the very spot where the workmen had been preparing the wood for making the cross; all was in readiness, and the men were asleep by its side. Judas was filled with horror at the sight: he shuddered and fled when he beheld the instrument of that cruel death to which for a paltry sum of money he had delivered up his Lord and Master; he ran to and fro in perfect agonies of remorse, and finally hid himself in an adjoining cave, where he determined to await the trial which was to take place in the morning.

Anne Catherine continues describing the Passion of Christ

When Jesus came up to the three Apostles, they were not lying down asleep as they had been the first time, but their heads were covered, and they had sunk down on their knees, in an attitude often assumed by the people of that country when in sorrow or desiring to pray. They had fallen asleep, overpowered by grief and fatigue. Jesus, trembling and groaning, drew nigh to them, and they awoke.

But when, by the light of the moon, they saw him standing before them, his face pale and bloody, and his hair in disorder, their weary eyes did not at the first moment recognize him, for he was indescribably changed. He clasped his hands together, upon which they arose and lovingly supported him in their arms, and he told them in sorrowful accents that the next day he should be put to death—that in one hour's time he should be seized, led before a tribunal, maltreated, outraged, scourged, and finally put to a most cruel death. He besought them to console his Mother, and also Magdalen. They made no reply, for they knew not what to say, so greatly had his appearance and language alarmed them, and they even thought his mind must be wandering. When he desired to return to the grotto, he had not strength to walk. Ann Catherine saw John and James lead him back, and return when he had entered the grotto. It was then about a quarter-past eleven.

During the agony of Jesus, Ann Catherine saw the Blessed Virgin also overwhelmed with sorrow and anguish of soul, in the house of Mary, the mother of Mark. She was with Magdalen and Mary in the garden belonging to the house, and almost prostrate from grief, with her whole body bowed down as she knelt. She fainted several times, for she beheld in spirit different portions of the agony of Jesus. She had sent some messengers to make inquiries concerning him, but her deep anxiety would not suffer her to await their return, and she went with Magdalen and Salome as far as the Valley of Josaphat. She walked along with her head veiled, and her arms frequently stretched forth towards Mount Olivet; for she beheld in spirit Jesus bathed in a bloody sweat, and her gestures were as though she wished with her extended hands to wipe the face of her Son. Ann Catherine saw these interior movements of her soul towards Jesus, who thought of her, and turned his eyes in her direction, as if to seek her assistance. Anne Catherine beheld the spiritual communication which they had with each other, under the form of rays passing to and fro between them. Jesus also thought of Magdalen, was touched by her distress, and therefore recommended his Apostles to console her, for he knew that her love for him was greater than that felt for him by anyone save his Mother, and he foresaw that she would suffer much for his sake, and never offend him more.

About this time, the eight Apostles returned to the arbor of Gethsemani, and after talking together for some time, ended by going to sleep. They were wavering, discouraged, and sorely tempted. They had each been seeking for a place of refuge in case of danger, and they anxiously asked one another, 'What shall we do when they have put him to death? We have left all to follow him; we are poor and the offscouring of the world; we gave ourselves up entirely to his service, and now he is so sorrowful and so dejected himself, that he can afford us no consolation.

The other disciples had at first wandered about in various directions, but then, having heard something concerning the awful prophecies which Jesus had made, they had nearly all retired to Bethphage.

Ann Catherine saw Jesus still praying in the grotto, struggling against the repugnance to suffering which belongs to human nature, and abandoning himself wholly to the will of his Eternal Father. Here the abyss opened before him, and he had a vision of the first part of Limbo. He saw Adam and Eve, the patriarchs, prophets, and just men, the parents of his Mother, and John the Baptist, awaiting his arrival in the lower world with such intense longing, that the sight strengthened and gave fresh courage to his loving heart. His death was to open Heaven to these captives—this death was to deliver them out of that prison in which they were languishing in eager hope! When Jesus had, with deep emotion, looked upon these saints of antiquity, angels presented to him all the bands of saints of future ages, who, joining their labors to the merits of his Passion, were, through him, to be united to his Heavenly Father. Most beautiful and consoling was this vision, in which he beheld salvation and sanctification flowing forth in ceaseless streams from the fountain of redemption opened by his death.

The apostles, disciples, virgins, and holy women, the martyrs, confessors, hermits, popes, and bishops, and large bands of religious of both sexes—in one word, the entire army of the blessed—appeared before him. All bore on their heads triumphal crowns, and the flowers of their crowns differed in form, in color, in odor, and in perfection, according to the difference of the sufferings, labors and victories which had procured them eternal glory. Their whole life, and all their actions, merits, and power, as well as all the glory of their triumph, came solely from their union with the merits of Jesus Christ.

The reciprocal influence exercised by these saints upon each other, and the manner in which they all drank from one sole Fountain—the Adorable Sacrament and the Passion of Jesus—formed a most touching and wonderful spectacle. Nothing about them was devoid of deep meaning—their works, martyrdom, victories, appearance, and dress—all, though indescribably varied was confused together in infinite harmony and unity; and this unity in diversity was produced by the rays of one single Sun, by the Passion of the Lord, of the Word made flesh, in whom was life, the light of men, which shined in darkness, and the darkness did not comprehend it.

The army of future saints passed before the soul of Jesus, which was thus placed between the desiring patriarchs, and the triumphant band of the future blessed, and these two armies joining together, and completing one another, so to speak, surrounded the loving Heart of Jesus as with a crown of victory. This most affecting and consoling spectacle bestowed a degree of strength and comfort upon the soul of Jesus. He so loved his brethren and creatures that, to accomplish the redemption of one single soul, he would have accepted with joy all the sufferings to which he was now devoting himself. As these visions referred to the future, they were diffused to a certain height in the air.

But these consoling visions faded away, and the angels displayed before him the scenes of his Passion quite close to the earth, because it was near at hand. Anne Catherine beheld every scene distinctly portrayed, from the kiss of Judas to the last words of Jesus on the cross, and she saw in this single vision all that she saw in her meditations on the Passion. The treason of Judas, the flight of the disciples, the insults which were offered Jesus before Annas and Caiphas, Peter's denial, the tribunal of Pilate, Herod's mockery, the scourging and crowning with thorns, the condemnation to death, the carrying of the cross, the linen cloth presented by Veronica, the crucifixion, the insults of the Pharisees, the sorrows of Mary, of Magdalen, and of John, the wound of the lance to his side, after death;--in one word, every part of the Passion was shown to him in the minutest detail. He accepted all voluntarily, submitting to everything for the love of man. He saw also and felt the sufferings endured at that moment by his Mother, whose interior union with his agony was so entire that she had fainted in the arms of her two friends.

✣ ✣ ✣

The Passion of Jesus, as presented by venerable Ann Catherine Emmerich, is a long and detailed story of the Crucifixion of Jesus. As the Passion of Jesus is the bedrock of spiritual development, it is my suggestion that everyone read *The Dolorous Passion of Our Lord Jesus Christ,* to personally receive the spiritual blessings imparted for tuning into this event.

✣ ✣ ✣

The procession again moved on; the road was very steep and rough between the walls of the town and Calvary, and Jesus had the greatest difficulty in walking with his heavy burden on his shoulders; but his cruel enemies, far from feeling the slightest compassion, or giving the least assistance, continued to urge him on by the infliction of hard blows, and the utterance of dreadful curses. At last they reached a spot where the pathway turned suddenly to the south; here he stumbled and fell for the sixth time.

The fall was a dreadful one, but the guards only struck him harder to force him to get up, and no sooner did he reach Calvary than he sank down again for the seventh time.

Simon of Cyrene was filled with indignation and pity; not-with-standing his fatigue, he wished to remain that he might assist Jesus, but the archers first reviled, and then drove him away, and he soon after joined the body of disciples.

The executioners then ordered the workmen and the boys who had carried the instruments for the execution to depart, and the Pharisees soon arrived, for they were on horseback, and had taken the smooth and easy road which ran to the east of Calvary. There was a fine view of the whole town of Jerusalem from the top of Calvary. This top was circular, and about the size of an ordinary riding-school, surrounded by a low wall, and with five separate entrances. This appeared to be the usual number of those parts; for there were five roads at the baths, at the place where they baptized, at the pool of Bethsaida, and there were likewise many towns with five gates. In this, as in many other peculiarities of the Holy Land, there was a deep prophetic significa-tion; that number five, which so often occurred, was a type of those five sacred wounds of our blessed Savior, which were to open to us the gates of Heaven.

About a hundred soldiers were stationed on different parts of the mountain, and as space was required, the thieves were not brought to the top, but ordered to halt before they reached it, and to lie on the ground with their arms fastened to their crosses.

Soldiers stood around and guarded them, while crowds of persons who did not fear defiling themselves, stood near the platform or on the neighboring heights; these were mostly of the lower classes—strangers, slaves, and pagans, and a number of them were women.

It was about a quarter to twelve when Jesus, loaded with his cross, sank down at the precise spot where he was to be crucified. The bar-barous executioners dragged him up by the cords which they had fastened around his waist, and then untied the arms of the cross, and threw them on the ground. The sight of our Blessed Lord at this mo-ment was, indeed, calculated to move the hardest heart to compas-sion; he stood or rather bent over the cross, being scarcely able to sup-port himself; his heavenly countenance was pale and wan as that of a person on the verge of death, although wounds and blood disfigured it to a frightful degree; but the hearts of these cruel men were, alas! Harder than iron itself, and far from showing the slightest commiseration, they threw him brutally down, exclaiming in a jeering tone, 'Most powerful king, we are about to prepare thy throne.'

Jesus immediately placed himself upon the cross, and they measured him and marked the places for his feet and hands, whilst the Pharisees continued to insult their unresisting Victim.

When the measurement was finished, they led him to a cave cut in the rock, which had been used formerly as a cellar, opened the door and pushed him in so roughly that had it not been for the support of angels, his legs must have been broken by so hard a fall in the rough stone floor.

Ann Catherine distinctly heard Jesus' groans of pain, but they closed the door quickly and placed guards before it, and the archers continued their preparations for the crucifixion.

The center of the platform mentioned above was the most elevated part of Calvary—it was a round eminence, about two feet high, and persons were obligated to ascend two or three steps to reach its top. The executioners dug the holes for the three crosses at the top of this eminence, and placed those intended for the thieves, one on the right and the other on the left of Jesus; both were lower and more roughly made than his. They then carried the cross of Jesus to the spot where they intended to crucify him, and placed it in such a position that it would easily fall into the hole prepared for it. They fastened the two arms strongly on to the body of the cross, nailed the board at the bottom which was to support the feet, bored the holes for the nails, and cut different hollows in the wood in the parts which would receive the head and back of our Lord, in order that his body might rest against the cross, instead of being suspended from it. Their aim in this was the prolongation of his tortures, for if the whole weight of his body was allowed to fall upon the hands, the holes might be quite torn open, and death would ensue more speedily than they desired. The executioners then drove into the ground the pieces of wood which were intended to keep the cross upright, and made a few other similar preparations.

The Nailing of Jesus to the Cross

The preparations for the crucifixion being finished, four archers went to the cave where Jesus had been confined and dragged him out with their usual brutality, while the most looked on and made use of insulting language, and the Roman soldiers regarded all with indifference, and thought of nothing but maintaining order.

When Jesus was again brought forth, the holy women gave a man some money, and begged him to pay the archers anything they might demand if they would allow Jesus to drink the wine which Veronica had prepared; but the cruel executioners, instead of giving it to Jesus, drank it themselves.

They brought two vases with them, one of which contained vinegar and gall, and the other a mixture which looked like wine mixed with myrrh and absinthe; they offered a glass of the latter to Jesus, which he tasted, but would not drink.

There were eighteen archers on the platform; the six who had scourged Jesus, the four who had conducted him to Calvary, the two who held the ropes which supported the cross, and six others who came for the purpose of crucifying him. They were strangers in the pay of either the Jews or the Romans, and were short, thick-set men, with most ferocious countenances, rather resembling wild beasts than human beings, and employing themselves alternately in drinking and in making preparations for the crucifixion.

This scene was rendered more frightful to Ann Catherine by the sight of demons, which were invisible to others, and she saw large bodies of evil spirits under the forms of toads, serpents, sharp-clawed dragons, and venomous insects, urging these wicked men to still greater cruelty, and perfectly darkening the air. They crept into the mouths and into the hearts of the assistants, sat upon their shoulders, filled their minds with wicked images, and incited them to revile and insult our Lord with still greater brutality.

Weeping angels, however, stood around Jesus, and the sight of their tears greatly consoled Ann Catherine, and they were accompanied by little angels of glory, whose heads alone she saw.

There were, likewise, angels of pity and angels of consolation among them; the latter frequently approached the Blessed Virgin and the rest of the pious persons who were assembled there, and whispered words of comfort which enabled them to bear up with firmness.

The executioners soon pulled off Jesus' cloak, the belt to which the ropes were fastened, and his own belt, when they found it was impossible to drag the woolen garment which his Mother had woven for him over his head, on account of the crown of thorns; they tore off this most painful crown, thus reopening every wound, and seizing the garment, tore it mercilessly over his bleeding and wounded head. Our dear Lord and Savior, said Catherine, then stood before his cruel enemies, stripped of all save the short scapular which was on his shoulders, and the linen which girded his loins. His scapular was of wool; the wool had stuck to the wounds, and indescribable was the agony of pain he suffered when they pulled it roughly off. He shook like the aspen as he stood before them, for he was so weakened from suffering and loss of blood that he could not support himself for more than a few moments; he was covered with open wounds, and his shoulders and back were torn to the bone by the dreadful scourging he had endured. He was about to fall when the executioners, fearing that he might die, and thus deprive them of the barbarous pleasure of crucifying him, led him to a large stone and placed him roughly down upon it, but no sooner was he seated than they aggravated his sufferings by putting the crown of thorns again upon his head. They then offered him some vinegar and gall, from which, however, he turned away in silence.

The executioners did not allow him to rest long, but bade him rise and place himself on the cross that they might nail him to it. Then seizing his right arm they dragged it to the hole prepared for the nail, and having tied it tightly down with a cord, one of them knelt upon his sacred chest, a second held his hands flat, and a third taking a long thick nail, pressed it on the open palm of that adorable hand, which had ever been open to bestow blessings and favors on the ungrateful people, and with a great iron hammer drove it through the flesh, and far into the wood of the cross. Jesus uttered one deep but suppressed groan, and his blood gushed forth and sprinkled the arms of the archers.

It was about a quarter to twelve when Jesus sank down at the precise spot where he was to be crucified. The barbarous executioners dragged him up by the cords which they had fastened round his waist, and then untied the arms of the cross, and threw them on the ground. The sight of Jesus at this moment was, indeed, calculated to move the hardest heart to compassion; he stood or rather bent over the cross, being scarcely able to support himself; his heavenly countenance was as pale as a person on the verge of death, although wounds and blood disfigured it to a frightful degree; but the hearts of the cruel men were harder than iron itself, and far from showing the slightest commiseration, they threw him brutally down, exclaiming in a jeering tone, 'Most powerful king, we are about to prepare thy throne.'

Jesus immediately placed himself upon the cross, and they measured him and marked the places for his feet and hands, whilst the Pharisees continued to insult their unresisting Victim. When the measurement was finished, they led him to a cave cut in the rock, which had been used formerly as a cellar, opened the door, and pushed him in so roughly that had it not been for the support of angels, his legs would have been broken by so hard a fall on the rough stone floor.

The executioners dug the holes for the three crosses at the top of Calvary and placed those intended for the thieves, one on the right of Jesus and the other on the left. They then carried the cross of Jesus to the spot where they intended to crucify him, and placed it in such a position that it would easily fall into the hold prepared for it. They fastened the two arms strongly on to the body of the cross, nailed the board at the bottom which was to support the feet, bored the holes for the nails, and cut different hollows in the wood in the parts which would receive the head and back of Jesus, in order that his body might rest against the cross, instead of being suspended from it. Their aim was the prolongation of his tortures, for if the whole weight of his body was allowed to fall upon the hands, the holes might be quite torn open, and death would ensue more speedily than they desired. The executioners then drove into the ground the pieces of wood which were intended to keep the cross upright, and made a few other similar preparations.

Although the Blessed Virgin had been carried away, fainting after the sad meeting with Jesus loaded with his cross, yet she soon recovered consciousness; for love, and the ardent desire of seeing him once more, imparted to her a supernatural feeling of strength,

Accompanied by her companions she went to the house of Lazarus, which was at the bottom of the town, and where Martha,
Magdalen, and many holy women were already assembled. All were
sad and depressed, but Magdalen could not restrain her tears and
lamentations.

They started from the house, about seventeen in number, to
make the way to the cross, to follow every step Jesus had taken in this
most painful journey. Mary counted each footstep, and being interiorly enlightened, pointed out to her companions those places which
had been consecrated by peculiar sufferings. When the holy women
reached the house of Veronica they entered it, because Pilate and his
officers were at that moment passing through the street, on their way
home. They burst forth into unrestrained tears when they beheld the
countenance of Jesus imprinted on the veil, and they returned thanks
to God for the favor he had bestowed on his faithful servant. They
took the jar of aromatic wine which the Jews had prevented Jesus
from drinking, and set off together towards Golgotha. Their number
was considerably increased, for many pious men and women whom
the sufferings of Jesus had filled with pity had joined them, and they
ascended the west side of Calvary, as the declivity there was not so
great.

The mother of Jesus, accompanied by her niece, Mary (the daughter of Cleophas), John, and Salome went quite up to the round platform; but Martha, Mary of Heli, Veronica, Johanna, Chusa, Susanna,
and Mary, the mother of Mark, remained below with Magdalen, who
could hardly support herself.

Lower down on the mountain there was a third group of holy
women, and there were a few scattered individuals between the three
groups, who carried messages from one to the other. The Pharisees on
horseback rode to and fro among the people, and the five entrances
were guarded by Roman soldiers.

Mary kept her eyes fixed on the fatal spot, and stood as if en-
tranced—it was indeed a sight calculated to appall and rend the heart
of a mother. There lay the terrible cross, the hammers, the ropes, the
nails, and alongside of these frightful instruments of torture stood the
brutal executioners, half drunk, and almost without clothing, swearing and blaspheming, while making their preparations. The suffer-

ings of the Blessed Virgin were greatly increased by her not being able to see her Son; she knew that he was still alive, and she felt the most ardent desire to behold him once more, while the thought of the torments he still had to endure made her heart ready to burst with grief.

A little hail began falling during the morning, but the sun came out after ten o'clock, and a thick red fog began to obscure it towards twelve.

The preparations for the crucifixion being finished, four archers went to the cave where they had confined Jesus and dragged him out with their usual brutality, while the mob looked on and made use of insulting language, and the Roman soldiers regarded all with indifference, and thought of nothing but maintaining order.

When Jesus was again brought forth, the holy women gave a man some money, and begged him to pay the archers anything they might demand if they would allow Jesus to drink the wine which Veronica had prepared; but the executioners drank the wine themselves. They had brought two vases with them, one of which contained vinegar and gall, and the other a mixture which looked like wine mixed with myrrh and absinthe; they offered a glass of the latter to Jesus, which he tasted, but would not drink.

The executioners soon pulled off Jesus' cloak, the belt to which the ropes were fastened, and his own belt; when they found it was impossible to drag the woolen garment which his Mother had woven for him over his head, on account of the crown of thorns; they tore off the crown, thus reopening every wound, and seizing the garment, tore it mercilessly over his bleeding head. Jesus then stood before his enemies, stripped of all save the short scapular which was on his shoulders, and the linen which girded his loins. His scapular was of wool; the wool had stuck to the wounds, and indescribable was the agony of pain he suffered when they pulled it roughly off. He shook like the aspen as he stood before them, for he was so weakened from suffering and loss of blood that he could not support himself for more than a few moments. He was covered with open wounds, and his shoulders and back were torn to the bone by the dreadful scourging he had endured.

Ann Catherine counted the blows of the hammer but her extreme grief made her forget their number. The nails were very large, the heads about the size of a crown piece, and the thickness of a man's thumb, while the points came through at the back of the cross.

When the executioners had nailed the right hand of Jesus, they perceived that his left hand did not reach the hole they had bored to receive the nail, therefore they tied ropes to his left arm, and having steadied their feet against the cross, pulled the left hand violently until it reached the place prepared for it.

The dreadful process caused Jesus indescribable agony, his breast heaved; his legs were contracted. The executioners again knelt upon him, tied down his arms, and drove the second nail into his left hand; his blood flowed afresh, and his feeble groans were once more heard between the blows of the hammer, but nothing could move the hard-hearted executioners to the slightest pity.

The arms of Jesus, unnaturally stretched out, no longer covered the arms of the cross, which were sloped; there was a wide space between them and his armpits. Each additional torture and insult inflicted upon Jesus caused a fresh pang in the heart of his Blessed Mother; she became white as a corpse, but as the Pharisees endeavored to increase her pain by insulting words and gestures, the disciples led her to a group of pious women who were standing a little farther off.

The executioners had fastened a piece of wood at the lower part of the cross under where the feet of Jesus would be nailed, that thus the weight of his body might not rest upon the wounds of his hands, as also to prevent the bones of his feet from being broken when nailed to the cross.

A hole had been pierced in this wood to receive the nail when driven through his feet, and there was likewise a little hollow place for his heels. These precautions were taken lest his wound should be torn open by the weight of his body, and death ensue before suffering all the tortures which they hoped to see him endure. The body of Jesus had been dragged upward, and contracted by the violent manner with which the executioners had stretched out his arms, and his knees were bent up; they therefore flattened and tied them down tightly with cords; but soon perceiving that his feet aid not reach the bit of wood which was placed for them to rest upon, they became infuriated. Some of their number proposed making fresh holes for the nails which pierced his hands, as there would be considerable difficulty in removing the bit of wood, but the others would do nothing of the sort, and continued to vociferate, 'He will not stretch himself out, but we will help him;' they accompanied their words with the most fearful oaths and imprecations, and having fastened a rope to his right leg, dragged it violently until it reached the wood, and then tied it down as tightly as possible. The agony which Jesus suffered from this violent tension was indescribable; the words 'My God, my God,' escaped his lips, and the executioners increased his pain by tying his chest and arms to the cross, lest the hands should be torn from the nails. They then fastened his left foot on to his right foot, having first bored a hole through them with a species of piercer, because they could not be placed in such a position as to be nailed together at once.

Next they took a very long nail and drove it completely through both feet into the cross below, which operation was more than usually painful, on account of his body being so unnaturally stretched out.

Ann Catherine Emmerich counted at least six and thirty blows of the hammer. During the whole time of the crucifixion Jesus never ceased praying, and repeating those passages in the Psalms which he was then accompanying, although from time to time a feeble moan caused by excess of suffering might be heard. In this manner he had prayed when carrying his cross, and thus he continued to pray until his death.

When the crucifixion was finished, the commander of the Roman soldiers ordered Pilate's inscription to be nailed to the top of the cross. The Pharisees were incensed at this, and their anger was increased by the jeers of the Roman soldiers, who pointed at their crucified king; they therefore hastened back to Jerusalem, determined to use their best endeavors to persuade the governor to allow them to substitute another inscription.

It was about a quarter past twelve when Jesus was crucified; and at the moment the cross was lifted up, the Temple resounded with the blast of trumpets, which were always blown to announce the sacrifice of the Paschal Lamb.

✢ ✢ ✢

I can best explain the sacrifice of the Paschal Lamb by telling the story of my baby sister, Shirley Ann.

Shirley was the last born of ten children. It was not long before mother and father realized Shirley was not going to walk or talk. Shirley was not toilet trained. She could not stand without assistance. She had to be carried wherever she went. When she was six years old Shirley was institutionalized for the remainder of her life.

When I was a boy I always wondered about the reason for Shirley's condition. Why did God allow this to happen to innocent Shirley?

Twenty years later I learned the reason for Shirley's condition in a Life Reading provided by The Religious Research Foundation, channeled by spirit counselor and guide, Dr. John Christopher Daniels.

In a period of history of cruelty and torment inflicted by man upon his fellow man, the soul of Shirley, then incarnate in the masculine form, brought blindness, dumbness, deafness, and maiming of limbs upon his fellow man. After the end of that incarnation, the soul received teaching on the spiritual planes concerning the brotherhood of man and the foolishness of using force against one's brother.

A teaching in theory had become a flesh and blood experience. The soul of the brutal man incarnated into the body of the lovely and innocent Shirley Ann to assume the karma of its brutal former incarnation. Shirley is the person who paid the price of her soul's former incarnation but the personality of Shirley did not commit the karma.

In Biblical terms, Shirley became the Paschal Lamb sacrificed for the good of her soul. Shirley didn't commit the crimes. A previous incarnation from her soul committed the crimes; but life is lived for the soul, the everlasting part of us. A lamb, or incarnate personality, is sacrificed for the good of the eternal soul. As Dr. John, Life Reading specialist for Religious Research has stated, "The good of the soul, the progression of the soul, must and does come first."

Jesus was the Paschal Lamb for the world. We all have lifetimes when we suffer for not what we do, but for what a previous incarnation from our soul has done. Jesus taught us to bear our cross without complaint, without self-pity, without bitterness, because a far greater glory awaits us when we do. Jesus' crucifixion is the example we are to follow when we assume an incarnation as a Paschal Lamb.

Erection of the Cross

When the executioners had finished the crucifixion, they tied ropes to the trunk of the cross and fastened the ends of the ropes round a long beam which was fixed firmly in the ground at a little distance, and by means of these ropes they raised the cross. Some of their number supported it while others shoved its foot towards the hole prepared for its reception—the heavy cross fell into this hole with a frightful shock—Jesus uttered a faint cry, and his wounds were torn open, his blood again burst forth, and his half dislocated bones knocked one against the other. The archers pushed the cross to get it thoroughly into the hole, causing it to vibrate still more by planting five stakes around to support it.

A terrible, but at the same time a touching sight it was to behold the cross raised up in the midst of the vast concourse of persons who were assembled all around; not only insulting soldiers, proud Pharisees, and the brutal mob were there, but likewise strangers from all parts.

The air resounded with acclamations and derisive cries when they beheld the cross towering on high, and after vibrating for a moment in the air, fall with a heavy crash into the hold cut for it in the rock. But words of love and compassion resounded through the air at the same moment; and these words, these sounds, were emitted by the most saintly of human beings—Mary—John—the holy women, and all who were pure of heart. They bowed down and adored the 'Word made flesh,' nailed to the cross; they stretched forth their hands as if desirous of giving assistance to the Holy of Holies, whom they beheld nailed to a cross and in the power of his furious enemies.

But when the solemn sound of the fall of the cross into the hole prepared for it in the rock was heard, a dead silence ensued, every heart was filled with an indefinable feeling of awe—a feeling never before experienced, and for which no one could account, even to himself; all the inmates of hell shook with terror, and vented their rage by endeavoring to stimulate the enemies of Jesus to still greater fury and brutality; the souls in Limbo were filled with joy and hope, for the sound was to them a harbinger of happiness, the prelude to the appearance of their Deliverer.

Thus was the blessed cross of Jesus planted for the first time on the earth; and well might it be compared to the tree of life in Paradise, for the wounds of Jesus were as sacred fountains, from which flowed four rivers destined both to purify the world from the curse of sin, and to give it fertility, so as to produce fruit unto salvation.

The eminence on which the cross was planted was about two feet higher than the surrounding parts; the feet of Jesus were sufficiently near the ground for his friends to be able to reach to kiss them, and his face was turned to the north-west.

The tremendous concussion caused by the fall of the cross into the hold drove the sharp points of the crown of thorns still deeper into his flesh, and blood ran down again in streams, both from it and from his hands and feet. The archers then placed ladders against the sides of the cross, mounted them and unfastened the ropes with which they had bound Jesus to the cross, previous to lifting it up, fearing that the shock might tear open the wounds in his hands and feet, and that then the nails would no longer support his body.

His blood had become stagnated by his horizontal position and the pressure of the cords, but when these were withdrawn, it resumed its usual course, and caused such agonizing sensations throughout his countless wounds, that he bowed his head, and remained as if dead for more than seven minutes.

A pause ensued; the executioners were occupied with the division of his garments; the trumpets in the temple no longer resounded; and all the actors in the fearful tragedy appeared to be exhausted, some by grief, and others by the efforts they had made to compass their wicked ends, and by the joy which they felt now at having at last succeeded in bringing about the death of him whom they had so long envied.

Anne Catherine Emmerick cast her eyes upon Jesus. She beheld him motionless, and almost lifeless. She felt as if she herself must expire; her heart was overwhelmed between grief, love, and horror; her mind was half wandering, her hands and feet burning with a feverish heat; each vein, nerve, and limb was racked with inexpressible pain; she saw nothing distinctly, excepting her beloved spouse, Jesus, hanging on the cross. She contemplated his disfigured countenance, his head encircled with that terrible crown of thorns, which prevented his raising his head even for a moment without the most intense suffering, his mouth parched and half open from exhaustion, and his hair and beard clotted with blood. His chest was torn with stripes and wounds, and his elbows, wrists and shoulders so violently distended as to be almost dislocated; blood constantly trickled down from the gaping wounds in his hands, and the flesh was so torn from his ribs that you might almost count them. His legs and thighs, and also his arms, were stretched out almost to dislocation, the flesh and muscles so completely laid bare that every bone was visible, and his whole body covered with black, green, and reeking wounds. The blood which flowed from his wounds was at first red, but it became by degrees light and watery, and the whole appearance of his body was that of a corpse ready for internment. And yet, notwithstanding the horrible wounds with which he was covered, there remained that inexpressible look of dignity and goodness which had ever filled all beholders with awe.

The complexion of Jesus was fair, like that of Mary, and slightly tinted with red; but his exposure to the weather during the last three years had tanned him considerably. His chest was wide, but not hairy like that of St. John the Baptist; his shoulders broad, and his arms and thighs sinewy; his knees were strong and hardened, as is usually the case with those who have either walked or knelt much, and his legs long, with very strong muscles; his feet were well formed, and his hands beautiful, the fingers being long and tapering, and although not delicate like those of a woman, still not resembling those of a man who had labored hard. His neck was rather long, with a well-set and finely proportioned head; his forehead large and high; his face oval; his hair, which was far from thick, was of a golden brown color, parted in the middle and falling over his shoulders; his beard was not any great length, but pointed and divided under the chin.

When Ann Catherine contemplated Jesus on the cross, his hair was almost all torn off, and what remained was matted and clotted with blood; his body was one wound, and every limb seemed as if dislocated.

The crosses of the two thieves were placed, the one to the right and the other to the left of Jesus; there was sufficient space left for a horseman to ride between them. Nothing can be imagined more distressing than the appearance of the thieves on their crosses. They suffered terribly, and the one on the left-hand side never ceased cursing and swearing. The cords with which they were tied were very tight, and caused great pain; their countenances were livid, and their eyes inflamed and ready to pop from their sockets. The height of the crosses of the two thieves was much less than that of Jesus.

First Word of Jesus on the Cross

As soon as the executioners had crucified the two thieves and divided the garments of Jesus between them, they gathered up their tools, addressed a few more insulting words to Jesus, and went away. The Pharisees, likewise, rode up to Jesus, looked at him scornfully, made use of some opprobrious expressions and then left. The Roman soldiers, of whom a hundred had been posted round Calvary, were marched away, and their places filled by fifty others, the command of whom was given to Abenadar, an Arab by birth, who afterwards took the name of Ctesiphon in baptism: and the second in command was Cassius, who, when he became a Christian, was known by the name of Longinus: Pilate frequently made use of him as a messenger

Twelve Pharisees, twelve Sadducees, as many Scribes, and a few Ancients, accompanied by those who had been endeavoring to persuade Pilot to change the inscription on the cross, came up: they were furious, as the Roman governor had given them a direct refusal. They rode round the platform and drove away the Blessed Virgin, whom St. John led to the holy women. When they passed the Cross of Jesus, they shook their heads disdainfully at him, exclaiming at the same time, '*Vah! thou that destroyest the temple of God, and in three days buildest it up again, save thyself, coming down from the cross. Let Christ, the King of Israel, come down now from the cross, that we may see and believe.*' The soldiers also made use of deriding language.

The countenance and whole body of Jesus became even more colorless; he appeared to be on the point of fainting, and Gesmas (the wicked thief) exclaimed, 'The demon by whom he is possessed is about to leave him.'

A soldier then took a sponge, filled it with vinegar, put it on a reed, and presented it to Jesus, who appeared to drink. 'If thou art the

King of the Jews,' said the soldier, 'save thyself, coming down from the Cross.'

These things took place during the time that the first band of soldiers was being relieved by that of Abenadar. Jesus raised his head a little, and said, *'Father forgive them, for they know not what they do.'*

Gesmas cried out, 'If thou art the Christ, save thyself and us.'

Dismas (the good thief) was silent, but he was deeply moved at the prayer of Jesus for his enemies.

When Mary heard the voice of her Son, unable to restrain herself, she pushed forward, followed by John, Salome, and Mary of Cleophas, and approached the Cross, which the kind-hearted centurion did not prevent.

The prayers Jesus obtained for the good thief a most powerful grace; the good thief suddenly remembered that it was Jesus and Mary who had cured him of leprosy in his childhood, and he exclaimed in a loud and clear voice, 'How can you insult him when he prays for you? He has been silent, and suffered all your outrages with patience; he is truly a Prophet—he is our King—he is the Son of God.'

This unexpected reproof from the lips of a miserable malefactor who was dying on a cross caused a tremendous commotion among the spectators; they gathered up stones, and wished to throw them at him; but the centurion Abenadar would not allow it.

The Blessed Virgin was much comforted and strengthened by the prayer of Jesus, and Dismas said to Gesmas, who was still blaspheming Jesus, *'Neither dost thou fear God, seeing thou art under the same condemnation. And we indeed justly, for we receive the due reward of our deeds; but this man hath done no evil. Remember thou art now at the point of death, and repent.'*

He was enlightened and touched: he confessed his sins to Jesus, and said: 'Lord, if thou condemnest me it will be with justice.'

And Jesus replied, 'Thou shalt experience my mercy.'

Dismas, filled with the most perfect contrition, began instantly to thank God for the great graces he had received, and to reflect over the manifold sins of his past life.

All of these events took place between twelve and the half-hour shortly after the crucifixion; but such a surprising change had taken place in the appearance of nature during that time as to astonish the beholders and fill their minds with awe and terror.

Eclipse of the Sun
Second and third Word of Jesus on the Cross

A little hail had fallen at about ten o'clock--when Pilate was passing sentence—and after that the weather cleared up, until towards twelve, when the thick red-looking fog began to obscure the sun. Towards the sixth hour the sun was suddenly darkened.

Ann Catherine was shown the exact cause of this wonderful phenomenon; but she has unfortunately partly forgotten it, and what she has not forgotten she cannot find words to express; but she was lifted up from the earth, and beheld the stars and the planets moving about out of their proper spheres. She saw the moon like an immense ball of fire rolling along as if flying from the earth. She was then suddenly taken back to Jerusalem, and she beheld the moon reappear behind the Mountain of Olives, looking pale and full, and advancing rapidly towards the sun, which was dim and over-shrouded by a fog. She saw to the east of the sun a large dark body which had the appearance of a mountain, which soon hid the sun. The center of this body was dark yellow, and a red circle like a ring of fire was round it. The sky grew darker and the stars appeared to cast a red and lurid light.

Both men and beasts were stuck with terror; the enemies of Jesus ceased reviling him, while the Pharisees endeavored to give philosophical reasons for what was taking place, but they failed in their attempt, and were reduced to silence. Many were seized with remorse, struck their breasts and cried out, 'May his blood fall upon his murderers!'

Numbers of others, whether near the Cross or at a distance, fell on their knees and entreated forgiveness of Jesus, who turned his eyes compassionately upon them in the midst of his sufferings. However, the darkness continued to increase, and everyone excepting Mary and the most faithful among the friends of Jesus left the Cross. Dismas then raised his head, and in a tone of humility and hope said to Jesus, *'Lord, remember me when thou shalt come into thy kingdom.'* And Jesus answered, *'Amen, I say to thee, This day thou shalt be with me in Paradise.'*

Magdalen, Mary of Cleophas, and John stood near the Cross and looked at Jesus while the Blessed Virgin, filled with intense feelings of motherly love, entreated her Son to permit her to die with him; but he, casting a look of ineffable tenderness upon her, turned to John and said, *'Woman, behold thy Son;'* then he said to John, *'Behold thy mother,'*

John looked at his dying Redeemer, and saluted this beloved mother (whom he henceforth considered as his own) in the most respectful manner. The Blessed Virgin was so overcome by grief at these words of Jesus that she almost fainted, and was carried a short distance from the Cross by the holy women.

Ann Catherine Emmerich does not know whether Jesus really pronounced these words, but she felt interiorly that he gave Mary to John as a mother, and John to Mary as a son. In similar visions a person is often conscious of such things which are not written, and words can only express a portion of them, although to the individual to whom they are shown they are so clear as not to require explanation. For this reason it did not appear to Ann Catherine in the least surprising that Jesus should call the Blessed Virgin *'Woman'* instead of 'Mother.' She felt that he intended to demonstrate that she was *that woman* spoken of in Scripture who was to crush the head of the serpent, and that then was the moment in which that promise was accomplished in the death of her Son. She knew that Jesus, by giving her as a mother to John, gave her also as a mother to all who believe in him, who become children of God, and are not born of flesh and blood, or of the will of man, but of God.

Neither did it appear to Ann Catherine surprising that the most pure, the most humble, and the most obedient among women, who, when saluted by the angel as *'full of grace,'* immediately replied, *'Behold the handmaid of the Lord, be it done to me according to thy word,'* and in whose sacred womb the Word was instantly made flesh—that she, when informed by her dying Son that she was to become the spiritual mother of another son, should repeat the same words with humble obedience, and immediately adopt as her children all the children of God, the brothers of Jesus Christ.

These things are much easier to feel by the grace of God than to be expressed in words. Ann Catherine remembered her celestial

Spouse once saying to her, 'Everything is imprinted in the hearts of those children of the Church who believe, hope, and love.'

Fourth Word of Jesus on the Cross

It was about half-past one o'clock when Ann Catherine was taken into Jerusalem to see what was going on there. The inhabitants were perfectly overcome with terror and anxiety; the streets dark and gloomy, and some persons were feeling their way about, while others, seated on the ground with their heads veiled, struck their breasts, or went up to the roofs of their houses, looked at the sky, and burst forth in bitter lamentations. Even the animals uttered mournful cries, and hid themselves; the birds flew low, and fell to the ground. She saw Pilate conferring with Herod on the alarming state of things: they were both extremely agitated, and contemplated the appearance of the sky from that terrace upon which Herod was standing when he delivered up Jesus to be insulted by the infuriated rabble.

'These events are not in the common course of nature,' they both exclaimed: 'they must be caused by the anger of the gods, who are displeased at the cruelty which has been exercised towards Jesus of Nazareth.'

Pilate and Herod, surrounded by guards, then directed their hasty trembling steps through the forum to Herod's palace. Pilate turned away his head when he passed Gabbatha, from whence he had condemned Jesus to be crucified. The square was almost empty; a few persons might be seen re-entering their houses as quickly as possible, and a few others running about and weeping, while two or three small groups might be distinguished in the distance.

Pilot sent for some of the Ancients and asked them what they thought the astounding darkness could possibly portend, and said that he himself considered it a terrific proof of the anger of their God at the crucifixion of the Galilean, who was most certainly their prophet and their king; he added that he had nothing to reproach himself with on that head, for he had washed his hands of the whole affair, and was, therefore, quite innocent.

The Ancients were as hardened as ever, and replied in a sullen tone, that there was nothing unnatural in the course of events, that they might be easily accounted for by philosophers, and that they did not repent of anything they had done. However, many persons were converted, and among others those soldiers who fell to the ground at the words of Jesus when they were sent to arrest him in the Garden of Olives.

The rabble assembled before Pilate's house, and instead of the cry of *'Crucify him, crucify him!'* which had resounded in the morning, the cry became 'Down with the iniquitous judge! May the blood of the just man fall upon his murderers!'

Pilate was much alarmed; he sent for additional guards, and endeavored to cast all the blame upon the Jews. He again declared that the crime was not his; that he was no subject of this Jesus, whom they had put to death unjustly, and who was their king, their prophet, their Holy One; that they alone were guilty, as it must be evident to all that he condemned Jesus solely from compulsion.

The Temple was thronged with Jews, who were intent on the immolation of the Paschal Lamb; but when the darkness increased, and it became impossible to distinguish the countenance of one from the other, they were seized with fear, horror, and dread, which they expressed by mournful cries and lamentations.

The High Priests endeavored to maintain order and quiet. All the lamps were lighted; but the confusion became greater every moment, and Annas appeared perfectly paralyzed with terror. Ann Catherine saw him endeavoring to hide first in one place, and then in another. Although not a breath of wind was stirring, the doors and windows of the houses were shaking as if in a storm, and the darkness became denser every moment.

The consternation produced by the sudden darkness at Mount Calvary was indescribable. When it first commenced, the confusion of the noise of the hammers, the vociferations of the rabble, the cries of the two thieves on being fastened to their crosses, the insulting speeches of the Pharisees, the evolutions of the soldiers, and the drunken shouts of the executioners, had so completely engrossed the attention of everyone, that the change which gradually came over the face of nature was not remarked; but as the darkness increased, every sound ceased, each voice was hushed, and remorse and terror took possession of every heart, while the bystanders retired one by one to a distance from the Cross. Then it was that Jesus gave his Mother to

St. John, and that she, overcome by grief, was carried away to a short distance.

The darkness continued to grow more dense, the silence became perfectly astounding; everyone appeared terror-struck; some looked at the sky, while others, filled with remorse, turned towards the Cross, smote their breasts, and were converted.

Although the Pharisees were in reality quite as much alarmed as other persons, yet they endeavored to put a bold face on the matter, and declared that they could see nothing unaccountable in these events; but at last even they lost assurance, and were reduced to silence.

The disc of the sun was of a dark-yellow tint, resembling a mountain when viewed by moonlight, and it was surrounded by a bright fiery ring; the stars appeared, but the light they cast was red and lurid; the birds were so terrified as to drop to the ground; the beasts trembled and moaned; the horses and the asses of the Pharisees crept as close as possible to one another, and put their heads between their legs. Thick fog penetrated everything.

Stillness reigned around the Cross. Jesus hung upon it alone; forsaken by all—disciples, followers, friends, his Mother even was removed from his side; not one person of the thousands upon whom he had lavished benefits was near to offer him the slightest alleviation in his bitter agony—his soul was overspread with an indescribable feeling of bitterness and grief—all within him was dark, gloomy, and wretched. The darkness which reigned around was but symbolical of that which overspread his interior; he turned, nevertheless, to his Heavenly Father, he prayed for his enemies, he offered the chalice of his sufferings for their redemption, he continued to pray as he had done during the whole of his Passion, and repeated portions of those Palms the prophecies of which were then receiving their accomplishment in him.

Ann Catherine saw angels around. She looked at Jesus again on his Cross, agonizing and dying, yet still in dreary solitude. He at that moment endured anguish which no mortal pen can describe—he felt that suffering which would overwhelm a poor weak mortal if deprived at once of all consolation, both divine and human, and then compelled without refreshment, assistance, or light, to traverse the stormy desert of tribulation upheld by faith, hope, and charity alone.

His sufferings were inexpressible; but it was by them that he merited for us the grace necessary to resist those temptations to despair which will assail us at the hour of death—that tremendous hour when we shall feel that we are about to leave all that is dear to us here below.

When our minds, weakened by disease have lost the power of reasoning, and even our hopes of mercy and forgiveness are become, as it were, enveloped in mist and uncertainty—then it is that we must fly to Jesus, unite our feelings of desolation with that indescribable dereliction, which he endured upon the Cross, and be certain of obtaining a glorious victory over our infernal enemies.

Jesus then offered to his Eternal Father his poverty, his dereliction, his labors, and above all, the bitter sufferings which our ingratitude had caused him to endure in expiation for our sins and weaknesses; no one, therefore, who is united to Jesus in the bosom of his Church must despair at the awful moment preceding his exit from this life, even if he be deprived of all sensible light and comfort; for he must then remember that the Christian is no longer obligated to enter this dark desert alone and unprotected, as Jesus has cast his own interior and exterior dereliction on the Cross into this gulf of desolation; consequently he will not be left to cope alone with death, or be suffered to leave this world in desolation of spirit, deprived of heavenly consolation.

All fear of loneliness and despair in death must therefore be cast away; for Jesus, who is our true Light, the Way, the Truth, and the Life, has preceded us on that dreary road, has overspread it with blessings, and raised his Cross upon it, one glance at which will calm our every fear. Jesus then (if we may so express ourselves) made his last testament in the presence of his Father, and bequeathed his last testament in the presence of his Father, and bequeathed the merits of his Death and Passion to the Church and to sinners.

Not one erring soul was forgotten; he thought of each and every one; praying, likewise, even for those heretics who have endeavored to prove that, being God, he did not suffer as a man would have suffered in his place. The cry which he allowed to pass his lips in the heights of his agony was intended not only to show the excess of the sufferings he was then enduring, but likewise to encourage all afflicted souls who acknowledge God as their Father to lay their sorrows with filial confidence at his feet.

It was towards three o'clock when he cried out in a loud voice, *'Eloi, Eloi, lamma sabacthani? Why hast thou forsaken me?'*

These words of Jesus interrupted the dead silence which had continued for so long; the Pharisees turned towards him, and one of them said, *'Behold, he calleth Elias;'* and another, *'Let us see whether Elias will come to deliver him.'*

When Mary heard the voice of her divine Son, she was unable to restrain herself any longer, but rushed forwards, and returned to the foot of the Cross, followed by John, Mary the daughter of Cleophas, Mary Magdalen, and Salome.

A troop of about thirty horsemen from Judea and the environs of Joppa, who were on their way to Jerusalem for the festival, passed by just at the time when all was silent round the Cross, both assistants and spectators being transfixed with terror and apprehension. When they beheld Jesus hanging on the Cross, saw the cruelty with which he had been treated, and remarked the extraordinary signs of God's wrath which overspread the face of nature, they were filled with horror, and exclaimed, 'If the Temple of God were not in Jerusalem, the city should be burned to the ground for having taken upon itself so fearful a crime.'

These words from the lips of strangers—strangers too who bore the appearance of persons of rank—made a great impression on the bystanders, and loud murmurs and exclamations of grief were heard on all sides; some individuals gathered together in groups, more feely to indulge their sorrow, although a certain portion of the crows continued to blaspheme and revile all around them.

The Pharisees were compelled to assume a more humble tone, for they feared an insurrection among the people, being well aware of the great existing excitement among the inhabitants of Jerusalem. They therefore held a consultation with Abenadar, the centurion, and agreed with him that the gate of the city, which was in the vicinity, should be closed, in order to prevent further communication, and that they should send to Pilate and Herod for 500 men to guard against the chance of an insurrection, the centurion, in the meantime, doing all in his power to maintain order, and preventing the

Pharisees from insulting Jesus, lest it should exasperate the people still more.

Shortly after three o'clock the light reappeared in a degree, the moon began to pass away from the disc of the sun, while the sun again shone forth, although its appearance was dim, being surrounded by a species of red mist; by degrees it became more bright, and the stars vanished, but the sky was still gloomy. The enemies of Jesus soon recovered their arrogant spirit when they saw the light returning; and it was then that they exclaimed, *'Behold, he calleth Elias.'*

Jesus' Death

The light continued to return by degrees, and the livid exhausted countenance of Jesus again became visible. His body was whiter from the quantity of blood he had lost. Jesus was almost fainting; his tongue was parched, and he said: *'I thirst!'*

The disciples who were standing round the Cross looked at him with the deepest expression of sorrow, and he added, *'Could you not have given me a little water?'*

By these words he gave them to understand that no one would have prevented them from doing so during the darkness. John was filled with remorse, and replied: 'We did not think of doing so, O Lord.'

Jesus replied: 'My friends and my neighbors were also to forget me and not give me to drink, that so what was written concerning me might be fulfilled.'

This omission had afflicted him very much. The disciples then offered money to the soldiers to obtain permission to give him a little water: they refused to give it, but dipped a sponge in vinegar and gall, and were about to offer it to Jesus, when the centurion Abenadar, whose heart was touched with compassion, took it from them, squeezed out the gall, poured some fresh vinegar upon it, and fastening it to a reed, put the reed at the end of a lance, and presented it for Jesus to drink.

Anne Catherine heard Jesus say several other things, but she only remembered these words: *'When my voice shall be silent, the mouths of the dead shall be opened.'*

Some of the bystanders cried out: 'He blasphemeth again.'

But Abenadar compelled them to be silent.

The hour of our Lord was at last come; his death-struggle had commenced; a cold sweat overspread every limb. John stood at the foot of the Cross, and wiped the feet of Jesus with his scapular. Magdalen was crouched to the ground in a perfect frenzy of grief behind the cross. The Blessed Virgin stood between Jesus and the good thief, supported by Salome and Mary of Cleophas, with her eyes riveted on the countenance of her dying son. Jesus then said: *'It is consummated;'* and, raising his head, cried out in a loud voice, *'Father, into thy hands I commend my spirit.'*

These words, which he uttered in a clear and thrilling tone, re-sounded through heaven and earth; and a moment after, he bowed down his head and gave up the ghost. Anne Catherine saw the soul of Jesus under the appearance of a bright meteor penetrate the earth at the foot of the Cross. John and the holy women fell prostrate on the ground. The centurion Abenadar had kept his eyes steadfastly fixed on the disfigured countenance of Jesus, and was perfectly over-whelmed by all that had taken place.

When Jesus pronounced his last words, in a loud tone, the earth trembled, and the rock of Calvary burst asunder, forming a deep chasm between the Cross of Jesus and that of Gesmas.

Ann Catherine said: The voice of God—that solemn and terrible voice—had re-echoed through the whole universe; it had broken the solemn silence which then pervaded all nature. All was accomplished. The soul of Jesus had left his body: his last cry had filled every breast with terror. The convulsed earth had paid homage to its Creator; the sword of grief had pierced the hearts of those who loved him. This moment was the moment of grace for Abenadar; his horse trembled under him; his heart was touched; it was rent like the hard rock; he threw his lance to a distance, struck his breast, and cried out: 'Blessed be the Most High God, the God of Abraham, of Isaac, and of Jacob; indeed this man was the Son of God!'

The words of Abenadar convinced many among the soldiers, who followed his example, and were likewise converted. Abenadar became a new man; he would no longer serve his enemies. He gave both his horse and his lance to a subaltern of the name of Longinus, who, having addressed a few words to the soldiers, mounted his horse, and took the command upon himself.

Abenadar then left Calvary, and went through the Valley of Gihon to the caves in the Valley of Hinnom, where the disciples were hidden, announced the death of Jesus, and then went to the town, in order to see Pilate. No sooner had Abenadar rendered public testimony of his belief in the divinity of Jesus, than a large number of soldiers followed his example, as did also some of the bystanders, and even a few Pharisees. Many struck their breasts, wept, and returned home, while others rent their garments, and cast dust on their heads, and all were filled with horror and fear. John arose; and some of the holy women who were at a short distance came up to the Blessed Virgin, and led her away from the foot of the Cross.

When Jesus, the Lord of life and death, gave up the soul into the hands of his Father, and allowed death to take possession of his body, this sacred body trembled and turned lividly white, the countless wounds which were covered with congealed blood appeared like dark marks; his cheeks became more sunken, his nose more pointed, and his eyes, which were obscured with blood, remained but half open. He raised his weary head, which was still crowned with thorns, for a moment, and then dropped it again in agony of pain; while his parched and torn lips, only partially closed, showed his bloody and swollen tongue. At the moment of death his hands, which were at one time contracted round the nails, opened and returned to their natural size, as did also his arms; his body became still, and the whole weight was thrown upon the feet, his knees bent, and his feet twisted a little on one side.

Words can not express the deep grief of the Blessed Virgin. Her eyes closed, a death-like tint overspread her countenance; unable to stand, she fell to the ground, but was soon lifted up, and supported by John, Magdalen, and the others. She looked once more upon her beloved Son—that Son whom she had conceived by the Holy Ghost, the flesh of her flesh, the bone of her bone, the heart of her heart—hanging on a cross between two thieves; crucified, dishonored, condemned by those whom he came on earth to save; and well might she at this moment be termed 'the queen of martyrs.'

The sun still looked dim and suffused with mist; and during the time of the earthquake the air was close and oppressive, but by degrees it became more clear and fresh.

It was about three o'clock when Jesus expired. The Pharisees were at first much alarmed at the earthquake; but when the first shock was over they recovered themselves, began to throw stones into the chasm, and tried to measure its depth with ropes. Finding, however, that they could not fathom its bottom, they became thoughtful, listened anxiously to the groans of the penitents, who were lamenting and striking their breasts, and then left Calvary. Many among the spectators were really converted, and the greatest part returned to Jerusalem perfectly overcome with fear. Roman soldiers were placed at the gates, and in other principal parts of the city, to prevent the possibility of an insurrection. Cassius remained on Calvary with about fifty soldiers. The friends of Jesus stood round the Cross, contemplated our Lord, and wept; many among the holy women had returned to their homes, and all were silent and overcome with grief.

Apparitions of the Dead in Jerusalem

Anne Catherine saw the soul of Jesus, at the moment he expired, appear under the form of a bright orb, and accompanied by angels, among whom she distinguished the Angel Gabriel, penetrate the earth at the foot of the cross. She likewise saw these angels cast a number of evil spirits into the great abyss, and she heard Jesus order several of the souls in Limbo to re-enter the bodies in which they once dwelt, in order that the sight might fill sinners with a salutary terror, and that these souls might render a solemn testimony to his divinity.

The earthquake which produced the deep chasm at Calvary did much damage in different parts of Palestine, but its effects were even more fatal in Jerusalem. Its inhabitants were just beginning to be a little reassured by the return of light, when their terror was reawakened with double force by the shocks of the earthquake, and the terrible noise and confusion caused by the downfall of houses and walls on all sides, which panic was still further increased by the sudden appearance of dead persons, confronting the trembling miscreants who were flying to hide themselves, and addressing them in the most severe and reproachful language.

The High Priests had recommenced the sacrifice of the Paschal lamb (which had been stopped by the unexpected darkness), and they were triumphing at the return of light, when suddenly the ground beneath them trembled, the neighboring buildings fell down, and the veil of the temple was rent in two from the top to the bottom.

Excess of terror at first rendered those on the outside speechless, but after a time they burst forth into cries and lamentations. The confusion in the interior of the Temple was not, however, as great as would naturally have been expected, because the strictest order and decorum were always enforced there, particularly with regard to the regulations to be followed by those who entered to make their sacrifice, and those who left after having offered it.

The crowd was great, but the ceremonies were so solemnly carried out by the priests, that they totally engrossed the minds of the assistants. First came the immolation of the lamb, then the sprinkling of its blood, accompanied by the chanting of canticles and the sounding of trumpets. The priests were endeavoring to continue the sacrifices, when suddenly an unexpected and appalling pause ensued; terror and astonishment were depicted on each countenance; all was thrown into confusion; not a sound was heard; the sacrifices ceased; there was a general rush to the gates of the Temple; everyone endeavored to fly as quickly as possible.

And well might they fly, well might they fear and tremble; for in the minds of the multitude there suddenly appeared persons who had been dead and buried for many years!

These persons looked at them sternly, and reproved them most severely for the crime they had committed that day, in bringing about the death of 'the just man,' and calling down his blood upon their heads.

Even in the midst of this confusion, some attempts were, however, made by the priests to preserve order; they prevented those who were in the inner part of the temple from rushing forward, pushing their way through the crowds who were in advance of them, and descending the steps which led out of the temple: they even continued the sacrifices in some parts and endeavored to calm the fears of the people.

The appearance of the temple at this moment can only be described by comparing it to an ant-hill on which persons have thrown stones, or which has been disturbed buy a stick being driven into its center. The ants in those parts on which the stones have fallen, or which the stick has disturbed, are filled with confusion and terror; they run to and fro and do nothing; while the ants in those parts which have not been disturbed continue to labor quietly, and even begin to repair the damaged parts.

The High Priest Caiphas and his retinue did not lose their presence of mind, and by the outward tranquility which their diabolical hardness of heart enabled them to preserve, they calmed the confusion to a great degree, and then did their utmost to prevent the people from looking upon these stupendous events as testimonies of the innocence of Jesus. The Roman garrison belonging to the fortress of Antonia likewise made great efforts to maintain order; consequently, the disturbance of the festival was not followed by an insurrection, although every heart was fixed with fear and anxiety, an anxiety the Pharisees endeavored, and in some instances, succeeded to calm.

Ann Catherine remembered a few other striking incidents: the two columns which were placed at the entrance of their Holy of Holies, and to which a magnificent curtain was appended were shaken to the very foundations; the column on the left side fell down in a southerly, and that on the right in a northerly direction, thus rending the veil in two from the top to the bottom with a fearful sound, and exposing the Holy of Holies uncovered to the public gaze.

A large stone was loosened and fell from the wall at the entrance of the sanctuary, near where the aged Simeon used to kneel, and the arch was broken. The ground was heaved up, and many other columns were thrown down in other parts of the Temple.

An apparition of the High Priest Zacharias, who was slain between the porch and the altar, was seen in the sanctuary. He uttered fearful menaces, spoke of the death of the second Zacharias (father of John the Baptist), and of that of St. John Baptist, as also of the violent deaths of the other prophets.

The two sons of the High priest Simon, surnamed 'the Just' (ancestors of the aged Simeon who prophesized when Jesus was presented in the Temple), made their appearance in the part usually occupied by the doctors of the law; they also spoke in terrifying terms of the deaths of the prophets, of the sacrifice of the old law which now was about to cease, and they exhorted all present to be converted, and to embrace the doctrines which had been preached by him whom they had crucified. The prophet Jeremiah likewise appeared; he stood near the altar and proclaimed, in a menacing tone, that the ancient sacrifice was at an end, and that a new one had commenced.

As these apparitions took place in parts where none but priests were allowed to enter, Caiphas and a few others were alone cognizant of them, and they endeavored, as far as possible, either to deny their reality, or to conceal them. These prodigies were followed by others still more extraordinary. The doors of the sanctuary flew open of themselves, and a voice was heard to utter these words: 'Let us leave this place;' and Ann Catherine saw all the angels of the Lord instantly leave the Temple.

The thirty-two Pharisees who went to Calvary a short time before Jesus expired were almost all converted at the foot of the Cross. They returned to the Temple in the midst of the confusion, and were perfectly thunderstruck at all which had taken place there. They spoke most sternly, both to Annas and to Caiphas, and left the Temple,

Annas had always been the most bitter of the enemies of Jesus, and had headed every proceeding against him; but the supernatural events which had taken place had so completely unnerved him that he knew not where to hide himself. Caiphas was, in reality, excessively alarmed, and filled with anxiety, but his pride was so great that he concealed his feelings as far as possible, and endeavored to reassure Annas. He succeeded for a time; but the sudden appearance of a person who had been dead many years marred the effect of his words, and Annas became again a prey to the most fearful terror and remorse.

While these things were going on in the temple, the confusion and panic were not less in Jerusalem. Dead persons were walking about, and many walls and buildings had been shaken by the earthquake, and parts of them fallen down. The superstition of Pilate rendered him even more accessible to fear; he was perfectly paralyzed and speechless with terror; his palace was shaken to the very foundation, and the earth quaked beneath his feet. He ran from room to room, and the dead constantly stood before him, reproaching him with the unjust sentence he had passed upon Jesus. He thought that they were the gods of the Galilean, and took refuge in an inner room, where he offered incense, and made vows to his idols to invoke their assistance in his distress. Herod was equally alarmed, but he shut himself up in his palace, out of the sight of everyone.

More than a hundred persons who had died at different epochs re-entered the bodies they had occupied when on earth, made their appearance in different parts of Jerusalem, and filled the inhabitants with inexpressible consternation. Those souls which had been released by Jesus from Limbo uncovered their faces and wandered to and fro in the streets and although their bodies were the same as those which they had animated when on earth, yet these bodies did not appear to touch the ground as they walked. They entered the houses of their descendants, proclaimed the innocence of Jesus, and reproved those who had taken part in his death most severely. Anne Catherine saw them passing through the principal streets; they were generally in couples, and appeared to glide through the air without moving their feet.

The countenance of some were pale; others of a yellow tint; their beards were long, and their voices sounded strange and sepulchral. Their grave-clothes were such as it was customary to use at the period of their decease.

When they reached the place where sentence of death was proclaimed on Jesus before the procession started for Calvary, they paused for a moment, and exclaimed in a loud voice: 'Glory be to Jesus forever and ever, and destruction to his enemies!'

Towards four o'clock all the dead returned to their graves. The sacrifices in the Temple had been so interrupted, and the confusion caused by the different prodigies was so great, that very few persons ate the Paschal lamb on that evening.

The Descent from the Cross

Nicodemus and Joseph placed the ladders behind the Cross, and mounted them, holding in their hands a large sheet, to which three long straps were fastened. They tied the body of Jesus, below the arms and knees, to the tree of the Cross, and secured the arms by pieces of linen placed underneath the hands. Then they drew out the nails, by pushing them from behind with strong pins pressed upon the points.

The sacred hands of Jesus were thus not much shaken, and the nails fell easily out of the wounds; for the latter had been made wider by the weight of the body, which, being now supported by the cloths, no longer hung on the nails. The lower part of the body now rested in a natural position, supported by a sheet fastened above to the arms of the Cross.

While Joseph was taking out the nail from the left hand, and then allowing the left arm, supported by its cloth, to fall gently down upon the body, Nicodemus was fastening the right arm of Jesus to that of the Cross, as also the crowned head, which had sunk on the right shoulder.

Then he took out the right nail, and having surrounded the arm with its supporting sheet, let it fall gently on to the body. At the same time, the centurion Abenadar, with great difficulty, drew out the large nail which transfixed the feet. Cassius devoutly received the nails, and laid them at the feet of the Virgin Mary

Joseph and Nicodemus placed ladders against the front of the Cross, in a very upright position, and close to the body, untied the upper strap and fastened it to one of the hooks on the ladder, they did the same with the other two straps, and passing them all on from hook to hook, caused the sacred body to descend gently towards the centurion, who received it in his arms, holding it below the knees; while Joseph and Nicodemus, supporting the upper part of the body, came gently down the ladder, stopping at every step, and taking every imaginable precaution, as would be done by men bearing the body of some beloved friend who had been grievously wounded. Thus did the bruised body of Jesus reach the ground.

When the body was taken down it was wrapped in linen from the knees to the waist, and then placed in the arms of the Virgin Mary.

The head, bosom, and feet of Jesus were washed; the body which was covered with brown stains and red marks in those places where the skin had been torn off, and of a bluish-white color, like flesh that had been drained of blood, was resting on the knees of Mary, who covered the parts which she had washed with a veil, and then proceeded to embalm all the wounds. The holy women knelt by her side, and in turn presented to her a box, out of which she took some previous ointment, and with it filled and covered the wounds. She also anointed the hair, and then, taking the hands of Jesus in her left hand, respectfully kissed them, and filled the large wounds made by the nails with this ointment or sweet spice. She likewise filled the ears, nostrils, and wound in the side with the same precious mixture. Meanwhile Magdalen wiped and embalmed Jesus' feet, and then again washed them with her tears, and often pressed her face upon them.

The Mother of Jesus, the holy women, the men—all were kneeling round the body of Jesus to take their farewell of it, when a most touching miracle took place before them. The body of Jesus, with all its wounds, appeared imprinted upon the cloth which covered it, as though he had been pleased to reward their care and their love, and leave them a portrait of himself through all the veils with which he was enwrapped.

The Resurrection of Jesus

Ann Catherine beheld the soul of Jesus between two angels who were in the attire of warriors: it was bright, luminous, and resplendent as the sun at midday; it penetrated the rock, touched the sacred body, passed into it, and the two were instantaneously united, and became as one. She then saw the limbs move, and the body of Jesus, being reunited to his soul and to his divinity, rise and shake off the winding-sheet: the whole of the cave was illuminated and lightsome.

Anne Catherine then saw the glorified body of Jesus rise up, and it passed through the hard rock as easily as if the latter had been formed of some ductile substance. The earth shook, and an angel in the garb of a warrior descended from Heaven with the speed of lightning, entered the tomb, lifted the stone, placed it on the right side, and seated himself upon it. At this tremendous sight the soldiers fell to the ground, and remained there apparently lifeless.

When Cassius saw the bright light which illuminated the tomb, he approached the place where the sacred body had been placed, looked at and touched the linen clothes in which it had been wrapped, and left the sepulcher, intending to go and inform Pilate of all that had happened. However, he tarried a short time to watch the progress of events; for although he had felt the earthquake, seen the angel move the stone, and looked at the empty tomb, yet he had not seen Jesus.

At the very moment in which the angel entered the sepulcher and the earth quaked, Ann Catherine saw Jesus appear to his Mother on Calvary. His body was beautiful and lightsome, and its beauty was that of a celestial being. He was clothed in a large mantle, which at one moment looked dazzlingly white, as it floated through the air, waving to and fro with every breath of wind, and the next reflected a thousand brilliant colors as the sunbeams passed over it. His large open wounds shone brightly, and could be seen from a great distance: the wounds in his hands were so large that a finger might be put into them without difficulty; and rays of light proceeded from them, diverging in the direction of his fingers. The souls of the patriarchs bowed down before the Mother of Jesus, and Jesus spoke to her concerning his Resurrection, telling her many things which Ann Catherine has forgotten. He showed her his wounds; and Mary prostrated to kiss his sacred feet; but he took her hand, raised her, and disappeared.

When Anne Catherine was at some distance from the sepulcher she saw fresh lights burning there, and she likewise beheld a large luminous spot in the sky immediately over Jerusalem.

The following week people were washing and purifying the Temple. They offered up expiatory sacrifices, cleared away the rubbish and endeavored to conceal the effects of the earthquake by placing planks and carpets over the chasms and fissures made by it in the walls and on the pavement; and they recommended the Paschal solemnities, which had been interrupted in the midst, declared that the disturbance had been caused by the presence of impure persons, and endeavored to explain away the apparition of the dead.

They referred to a vision of Ezechiel. They threatened all who dared to say a syllable concerning the events which had taken place, or who presumed to murmur, with excommunication and other severe punishments. They succeeded in silencing some few hardened persons who, conscious of their own guilt, wished to banish the subject from their minds, but they made no impression on those whose hearts still retained some remains of virtue; they remained silent for a time, concealing their inward belief, but later, regaining courage, proclaimed their faith in Jesus loudly to the world.

The High Priests were much disconcerted, when they perceived how rapidly the doctrines of Christ spread over the country. When

Stephen was deacon, the whole of Ophel and the eastern side of Zion was too small to contain the numerous Christian communities, and a portion were obliged to take up their residence in the country between Jerusalem and Bethania.

The High Priest Annas was in such a state of frenzy as to act like one possessed; he was at last obliged to be confined, and never again to make his appearance in public. Caiphas was outwardly less demonstrative, but he was inwardly devoured with such rage and extreme jealousy that his reason was affected.

On Easter Thursday Pilot was instituting a search for his wife in every part of the city, but his efforts for her recovery were fruitless; she was concealed in the house of Lazarus, in Jerusalem. No one thought of looking there, as the house contained no other female; but Stephen carried food to her there, and let her know all that was going on in the city. Stephen was first-cousin to St. Paul. They were the sons of two brothers. On the day after the Sabbath, Simon of Cyrene went to the Apostles and begged to be instructed and to receive baptism.

The visions of Sister Emmerich, which had continued from the 18th of February to the 6th of April 1823, came to a conclusion.

MYSTICS

Since the death of Jesus, the Catholic Church has been the ac-knowledged body for the determination of a saint. The Catholic Church's investigative procedures have been honored and accepted through the years of its existence.

There have been saintly people who will never be acknowledged as a saint for the simple reason they were not a member of the Catho-lic Church. And this is understandable, considering the history of religion; but many individuals have been endowed with spiritual gifts equal to saints.

A more democratic method of determining a saint would be to base an individual's worthiness upon their spiritual contributions to humanity as a whole, and not upon their membership in any reli-gious organization.

Edgar Cayce was not a Catholic, but seldom has a man lived that was more spiritually tuned and psychically gifted than the man known as the mystery man of miracles.

I first learned of Edgar Cayce from the book *The Search for Bridey Murphy.* I then read his biography, *There Is A River,* by Thomas Su-grue, and was astounded. His life had allowed me to see the type of gift a next door neighbor type of person was capable of possessing. I have always considered Edgar Cayce to be a saint. He certainly was a saintly man.

The first person I gave thought to upon reading the story of Ed-gar Cayce was my father. My father was no saint, nor was he an Edgar Cayce. Father was raised a Catholic but he left the Church when he was twenty years of age due to the death of his beloved first born, adorable Baby Paul, who had been named after my father. Father's faith in his Church was surely tested during this time. The Church was his spiritual authority and he turned to his Church for the ulti-mate solution, for he believed the Biblical teaching, *Ask and ye shall receive; Pray and it shall be given unto you.*

Baby Paul contacted pneumonia and scarlet fever when he was

two. Father's prayers were left unanswered. My father was devastated when Baby Paul died. The child he had held in his arms and rocked to sleep was taken from him. Father couldn't even kiss his son good-bye nor could he even touch him again. Baby Paul was encased under glass as a preventive measure against contamination. Before the lid of the casket was closed Father leaned over the casket and kissed the glass that separated them; then with eyes filled with pain Father watched as the casket was lowered into the ground. He would never forget that image. .

I was living in Hawaii and on Welfare when I read *There Is A River.* The book was priced at $5.00. I had to send a copy of the book to my father. I got $5.00 for donating a pint of blood at the blood bank. The story could change his life - I thought. He could use some enlightenment into the purpose of life and death and reincarnation - I thought. It could be a turning point in his life, again - I thought. What greater gift to present to a father who had lost his faith?

Father never thanked me for the gift, nor did he even acknowledge receiving it. Mother said he was reading it but kept falling asleep. Mother read it. Sister-in-law Annie read it, but she didn't believe the story was true.

It took a long time for the story of Edgar Cayce to bear fruit regarding my father's mental and emotional well being – but my gift did bear fruit – at a most opportune time – and none too soon.

Fifteen years later Father lay upon his death bed. Father lost control of his nerves. His body became spasmodic, quivering and trembling from the fear that raged throughout his body. He had blamed God for the death of his beloved first born, the pride of his young manhood, adorable Baby Paul. And now the death that had come for his child was coming for him, haunting him with the age old questions that have humbled the mightiest of men: Does God exist? Will I be condemned to the eternal fire of Hell?

Father asked my brother Leo to get the hospital priest, an almost unbelievable request for Father had been strongly anti-Catholic. Father then gave his confession, received absolution, and died in peace soon after. Father may have thought Baby Paul had decayed in the ground. Father never visited the grave more than twice to my knowledge. It was through his own death that Father would learn the truth.

I am sure his first born, adorable Baby Paul, welcomed Father into the bright light of life on the other side with a welcoming smile on his face.

The reaction of my family to the story of Edgar Cayce was no different than the reactions Cayce received from many individuals. There were those who were open minded, and those who were close minded. Cayce received all types of reactions, and he laid the ground-work to reply to those various reactions.

The following material is a modified version of the gifts of Edgar Cayce and explains why my father probably felt trapped by his limited and negative beliefs.

Cayce was an uncomplicated man. He was born and reared on a farm in western Kentucky. He attended the local schools and was considered rather dull until he began to read. A woodcutter told Edgar the first Bible story that made a lasting impression. The wood-cutter admitted being as strong as Samson. This introduction to the Bible caused Edgar Cayce to ask his father to buy a Bible for his own, that he might read it, and he read the Bible once a year for every year of his life. Edgar Cayce believed in its promise of being able to commune with the One God.

However, the promise received at that time did not prevent his missing his lessons in school, as usual, the following day. In the evening he had the same hard time in preparing his spelling lesson. Each time he studied the lesson he felt that he knew it, yet when he handed the book to his father and he was given words to spell Edgar couldn't spell them. After wrestling with his problem for two or three hours, receiving many rebuffs for his stupidity, something inside of him seemed to say, "Rely on the promise". He asked his father to let him sleep on his lesson just five minutes. His father eventually consented. Edgar closed the book, and leaning on the back of the chair went to sleep. At the end of five minutes Edgar handed his father the book. He not only knew his lesson, but he could then spell any word in the book; not only spell the words but could tell on what page and what line the word would be found. From that day on Edgar had little trouble in school, for he would read his lesson, sleep on it a few minutes, and then be able to repeat every word of it.

Edgar could not explain his ability. It was a wonder to his parents, to his associates, and his teachers. He did not attempt to reason why this happened. His life became a combination of literally thousands of such experiences. Although he understood many of the laws associated with these phenomena, his understanding was born of experience; he left the technical explanation to others.

Edgar began suffering from severe headaches. One day he had a very severe attack and became unconscious. A friend found him wandering about the streets and carried him home. For days he knew nothing. When he became conscious again he had no control whatever of his voice and for twelve months or more he could scarcely speak above a whisper. Every remedy they knew of was tried, but Edgar continued to fail in health.

Among those who treated him was a hypnotist—not a highly educated man—just a plain business man who was interested in the phenomenon of hypnotism. While under the hypnotic influence, Edgar Cayce was able to speak, yet when brought from under it, he could not. Successive attempts to hypnotize him got on his nerves and he was unable to sleep. The hypnosis sessions were discontinued for a time. He had received a good deal of newspaper publicity which prompted a noted physician from New York to visit him. Hypnotism was tried again, but this time with no results. Then Edgar told the physician of his experiences as a child, and that he felt sure he could make himself unconscious. He felt within himself the same condition taking place when being hypnotized as he felt when putting himself to sleep. He suggested that this was why the hypnotist was unable to give him a post-hypnotic suggestion. If he put himself in the unconscious condition and have someone talk with him, he would be able to tell the person the trouble and how to get rid of it.

Edgar's parents had little faith in hypnotism and were afraid to try further suggestions, but after several months Edgar was unable to even whisper, and many declared he had galloping consumption. Edgar pleaded with his mother and father to at least let the man who had first hypnotized him try the experiment the specialist had suggested. They finally agreed. On a Sunday afternoon, March 31, 1901 this man came to the Cayce home. No one was present except his mother, father, and this gentleman. Edgar lay on the couch and gave the first of what is now called a "reading". In a few minutes Edgar lost consciousness. After the hypnotists suggestion Edgar said that he could see himself: "Yes, we can see the body," Edgar said. "In the normal physical state this body is unable to speak, due to a partial paralysis of the inferior muscles of the vocal cords, produced by nerve strain. This is a psychological condition producing a physical effect. This may be removed by increasing the circulation to the affected parts by suggestion while in this unconscious condition."

In five to ten minutes Edgar said, "It is all right." Then the man told him to wake up at a given time. When Edgar was conscious again he knew that he could speak.

That was Edgar Cayce's first reading.

Since that time he had given more than fifteen thousand individual readings. The gentleman who assisted in this first reading believed that if he could describe what was wrong with himself he might also help others. The hypnotist asked Edgar to try, and so he began spending much of his time in an unconscious state giving information for those who, hearing of this unusual power, sought help.

Edgar was still ashamed to talk about his readings. People thought him odd and he resented for a time the little slights and slurs of his associates who took pleasure in laughing at him. Edgar realized it is hard to be "different. He eventually selected photography as a life work and gave only his spare time and evenings to the increasing number of requests for readings. It was only when he began to come in contact with those who received help from following the suggestions given in readings that Edgar began to realize the true nature of the work which lay before him. Indeed, he did not even decide to give his whole time to the work until situations in his own family brought him face to face with facts.

One day a man phoned Edgar at his photography studio: "I have heard of what you, with the assistance of a certain man, have been able to do for those who are very sick. I have a little girl whose condition is said to be hopeless. Won't you come and see what you will say about her condition?"

Edgar never forgot his feelings on that occasion. He journeyed to the little city where this professor lived. The man met Edgar at the train station with his carriage, then drove him to his home, introduced him to his wife, then asked Edgar if he would like to see the little girl and examine her. He felt foolish and didn't know whether he wanted to or not. He knew that of himself he could tell nothing. He had never studied anything of the kind and didn't know what it was all about. Edgar agreed to look at the little girl but he did not suppose it would make any difference. He was led into a room where the little girl was sitting on the floor rolling blocks. A nurse was attending her. She looked as well as any child Edgar had ever seen, and he couldn't imagine what in the world would be said regarding such a perfect looking little girl.

When Edgar was conscious again, the little girl's father and mother were in tears. The mother gripped Edgar by the hand and said, "You have given us the first hope we have had in years respecting Annie's condition."

The following affidavit was secured from the father for research purposes:

"Personally appeared before Gerrit J. Raidt, a notary public in and for said county, C. H. Dietrich, and after being duty sworn, deposes and says that:

"Annie L. Dietrich, born January 7, 1897, at Hopkinsville, Ky., was perfectly strong and healthy until February, 1899, when she had an attack of LaGrippe, followed by two violent convulsions, each of twenty minutes' duration. Dr. T. G. Yates, now of Pensacola, Florida, was the attending physician. Convulsions returned at irregular intervals with increasing severity. She would fall just like she was shot, her body would become perfectly rigid, the spells lasting from one to two minutes.

"This went on for two years, or until she was four years old. At this time she was taken to Dr. Linthicum in Evansville, Indiana, and Dr. Walker, also of Evansville, They said a very peculiar type of nervousness was all that ailed her and proceeded to treat her accordingly, but after several months' treatment, with no results, the treatment was stopped.

"In a few months, Dr. Oldham, of Hopkinsville, Kentucky, was consulted and he treated her three months, without results. Later he took her for four months more treatment, making seven months in all, but without results. She was now six years old and getting worse, having as many as twenty convulsions in one day. Her mind was a blank, all reasoning power entirely gone.

"March 1st, 1902, she was taken to Dr. Hoppe, of Cincinnati, Ohio, who made a most thorough examination. He pronounced her a perfect specimen physically, except for the brain affection, concerning which he stated that only nine cases of this peculiar type were reported in medical records, and every one of these had proved fatal. He told us that nothing could be done, except to give her good care, as her case was hopeless and she would die soon in one of those attacks.

"At this period our attention was called to Mr. Edgar Cayce, who was asked to diagnose her case. By auto-suggestion he went into a sleep and diagnosed her case as one of congestion at the base of the brain, stating also minor details. He outlined to Dr. A. C. Layne, now of Griffin, Ga., how to proceed to cure her. Dr. Layne treated her accordingly, every day for three weeks, using Mr. Cayce occasionally to follow up the treatment, as results developed. Her mind began to clear up about the eighth day and within three months she was in perfect health, and is so to this day. This case can be certified by many of the best citizens of Hopkinsville, Kentucky, and further deponent saith not.

"Subscribed and sworn before me this 8th day of October, A.D. 1910.

(Signed) C. H. Dietrich
"Gerrit J. Raidt, Notary Public
Hamilton County, Ohio."

Following the Dietrich case a growing demand came from all classes and kinds of people for readings on every possible subject. Edgar was still skeptical of his ability and entered only half-heartedly into giving readings under any kind of circumstance. Some of his experiences during this period were most trying. It was a wonder to him that his attitude did not destroy the effectiveness of the readings.

In 1910 and 1911 a series of unusual cases were brought to the attention of newspapers. A great deal was written in the papers throughout the country, some very glowing accounts, some very scathing. Edgar was called everything from a prevaricator and a charlatan to a second Messiah.

The time came when the true nature of the readings was brought home to him. He had given hundreds and hundreds of readings for other people through the years, but none for his own family. His wife became very ill. After several months under the care of three or four physicians, the physician in charge of the case called Edgar to his office one morning and said, "Cayce, I am sorry to tell you, but your wife cannot possibly live another week. Everything possible that I know has been done. One lung is choked. No air has been going through it for months. The other is now affected and you must know from the hemorrhages it is bleeding. With the high temperature, with the little resistance, she can not hold out. I will come whenever she wants me, but if there is anything in this monkey business you are doing you have better try it."

Edgar was crushed. He was going to take the life of one near and dear to him into his own hands, and the very force and power he had been wishy-washy in using would now be put to a crucial test.

When the reading was over, the physician who had been called in for the case, said, "Cayce, that was the most beautiful lecture I ever heard on tuberculosis, and I have lectured both here and abroad on the subject. You say there is hope, but with my examination and experience, I can not see how there can be."

Suggestions were made in the reading for her improvement. One of the physicians followed the suggestions very closely. Many, many years had passed since the reading, and Edgar Cayce's wife was in better health than she had ever been in her life.

It was during Edgar's wife's illness that a very famous psychologist from Harvard University visited to investigate his work. In a very gruff manner the Harvard psychologist told Edgar that he had come to expose him. He said, "I have exposed more fake mediums than any man in this country, and there has been too much written recently about you in the papers. Where is your cabinet? What is hour modus operandi?"

Edgar Cayce didn't know what the man was talking about. Edgar explained that no special preparations were necessary, that he had just as soon lie on the street or the roadside as in an office. Edgar said, "Doctor, the preparations evidently must be in the minds and hearts of those who seek information. Here is my wife. Just a few days ago she was given up by doctors in charge of her case. Information was given through a reading. Today there is hope. Here is the reading. Here is the patient. Examine her. Read this. Go and ask Professor Dietrich, or Mrs. Dabney, about their experiences. Then explain the work to me. Tell me if I am fooling myself, for I claim nothing."

The following day this psychologist came and listened to information which was given for some man who sought aid. For several days he talked with those who came for readings, listened to the information as it was given and talked with people about Edgar and the work. Finally the professor said, "Cayce, this is no fake. You are mixed up with the wrong type of people. Keep your feet on the ground. Always be sincere. Do not attempt to force anything. If you never do another case than that of the little Dietrich girl, your life will not have been in vain."

Since that time practically every member of Edgar's own and his wife's family had had readings. Edgar knew the information through the readings was not a cure-all. His mother, the most wonderful mother a man could have, passed on. During the last few hours of her illness, she called Edgar to her bed. "Son, your mother is going now. You have kept her alive for years through your work. Now she must go, but you must so live your own life that you may bring to others that comfort, that ease, which has so often come to your mother through those readings in which God speaks to those who will listen."

Even after those experiences Edgar could not make up his mind to give his whole time to the readings. He moved to another state and set about to build up a business as a photographer. But the stories of the readings followed him to Alabama and finally to Selma, a small town near Montgomery, where he settled with his family.

The information which has come through Edgar Cayce's readings has always stimulated him to greater studies of the Scriptures and applications of the truths which they contain. It was in Alabama that he became very active in Sunday School, and Christian Endeavor work. During ten happy years his young men's classes and groups of Junior Christian Endeavor Experts made fine records. As he looked back over the many years of church work there were few periods during which he did not have a Sunday School class; but the years in Selma, Alabama, brought greater opportunities to work with young people.

One of the finest Christian gentlemen Edgar ever knew made this report:.

"State of Alabama
Jefferson Co.

"Before me the undersigned authority, Notary Public in and for said County and State, personally appeared Wm. K. Schanz who is known to me, and who, being first duly sworn, deposeth and saith as follows:

"In the five years that I have known Mr. Edgar Cayce, of Selma, Alabama, it has been to my great personal pleasure and benefit; meeting him through Christian Endeavor, he being Superintendent of the best Junior C.E. Society it has been my pleasure to meet and talk to, I being State Treasurer of the Alabama C.E. Union and Field Worker. I first came to know him as a deep, earnest, sincere Christian man. Naturally we met at different times and talked about Christian Endeavor work, and religion, until we became close friends. Visiting in Selma quite frequently, I came to hear, from others, of the great work Mr. Cayce had done in Selma and other places with his psychic power, and it has been my pleasure to meet quite a few people who have benefited by Readings given by Mr. Cayce, and who have personally told me of the good Mr. Cayce has done for them. I, however, do not wish to speak from hearsay, but from personal knowledge, it having been my pleasure to be present at the following Readings, uttered during these Readings, and which I afterwards transcribed, a copy being given to Mr. Cayce of each Reading, and a copy of which I have here in my office, and which I will forward, if necessary.

"While on a vacation to my mother's home in Reading, Pa., this summer just past, I had the misfortune, while bathing to get water in both my ears, which later resulted in abscesses forming and making me wretched. I consulted and was treated by a doctor in Atlantic City, N.J., and also by a doctor at Reading, Pa.; the abscesses opened and left me with running ears. From this trouble my nose and throat became affected, and through taking treatment from an ear, nose and throat specialist in Bessemer, Alabama, upon my return South, I got gradually worse, until in the middle of October I could hardly hear and had great difficulty in breathing and speaking. I got in touch with Mr. Cayce, and he came to Birmingham and gave me a Reading upon his arrival here. Mr. Cayce knew very little of my trouble in my head, but in the Reading went thoroughly into the trouble, explained where the trouble was, and how it could be cured, telling me to stop treatment with the ear specialists and take up osteopathy and electric violet ray treatment. I have followed his advice as closely as it was possible for me, and am still following the treatment, and today my hearing is entirely restored, my ears have stopped running since that beginning of December, and I have again started singing; with the exception of a little trouble with my nose (which I know will disappear in time), I am perfectly well.

"During Mr. Cayce's stay in Birmingham I was present and reported verbatim Readings on the following persons: Oct. 15, Mrs. Fannie Kahn; Oct 19, Louis Halbert Tinder; Oct 20, Mrs. Lorena Tinder; Nov. 2, a second Reading on myself, the first having been given on Oct. 15; Nov, 3. Phillip Pendleton, and Nov. 5, Mrs. Willie Vandefrig. All of these Readings were on diagnosis and given in the Hotel Tutwiler. Birmingham, Alabama; however, Mrs. Fanie Kahn was in Lexington, Kentucky, when the Reading was given for her; Louis Halbert Tinder was sitting in an automobile in front of the Tutwilder Hotel while his Reading was given; and Mrs. Lorena Tinder was visiting at Irvine, Kentucky, at the time the reading on her was given. The others were present in the room. At most of these Readings the room where the Reading was given was full of spectators, and at nearly every one there were from one to three doctors present and asking questions. I know personally that all of the above mentioned people have been greatly and wonderfully helped by following the diagnosis and treatment given in the Readings by Mr. Cayce, and all are loud in their praise of Mr. Cayce and the help he has given them. I know also that the doctors and professional and business men present at the Readings were amazed at Mrs. Cayce's revelations, but one and all have confessed that there was no doubt but that Mr. Cayce had a power that few, if any, possess; and that his practice of using his power for the benefit of humanity was noble and princely.

"For myself, I believe in Mr. Cayce and his power, for seeing and experiencing is believing. I know not whence comes his power, but I do know that he is using it for good, hence it must come from good, the All Good, which is God. May he never lose his power.

(Signed) Wm. K. Schanz.

"Subscribed and sworn to before me this 22nd day of January, 1921.

(Signed) G. P. Benton,

Notary Public

Far from discouraging his work in giving readings Edgar's studies of the Bible had given him greater understanding of the true meaning and significance of his experiences, and he believed that the information contained in hundreds of readings helped to clarify and explain his Bible for him. Edgar considered the Bible the greatest of all records of psychic experiences.

Individuals continually sought Edgar for help, asked that he try to help them through his readings. He began to realize that his greatest field of service to his fellow men lay in trying to be of assistance to those who desired help. It was then that he began to seek others who believed the readings worthy of study. The first attempts were made to form an organization to preserve and examine the daily readings which were given.

Ignorant of the laws governing the vast realm of the "psychic" many mistakes were made. Edgar learned that holding to an ideal does not insure an individual's being protected from the hard knocks of experience, especially when that ideal involves studies in advanced fields of thought.

Upon repeated attempts to establish a hospital the information that came through continued to insist upon Virginia Beach, Virginia, as the best place from which to conduct the work. Finally, where readings could be followed carefully, Edgar Cayce moved in 1925, with his family, to the little coastal town, then only a small, insignificant resort. It is here that they lived and worked since that time.

A hospital was built under their first organization, the Association of National Investigators, Incorporated. During the few years of its operation, some remarkable cases were handled and some unusual records secured.

This is the story of a man who was brought to the hospital after he had followed readings given for him while in a very serious condition. The following report is his own story:

"Since returning to my duties as Superintendent of the Carolina Wood Products Company at Ashville, N.D., I felt it my duty to write and thank you for the courteous treatment that I have received at your institution, to which I owe my life.

"It might be interesting for me to review just what happened to me. We work nearly one thousand men and owing to the stress of my duties, I was in a very run-down condition. I became very ill, which led to unconsciousness for several days. My associates obtained the best doctors possible in the South under the direction of Dr. Bernard Smith, of Asheville, who is reputed to be one of our leading men.

"Some of the doctors felt I had a strange fever. A very prominent Atlanta doctor took an X-ray which showed a clear case of advanced tuberculosis. My family wired you for a reading. The diagnosis came back that I had bacilli in the blood stream. Upon further examination it proved to be streptococci. The doctors had given me a transfusion of one quart of blood which the reading said would save my life provided certain other medicines were taken and certain treatment followed out.

"The doctors had given me up to die, but one week later when Dr. Paullin from Atlanta arrived again for the second examination, upon examining the plates of the X-ray he agreed with Dr. Murphy, the X-ray physician, that it was a mild case of bronchitis, if the plates were to be believed. Three weeks later I was taken on a cot to your hospital where daily readings were given and their suggestions followed. Soon I was strong enough to sit on the sand at Virginia Beach.

"Later I was permitted to go in the water and five weeks from the day I arrived at the beach I was permitted to return to New York to report to the president of our firm for duty.

"I have never felt better in my life than I have felt in the past eight months and I agree with Dr. Smith who in a letter to me stated that I was out of the hands of the doctor and in the hands of God, and you no doubt have been the means for the information to come from God Himself to save my life and to you again I say I own my thanks. I certainly enjoyed the personal attention received from you, your doctors and nurses at the institution and if at any time I can be of service to you or yours, you have but to command.

"I am, with kindest personal regards,

"Very sincerely,

(Signed) L. Francis."

Complete records of this case along with hundreds of others are in the files of the Association for Research and Enlightenment, Inc., which is making a study of Edgar Cayce's earnest desire to be of help whenever and wherever possible. An investigative reporter could go on and on with records of case after case; for, indeed, the work of Edgar Cayce's life is written plainer in others' experiences, in others' results from following the information given in readings. Individuals who desire to study it further must seek it there.

Many questions arose in people's minds, such as, "If this is true why haven't I heard of it long ago?"

For several years a great many papers carried articles concerning the phenomena of Edgar Cayce, especially at a time they were reported to the research society, and in New York where he was accused of "attempting to tell fortunes".

It was Edgar Cayce's conviction that man's pageant must pass and fade, but God works in slower and more secret ways; His wondrous works to perform. He blows no trumpet. He rings no bell. He begins from within, seeking His ends by quiet growth. There is a strange power that men call weakness, a wisdom mistaken for folly. Man has one answer to every problem—power, but that is not God's way.

Cayce has had successes and Cayce has had failures. Cayce admitted that he would be afraid there was something supernatural about him if he did not have failures. "Humanity is doomed to failure," said Cayce, "when it trusts in its own weak self, and most of us have that failing."

Besides giving two readings every day and talking with hundreds of people who came asking for readings and inquiring about the hospital, he attempted to handle for a time much of the business details of the institution. Yet as he looked back over the turmoil and tribulations, the disappointments and periods of despair, the good which was accomplished stood out above everything else.

In February, 1931, with the increasing economic pressure, the Association of National Investigators, Incorporated, through some of its directors, felt it necessary to close the hospital and discontinue the program of the organization. Edgar tried to take stock of him-self and the work. Even then he wondered, "Am I all wrong?"

A few weeks later individuals from every walk of life who had had experience with readings gathered in his home. They came from all parts of the country and crowded into every available space extending onto the porch and lawn. There were literally hundreds of letters and telegrams from those who could not be present. Edgar Cayce spoke:

"Friends, I have nothing to sell. I am not attempting to spread propaganda. Each one here has had personal experience with the information, or phenomena, as manifested through me; some of you know of my own shortcomings, as well as shortcomings of others. It isn't a question as to whether I want to go on, but the question is, do you as a group, as individuals, want to see a study of phenomena, or the information, continue? Is it worth while? My position is this: Some years ago, when through the information my wife's life was spared, a little later my boy's eyes received their sight and the younger boy was healed also, I could only say, 'God, I don't understand, but for the good that has come to me, may I be able to help others when they ask'. You all know from your own experiences whether this is worth while. Do not consider my experience, but your experiences."

Each and every one gave testimony of their personal experience, indicating a desire to see the work go on. From this meeting the Association for Research and Enlightenment, Incorporated, was organized, a philanthropic organization, chartered under the laws of the State of Virginia, to carry on psychical research. There are no barriers to prevent any individual from taking part in the work of this association.

More complete records are kept today than ever before. A number of case studies are available in pamphlet form for those desiring to know something of the results obtained in following readings given.

The life of a person endowed with such powers is not easy. For more than forty years Cayce gave readings for those who came seeking help. Seventy-five years ago the jeers, scorn and laughter were even louder than today. He had faced the laughter of ignorant crowds, the withering scorn of tabloid headlines, and the cold smirk of self-satisfied intellectuals. But he had also known the wordless happiness of little children who have been helped, the gratitude of fathers and mothers and friends. There were few letters that had not brought Edgar expressions of appreciation for new life, new hope, and new ability stimulated through the readings which have been applied in some individual's life. Trouble and worry and criticism meant very little at such times.

Edgar believed the attitude of the scientific world is gradually changing toward these subjects. Men high in their respective fields are devoting time and effort to studying the laws that govern all kinds of psychic phenomena. Universities in this and other countries are carrying on advanced experiments. Psychical research must have open-minded, intelligent cooperation from scientists in many fields in order to be ultimately of lasting value in human experience. Their Association hoped to have some part in bringing about such cooperation.

The Association for Research and Enlightenment, Incorporated, is attempting to make a careful study of the phenomena of the readings and at the same time pass on to others that which has proved helpful in each member's experiences. It was the desire of Edgar Cayce to give him-self to the studies and experiments of the readings, knowing that many had been helped, and he hoped to be a "channel of blessing" to each individual who came with some physical, mental or spiritual burden. This was his life.

✝ ✝ ✝

For a man with such a unique ability Edgar Cayce sure had his ups and downs. His own Life Reading informed him that several life-times ago he had developed his clairvoyant ability after he had been wounded and left to die on the battlefield. He lived for several days in extreme agony; unable to move or help himself; he had only his mind as a weapon against pain. Just before he died he overcame his pain through the power of his mind. This achievement set the stage for future clairvoyance - as no self-development is ever lost. But, like all of us, we are tempted, and many times we give in to temptation - as did the soul of Edgar Cayce.

In Cayce's following incarnation he was a gambler and card shark with psychic ability. Although it was never stated in what country or century he lived as a gambler, in my mind's eye I visualized Cayce as a loner, a sort of Maverick, making his way in gambling saloons across the American West, from Colorado to San Francisco, using his psychic ability to read his opponents cards and came out the winner each time. In that lifetime he used his psychic ability for material gain. In this lifetime he was given the opportunity to overcome the greed expressed in his past life as a gambler and was again given psychic ability to see which direction he would go. Cayce learned from the past and chose the Way of the Cross. He sacrificed his life for the good of others and chose not to make money using his gift. In this lifetime he was as saintly a man as one could hope to be.

While studying some material on Edgar Cayce I was struck by the many individuals who had lived during Biblical times, as had the soul of Edgar Cayce. I really couldn't keep up with all of those Biblical names: Uhilda, and Uhjltd, or Ujdelda, sister of Uhjltd. The Cayce-soul had incarnations with the Jesus-soul in Atlantis, which then followed incarnations in ancient Egypt after the destruction of Atlantis. The soul of Cayce had an incarnation as the Egyptian High Priest Ra-Ta; the soul of Jesus had an incarnation as the legendary philosopher Hermes.

The knowledge one can receive from studying the Edgar Cayce material, on file at the Association for Research and Enlightenment, equals and in some areas surpasses knowledge received from a university. Cayce learned from his Life Readings that his soul came from the star Uranus. To use every day language, the planets are where we go after we die. We do not live in a physical body-form on the other planets; we live in a body-form appropriate to that planetary vibration. Each planet has a separate and unique vibration. The Earth is the third planet from the sun, so the Earth is the third dimension. Every planet vibrates at a dimension appropriate to its purpose. The inner planetary sojourns may be referred to as dimensions, or planes, or realms. We do not live on the planets physically. My deceased brother had been told in his Life Reading that he came from the Realm of Creativity. Every realm has a distinct purpose. Souls then incarnate into planet Earth and provide planet Earth with its various cultures developed from sojourns on other planets, with their likes and dislikes: musicians and dancers, doctors and lawyers, scientists and astrologers, its carpenters and bricklayers. And because our post-physical body studies, or goes to school on the other planets in our solar system, the planets have astrological influences in our lives - but no force is greater than our free will.

When we, as souls, complete our development in our solar system, we go to Arcturus, the star directly opposite the exit chamber of the Great Pyramid in Egypt. At least this is the way I understand the situation from my study of the Edgar Cayce readings.

Edgar Cayce had been dead over ten years when I first learned of him. Approximately a year later I received a Life Reading from a newly developed source in Los Angeles, named The Religious Research Foundation, founded and directed by Dr. Franklin Loehr, a Presbyterian Minister who had done scientific research into the power of prayer on plants; the results of this prayer-plant research were published by Doubleday in a best selling book, The Power of Prayer on Plants.

When I entered a general store in Escondido, California, I noticed a paper-back book on the rotating book rack titled *Edgar Cayce, Mystery Man of Miracles*. The story brought me to tears and I tried to hide my emotions behind the pages of the book. Every time I entered the store I picked up the book and re-read some of its inspiring passages. I was always brought to tears. I couldn't get enough of Edgar Cayce.

I often wondered what kind of Life Reading Edgar Cayce would have given me. After all these sixty years of studying Cayce material, and Dr. John material, I know now, as good as Edgar Cayce's Life

Readings were, I received the best Life Reading for myself. My Reading was straight forward and to the point. It spoke in my language. Grace Wittenberger was the medium. The voice speaking was called John, but the sound of the voice was feminine. I didn't understand how the operation worked. I only knew that it worked for me. When I finished reading the last page of my Life Reading, I knew the Reading's message was correct; it was for me and me alone. It provided the understanding and guidance to carry me through my remaining years. The story of my life and Life Readings are told in my first book, *Life Stories Life Readings*.

D r. Loehr used the scientific method to verify the authenticity of Religious Research's Life Readings, evidenced by his work on the power of prayer on plants. Edgar Cayce used the scientific method to verify the accuracy of his Life Readings through his amazing medical diagnoses. Jesus Christ used the scientific method to prove his spiritual message was correct by walking the countryside among the poor and unlearned, healing the sick, casting out devils, purifying lepers, allowing the blind to see, the lame to walk, and he even raised the dead. How much more scientific evidence would anyone need to prove that "this" human-being was the "ultimate" human-being with the true message?

In each of the separate schools of teaching, a version of the scientific method has been used as proof of their authenticity.

Venerable Anne Catherine Emmerich read the records of the Immortal Truth regarding the Passion of Jesus, the Christ, and was given the stigmata as evidence of Divine approval.

Edgar Cayce read the records of the Immortal Truth and revealed much of Jesus' life, which are on file at the Association for Research and Enlightenment in Virginia Beach, Va.

John Christopher Daniels, spirit guide and counselor for the Life Readings of the Religious Research Foundation, also read the records of the Immortal Truth and has left some inspiring, if not unusual, understandings regarding Jesus Christ. The following comments were given by Dr. John in reply to questions from Dr. Loehr. Dr. John was not reading the Akashic Records at this time.

Dr. John:

A. And in the Jesus life the Christ soul accomplished something which no other soul has ever accomplished. He accomplished the complete eradication of evil from the personality life. The soul denied a toehold for evil in his personality life. There is no other soul that has yet accomplished this to perfection. And it is for that reason that the Christ soul is honored and respected by all other souls who have been spiritual teachers in the earth framework at various times.

Of course the accomplishment by the Christ soul, in the Jesus incarnation, of demonstrating the power of life attuned to God over the death experience, which is evil's greatest weapon, is an accomplishment for which, in a manner of speaking, puts him at the head of the list. And he should be revered and honored, respected and loved in that framework - and he is by all other souls who have been the founders of other world religions.

There has been a place and a contribution for each world religion in its time. The emphasis of each one has been important. And because of that, each soul who was the vehicle by which an earth religion was established is to be honored and respected and learned from. Now the accomplishment of the Christ soul, in the Jesus incarnation, in breaking the hold of evil makes it possible for that soul in the continuing personality expression of Jesus to pass through all realms of evil in other planes. 3450:15

In the time of Atlantis, civilization was brought to a high point of mental development and power. It lacked love – that was the missing element – that is what destroyed it. The Jesus Christ incarnation supplied in living example that missing element for earth-beings to use, to develop, to cultivate, as once again civilization grew to the point of high attainment it had in Atlantis.

The Jesus One is the Christ Soul, the Special One. We feel that he is the individuated God-being who has gone the farthest of any of those associated with planet Earth in its functioning, its mission. He is the Highest One to whom we report and whether he reports to a higher council or directly to the Father, I do not know and I do not ask. I believe this ascribes to him sufficient uniqueness and divinity, and although it may not please some, I think it pleases him and correctly describes him to human understanding at the present time.

He is the one to show us what God is, what we are, what the soul is, what is really happening upon Earth – this great drama of redemption of evil.

The Christ shows us both God's love and God's decisions, what is God's way, how God's spiritual universe is structured. We gladly acknowledge him to be Master because we are glad to have one of his spiritual caliber to lead us." 8012:4

The Jesus Team took over the project of redemption in this eon to clear the spiritual universe. To clear away the un-Godlike elements produced by non-understanding and non-following of the ways and will of God - even more, to clear away the willful flaunting of the ways and will of God. 7486:8

A special kind of individuated God-being-ness known as the soul was evolved by God. The prototype soul is the one we know as Jesus, the Christ. The soul is a spiritual being with a particular nature and purpose.

The human being has the spiritual intelligence to know the difference between good and evil, and then choose that which it will serve. In this way the human can transmute spiritual energies out of physical energy, deciding whether to feed evil with those energies (as in anger, lust, envy, selfishness, etc.) or to feed good with them, as when endeavoring to be truly a child of God in the world.

This individuated God-being known as the soul is very definitely close to the loving heart of God, because this is the child of God to redeem the spirit beings who have strayed from God or even turned against Him. 7389:4-5

Jesus is not God in the sense of being "The God." Jesus is God in the sense of being a God-child, an individuated God-being, who has developed his God-being-ness, his God nature and his God powers, and who has so won the confidence of God that he is a spokesman for God, a trusted, beloved elder son of God. 8043:7

He was the son begotten by God the Father, and every soul in Earth-living is begotten by God, the Father, and therefore is a Son of God. 990:18

Q. What is meant by the "Only Begotten Son?"

A. Only in the sense of "first," the first perfected man. He was born of a virgin and was the first soul in Earth-living to bring into one specific

Earth-life the soul wisdom and growth from all previous lives to bear upon the personality expression such as to achieve perfection. 1192:15

Q. What is the relationship of Jesus to God?

A. The relationship of Jesus to God is no different than the relationship of man to God except that Jesus has achieved what man in general has not but can achieve in that relationship.

Q. Is he then the Firstborn, the first one to come to that Son-ship, the first among many?

A. Right. 2034:11-2

Q. What is meant by the words "believe that Jesus is The Christ?"

A. Believe that Jesus is The Christed Man, the man perfected in that sense. Christ is a degree conferred upon a soul perfected. 1192:15

Q. Does God mean that we should worship Jesus?

A. No. Jesus, himself, taught that men should worship God, not him. The teaching of the worship of Jesus is not God's teaching. It is the teaching of the Church as it has come down through the ages.

Naturally, in the New Testament, and in the Bible as a whole, although it's a rather thin line, the teaching is respect, affection and the veneration of Jesus. To follow him as guide and Master, not only the Shower of The Way, but the actual Incarnation of The Way; and yet not worshiping him but finding God through him, and finding God through Jesus with such glory and fullness that some of this glory and fullness spills over into the vessel, Jesus, as well. 1688:12

So we are told some of the previous lives of Jesus on Earth were:

Melchizedek, in the Old Testament:

Jeshua, a scribe, not one of the great leaders but a scribe during the time of Ezra and Nehemiah:

A Sumerian Priest, who was chosen for the blood sacrifice rite, which was an annual rite then. Some recovered, but he did not. He really did give his life, and his blood was shed at that time too for the redemption, as the nation conceived it, of his people:

Jonathan, during the time of King David 1000 B.C.:

Joshua, who took over for Moses and led the children of Israel into the Promised Land:

The Buddha - that is really the same soul that came to the Eastern people in their framework of experience as The Buddha and 500 years later he came to the Jews in the framework which combined the Orient with the forthcoming Occident – came there as The Christ – his climatic life. We have been told that this is the final incarnation of Jesus.

However, the soul-mate, the feminine half of that soul, has had previous incarnations of course and has had subsequent incarnations; that the soul-mate was John the Beloved Disciple, for instance. Also, the soul-mate of Jesus had the incarnation as Joan of Arc and this was a martyrdom life of course for that soul.

We are told that the soul-mate is to come in a new incarnation somewhere from 300 to 800 years from now, in masculine incarnation; and that this will be its climactic life, its life of great world-wide spiritual significance. 1192:16

Q. Was Jesus, Buddha, and Mohammed all of the same spirit, or soul?

A. Jesus and Buddha were; not Mohammed. 3957:16

Q. Was Jesus aware he had been Buddha?

A. As the Christ soul, yes, we would say he was aware. As he came into that estate of Christhood, as it is related in the Bible, all knowledge was given unto Him. 3957:16

Q. How can one put Jesus first and push Buddha out?

A. You don't need to push Buddha out in the sense of him being a negative force or influence; you use him as a stepping stone; you can go through Buddha to Jesus. Buddha can show you the Christ Light, but as for making contact and making a vital and real contact, all you have to do is sincerely want it and ask for it. And then deliberately build up a relationship with Jesus the Christ as a personal friend. Read the book *The Transforming Friendship,* by Leslie Weatherhead; and don't rebel against it; give the book a chance to talk to you. 148:11

Q. What was the purpose behind that soul having those two particular incarnations?

A. That soul's destiny, as it came from the Being-ness of God, was to show that in the framework of Earth experience a soul in human-being-ness could so hold to spiritual being-ness that it could manifest a physical life in which evil had found no foothold. This is the destiny of all souls in the Earth experience. 3957:17

Q. Was Jesus aware of Buddhism? Did it influence him?

A. Yes, it is our understanding that the Jesus-soul had a previous incarnation as the Buddha and brought many teachings. It is my understanding that in the Jesus lifetime in Palestine, he had the good friend Lazarus, who was an older man with an education and some means. 7506:15

Lazarus traveled and studied in the East and knew the universal wisdom the masses did not know, even as the Magi who came from Persia at the time of Jesus' birth knew. Lazarus helped to prepare the way for Jesus' own travels and studies as he came into his young manhood. His personality and mind had to be prepared, and was. 8132:14

He traveled to India and he took the younger man, Jesus, with him. This was so Jesus could see in person what had happened to his teachings there; and this is one reason that he did not bring the teaching of reincarnation too openly into his teachings in Palestine. He saw how it had been misunderstood and misused and how one had to temper one's message to the persons receiving it if he was really to communicate his teachings. So often he said to them, "I have more for you but you are not ready to receive it."

This is one of our hopes, we who work to prepare the way for His next coming, that when he comes there will be more people much better prepared to receive it in the world. Then the Kingdom of God may be advanced by his second coming even more than it was by his first coming. 7506:15

In his first coming as Jesus he did not fulfill the role of Messiah as that role is generally portrayed in the Old Testament in the Jewish tradition; however, some of the prophets of Israel had seen that the Messiah, the Anointed One, would come as the 'suffering servant.' In the prophecy of Isaiah this is beautifully foretold.

Others have seen that he would come as the 'King of Kings and Lord of Lords,' and that the governments of the world should be upon his shoulders. That portion, of course, was not fulfilled by Jesus of Nazareth nearly two thousand years ago. But the soul in the Jesus lifetime passed certain final tests, and earned the right then to fully come as God's agent, in the active intervention in the affairs of men, to establish with power certain principles. 8004:2

Q. How is the Virgin Mary cosmically related to Jesus?

A. A cosmic family member. The Virgin has been used in many religions as one of the potent symbols and aspects of mysticism. This is true in certain mystical aspects of the Christian religion centering around the Virgin Mary.

Q. Is she manifesting as the feminine aspect of God, and has she done so throughout history, such as the Goddess Isis in Egypt or the Divine Mother Kali in India, and so forth?

A. Only as all women, and especially advanced spiritual women so manifest the mother aspect of deity. The Mary who was mother of Jesus was a soul, even as He is a soul. She had past lives; she's had future lives since the Mary life. I have placed her as having a very recent incarnation as the great spiritual leader whom you knew as Mahatma Mohandas Gandhi. 7095:24

The Mother Mary is remembered and honored as a channel used by God to bring forth His son into personality expression. This is universally recognized by Earth-lings. That soul having the expression of the Mary personality could be used as God's channel because of what the soul had become in its own being-ness. Mary was more than a reflection of God in action; she was God in action in her motivation, in the manner in which she lived, in her personality qualities. She became, and thus was used, but she had no particular uniqueness that caused God to select her as His channel, which others do not have the opportunity of having. She was elected because of her being-ness, what that soul achieved through many lifetimes of practice, of personality being-ness, every other soul in personality living has the opportunity of achieving. All have the ability to become, as a person, in their thinking and feeling and their expression of thought and feeling, the opportunity to become - to be.

You might think of it just as Jesus himself, or Saint Francis, or Saint Theresa become archetypal patterns for people, according to the particular background of Earth experiences; the particular make-up of soul forces feeding into the personality. A given personality will be challenged or inspired by someone who represents the archetypal pattern of being-ness for that personality to work toward. 3611:6

Q. The Catholic Church maintains Mary was without sin. Was the magnitude of her role on Earth accurately recorded in the Bible?

A. This is a question that depends upon what one means by various words. She was the chosen mother for the physical instrument of the Person Jesus, that incarnation of the Christ soul. She did not understand her son completely. She once came with some of her other children to take him back home, fearing that he really had 'gone off the deep end' in his teaching and his traveling around.

She was fine. In the Catholic Church and some other churches she has been made into a symbol of the ideal feminine mystique, and that has been good. So that the feminine part was kept within that religion better than it was kept certainly in the Scottish Church, and that was a good service. But almost no human concept of something as great as God is complete, nor wholly accurate. 7177:26

Q. Was the appearance of Mary, the mother of Jesus, at Fatima and at Lourdes, authentic?

A. Yes. 990:18

Q. What was Jesus' everyday life like among people?

A. The Jesus-one, in his own life, was not such an esoteric, mystical experience as many people have attributed to him now. He was a man. He lived. He was born in Bethlehem. He was brought up in Nazareth.

With his good, somewhat older and fairly affluent friend, Lazarus, he visited India where he could observe the Buddhist religion which the Jesus-soul in the incarnation of Buddha had founded. From this practical observation the Jesus-person, as well as the Jesus-soul, gained certain insights guiding him in his public ministry, and learned from the Buddha time.

Jesus was a person, a human being. This was very essential to the whole pattern and plan. He did not go around with a bright halo around his head. He did not go dripping either sanctity or mysticism. Many passed him by, heard him, and even touched him, with no sense at all of the majestic divinity ascribed to him by later theologians and by the love of later generations of his followers. This visitor had a commanding presence. He didn't draw himself up and look commanding at all. He just was. The integrity of him, the essential being-ness of him, was there, and people noticed it; also a reputation grew up around him.

Those who saw him in their own lives never forgot this strong man with the eyes that saw them, not just see through them, but could see them. He saw everyone in his audience, and those that were perceptive knew that he saw them. So they never forgot him. He made deep impressions on their lives. 7026:13

So to be in a city and to come into contact with some of those who had heard Jesus and were spreading the word of him, and to talk with some of the disciples, the Apostles, was almost as impressive as to have heard and seen Jesus in person in Palestine.

This should be recognized as part of the real humanity of Jesus. The divinity of Jesus was expressed in his humanity and humanity includes divinity and each soul must make it so because the soul is divine and brings the divine element into the human element.

Now one might also say that all life is divine and even that all matter is divine because all those come from God. Yes; but the soul has a particular kinship with God. An individuated portion of God is closer to God in its being-ness than is a creation by God, and thus is the soul.

So divinity in humanity is what the soul brings. Not just Jesus, although Jesus as the proto-type soul might be said to be the initiator of this process. 7293:8-9

Some had particularly prepared and incarnated for it – especially the Master's own soul-mate, John the Beloved Disciple. 7279:8

Q. What specific kinds of teachings did Jesus learn in the East, and are these teachings and abilities engendered by them available in one form or another now?

A. It was not, in a sense, learnings, as it was the re-establishment of contacts with teachings in existence in the Earth plane since the times of Atlantis. Jesus' travels gave the opportunity for the synthesis of knowledge in that specific personality, as well as he being the synthesizer for the many areas where he visited. He came to them specifically to establish mystery schools as the synthesizer for them with the schools established in other parts of the world. 3981:22

What was called "Temples of Wisdom," in Egypt was visited by Jesus in the preparatory years before his Earth mission became evident. 3959:13

Q. How did the resurrection of Lazarus fit in the picture?

A. It was a special phenomenon. It was not a natural part of human life. Actually, as we understand it, Jesus, as he approached his climatic test, which would be to resurrect him-self or to be resurrected, was given this practice. His good friend and follower, Lazarus, died, and four days later, when there was no doubt about Lazarus being dead, Jesus brought resurrection, restored the spirit of Lazarus (which stayed close) to a living, vital contact with the body of Lazarus, and thus restored the vital life processes within the body.

When Jesus did this, he was convinced that he could go through death and then resurrect himself. It was a fine service of Lazarus. If Jesus had failed, Lazarus would have stayed dead; but Jesus did not fail. If Jesus had failed, the whole picture of the cross and the resurrection would not have taken place, at least not then. 7317:28

These methods and powers were known to Jesus and to Lazarus, and were tried out in the deliberate experiment of Lazarus dying, being completely dead, being buried, and then brought back to physical life. This was the service of a good friend to Jesus. This was a part of the grace of God.

The personality of Jesus of Nazareth, knowing these things were to be, still was very human, even as you and I, and knew the force of wondering and doubt. So this good friend (Lazarus) died; and had Jesus not been able to raise him from the dead, Lazarus would have stayed dead, and Jesus would not have been ready for his own death and resurrection.

The raising of Lazarus was a close-linked prelude to Jesus' own resurrection; and it shows how a great team was working with Jesus, to bring him through a complete incarnation experience without giving in to temptation in any way, so that evil has no hold in him, was no part of him.

The victory of Jesus' sinless life, tempted as are all human beings, but victorious over all evil, was a team victory, as well as his own tremendous victory. While on the cross, Jesus found other evidence of the love that sustained him, even as love sustains you and me. Remember how the thief on the cross beside Jesus who said, 'This man is sinless – Remember thou me when thou cometh into thy kingdom.'

And Jesus replied, 'This day shalt thou be with me in Paradise.'

This one beside Jesus at that final testing time was a cosmic family member who had incarnated and lived a life which would cause him to be arrested, convicted, and crucified.

In the final trial where Jesus faced and conquered the shame, the seeming failure, the intense physical pain of crucifixion, without allowing evil to get the least little hold upon him, there was this cosmic family member supportive at his side. Jesus, looking, recognized him and knew what had happened. Although Jesus well may not have needed any extra help, the fact that one other would love him and God so much as to do even this, one who knew the cosmic significance of Jesus' victory so as to be there on a cross at his side, was all the extra help Jesus might have needed to assure the complete victory of a person, a human being, over all the forces of evil. And in attaining that victory, to show us that it can be done, and show evil that it has been mastered. 8132:13

Q. What was the purpose of Jesus raising Lazarus from the dead?

A. Lazarus and his sisters Mary and Martha, and the married sister Ruth, who dwelt in Joppa, were among the closest of Jesus' friends. Lazarus' home in Bethany was a short two-hour walk from Jerusalem, and Jesus stayed in that home on many or most of his trips in that area.

Lazarus was a little older than Jesus. Lazarus, who had independent means, who had traveled and studied in the East, knew the universal wisdom the masses did not know, even as the Magi, which came from Persia at the time of the Christ's birth, knew. Lazarus had helped to prepare the way for Jesus' own travels and studies in the East as he came into his young manhood; those hidden years from 12 to 30 were not spent in a carpenter's shop entirely. The Jesus of Nazareth personality and mind had to be prepared, and was. Then, knowing that the last enemy to be overcome is death, and that the total victory was to be demonstrated by the Master in this consummate incarnation of the consummate soul, the ways in which the physical body could be repaired of its physical damages incidental to death, as a living spirit associated with that body were studied. 8132:13

Q. Can you shed some light on the crucifixion and resurrection of Jesus Christ?

A. In Jesus you had a highly evolved soul who came very definitely with the mission of letting other souls in personality expression, know and discover, while still in Earth-living, that they could be at one with the Source of Life.

He was attacked by the forces of evil. The crucifixion, and the resurrection, is historically correct. It is historically documented. It was not his life, it was not his teaching, it was not the crucifixion that established the Christian Movement. That which established the Christian Movement in the Earth realm is the fact of the resurrection. It was the discovery by the disciples that he who was dead had risen from the dead; that set them on fire to tell of his life and teachings to all the nations.

There is deep significance in what is called 'The Atonement,' in being a burden bearer for another; in one soul bearing the karma of other souls. "The Aquarian Gospel" will help in the understanding of this. 2944:13

Q. Do we have to incarnate until we can tolerate even being crucified, as Jesus did?

A. The experience of crucifixion is a different experience for every soul. It represents the complete obliteration of self-will in favor of cosmic-will. That experience needs to be attained by every progressing soul.

Now "the complete experience" – there are bits and pieces of that experience gained by the soul within the framework of various Earth-lives in its development; but there comes a time when there has to be the completed process of obliteration of self-will.

Q. Well this would be as St. Paul would say, I die so that it is no longer I that lives, but Christ lives in me - even though Paul continued to operate very effectively as a very distinct individual.

A. Yes. 1242:24

By following the most advanced God-child in our midst in human history, the person, Jesus of Nazareth, rightly called The Christ; there is a pathway and a hand to help at all stages of the journey. But the journey must be made by each one. 7281:15

One of the great spiritual laws is that no one does the growing for anybody else. Yes, there is a forgiveness, there is a vicarious suffering aspect, and this is well exemplified by Jesus and his death upon the cross to 'save us from our sins' and such; however, we also must save our own selves from our sins. We must also discover and correct our own doings in whatever plane of being and growth in which we may happen to be. 7011:7

No one can do our growing for us because we are each one an individual child of God, possessed of God potential. Each one must develop his own God potential, which in every case is a little different than any other person's nature. 7011:8

Q. Could not the death of Jesus be a normal one instead of the crucifixion?

A. Oh, but so much would have been lost! The crucifixion of Jesus was one of the marvelous ways of fixing the attention of mankind upon the Jesus one, and until now the Jesus one is probably the best known personage of all history - which is in purposeful preparation for his coming again. The same Jesus, coming from the spirit realms into physical manifestation, this time to use the Great Powers in the climatic battle against evil for the redemption of Earth and the redemption of as much as possible of evil itself. 7385:20-1

Q. It seems a shame, a personality that has much vibrancy, much ability, should be taken out of our realm simply because of mistakes of the far past.

A. Sacrifice of good for a better is something not well understood on the Earth plane, but is something which is a part of Earth-living.

Sacrifice – giving up a good for a better – is a part of Earth-living. The sacrifice of an eagerness for life, an ability to serve for the purpose of clearing and freeing the soul that it might at another time and with greater vision and understanding, serve – is a sacrifice with a purpose. It was too bad that Jesus went to the cross. He had so much to give. He brought healing and comfort. He had a joy of living. It was too bad to have to give it up.

Q. Now I see the point.

A. The sacrifice in itself was a greater service for others, but for that soul also.

Q. It takes a good coin to buy precious jewels.

A. And it takes good to overcome evil. 259:2-3

Now, certain events in history - the crucifixion being one – are events which, as it were, are still alive. In psychic experience you can go back to a time in history and see it happening. Now you go back sometimes as the Earth character you were at the time of the event; or you can also go back psychically and from this psychic plane of reverie you observe the event in a psychic state.

Q. If this is an experience which is still alive in the psychic realm, is the suffering of the crucifixion still going on?

A. In a sense, yes.

Q. You take the experience like the crucifixion and we would rather think the transition would come to an end, historically, in time.

A. People's consciousness enters in here. People's consciousness plays a part in keeping alive the event. In churches, the event of the crucifixion is re-established so often that it is maintained in consciousness.

Q. Well is this a good thing?

A. But now there are many other experiences. For example: you take a mother who perhaps stands by the bedside and watches an only child slip away from her. She may reinstate that experience over and over in memory, first week by week, then it becomes months, then it becomes years; but always the theme is reinstated by the grief and the holding to the incident by the mother.

Now in a case like that it very often does happen that the soul (of that child) which has gone over is held in bondage and is not freed.

Q. Well not only would the mother be holding herself in that sorrowful suffering picture, but she would be holding the child also to it to some extent.

A. Yes. Now here again there are many factors feeding in. The length of time the soul is held is determined not only in this example by the mother's grief, but also by the karma of the soul; and by the openness of the soul and responsiveness to higher spiritual influences. There is more than one deciding factor.

Q. So the one held in a suffering picture, so to speak, or held to a particular event in time not too pleasant, is not held only because of the ignorance and misuse of a creative power and emotions.

A. Not entirely.

Q. Is Therese Neumann, who experiencing the stigmata, in one sense, holding the experience of the Crucifixion alive?

A. Yes. There is something else in that experience. As a soul she is demonstrating on the human level how the body can be kept alive and in good health without being dependent on physical food. Now she is in a body, which is in good health, in between times when she is not under the stigmata. She comes and goes. She travels about. She is healthy, radiant and well; but she does not eat. She lives in The Light. 1588:4-6,

Q. What happened to those two other men crucified with Jesus?

A. Jesus stepped out and away from the experience. Now the thief who asked for forgiveness and was told by Jesus, "This day thou shall be with me in paradise," was instantly released from the experience even as Jesus was. The other thief was held in the crucifixion picture for some time before his release. This was, in part, karmic for that individual soul. 1589:4

Q. I have heard or read somewhere that the two thieves who died on the cross when Jesus was crucified were two friends who incarnated when Jesus was born so that they could die with him. Is this correct?

A. I understand this is true of one of them. That he was actually a cosmic family member of Jesus. Was there to be a loving, strong support in the final climatic test whereby Jesus established his complete mastery over the forces of evil and it was a marvelously wonderful loving strong thing to do. Jesus recognized that one and said, "This day thou shall be with me in paradise." 8068:26

Q. Why did Jesus have to suffer on the cross and die in order to help people, and how is that a good example or role model?

A. Well, this is a good question. One answer might be that he did not have to suffer on the cross and die, but in so doing he met the worst that evil could bring to him and he did not let evil get into him. He maintained his complete allegiance to and alignment with good.

Also, the cross has proved to be a tremendously effective way of reaching the attention of human beings, which is what he wants to do. So from that aspect this was certainly a profitable thing for Jesus to do. 8076:2

Q. Where did Jesus go in spirit after he was crucified?

A. The Christ, after the crucifixion, was taken into realms that are not good, to show them the man who took all that evil could bring, and was not swerved out of the God Path thereby. Therefore he is Master, the Christ, in a victory celebration, was taken by High Beings, by God, in many ways, into these other realms as a Winner, and they saw their Conqueror. 8045:17

Q. Then the crucifixion was the final testing of Jesus?

A. The Jewish tradition said that there would be a Messiah sent to restore the Kingdom to Israel, and to accomplish many other prophetic aspects of that great nation. They rejected Jesus of Nazareth as not meeting that pattern; and they were quite right in so doing; but there is a double aspect to this.

The one that would restore the Kingdom, and in a much larger sense, establish the Kingdom of God upon Earth, was thoroughly tested. He was subject to temptations, and suffered as we do.

Under that great climactic public testing and trial, arrest, betrayal, desertion, torturing, and crucifixion, he would say, "Now is the Prince of darkness come but he has nothing in me."

He earned the right to return in the fullness of time to truly become God's vicar upon Earth, to exercise the Great Powers, to administer judgment. 7213:9

The fact that his was shorter and more dramatic and more intense in its duration, does not mean that he does not know of the long and slow crucifixions which so many of his followers go through, which temper them, which add to their consciousness and their being-ness, and which help to prepare the person to be a more effective tool in this service.

After each crucifixion for the Christ, there is a resurrection with the Christ. As he said, 'Blessed are ye when men speak ill of you and do evil things unto you for my sake. They did that to me and to the other prophets in the service of God also.'

The ones called saints have often blessed and thanked God more for the difficulties that they went through than for the comforts they had. They knew the difficulties were preparing them to be of more effective and better service to their Master.

Anything that prepares us, at whatever stage in our soul development we may be, for better service to the Master, more effective expression of our being-ness with and for God, that is good.

In the strange alchemy of the spirit's force to transmute that into good, even the work that evil does upon us can be made to praise God if we react to it in such a way that we are larger beings in our personal and soul being-ness, and more knowledgeable and effective instruments for God's use and under the direction of the Master. 7211:24-5

The rending of the veil at the death of Jesus was a natural event and a powerful introduction of a thrust into human history of further events to come to bring about the rending of the veil between the spiritual realms and the physical realm. The time may well come when those from the astral realm may walk among and be known and seen, and some of you will, upon occasion, walk in the astral realm with them, and return in full consciousness and with at least a knowledge of the method employed. Do not under-rate the unexplained phenomena in Earthly skies. Wait patiently for the correct understanding. That is, do not jump in your own minds to a pattern which you feel they must fit. They will fit their own pattern. One can study avidly and still await patiently. 8132:7

Q. Why was it necessary for the body of Jesus to be resurrected? Surely a decayed physical body had nothing to do with the reincarnation or the resurrection of the spiritual body, does it?

A. That is quite correct that the dissolution of the physical body really has no effect. However, the resurrection of the physical body of Jesus, the Christ, in Palestine was a very special case. It was a victory over the forces of evil which had killed the body. It was a bold announcement of the victory of good over evil and of the forthcoming larger victory, which Christ will lead over the forces of evil.

People in those days mostly were illiterate (would be considered in your day rather primitive). This was something that was seen which made a very great impression upon those who did see it; so it was a philosophical, psychological, and theological advent of significance, and hence was used. It was part of the plan from the beginning, and we must say it did add quite a bit to that plan. A mere spiritual appearance after the death of Jesus would have reduced the event to just another psychic phenomenon.

Doubtless, there were other reasons, as well, but these are some that I can see. 8011:5

Q. What happened to the physical body of Jesus in his ascension, his going from the physical to spiritual planes, without going through the doorway of death?

A. This comes into the framework of the phenomenon of dematerialization; the changing of the vibrational rate will put the body into a form of being not discernable by the three dimensional eye of the material world. This is not a phenomenon unique to the Jesus personality. There are numerous happenings of this nature, particularly in the framework of esoteric and occult practices as known in the Hindu religious pattern, for example. The laying down and taking up of the body at will is "phenomenal" only in terms of the limited understanding of those to whom it appears as a phenomenon.

A great deal more can be done with the body than is recognized by an Earth consciousness settled and rooted in the reality of the material.

This taking up of the body for the purpose of appearing in human form among Earth people is practiced, has been practiced, through the ages. Even in the present on occasion there will be the appearance in human form in the original body of a soul from perhaps centuries past who mastered this learning and who can appear among Earth-beings, holding to the original bodily form for the purpose of identification by those Earth-beings. 3749:10

The powers Jesus demonstrated in the way that he demonstrated them are available to other souls who attain the unique relationship that the Jesus-soul had with God. We do not find any records of any other soul having attained the same position, but innately there is room in the expansion of individual soul-being-ness for all souls to attain that God estate which Jesus had.

Jesus himself indicated that, too. He said that because he goes unto the Father we can come into his power in his name. He said, 'And the things that I do ye shall do also, and greater things shall ye do.' 3997:32

Q. Since Jesus did have an incarnation in Atlantis, is it possible that he had the knowledge and mastered the use of levitation, dematerialization and de-massing, that this is how the ascension took place?

A. Yes. There is a little more to it than that, but essentially this is correct. These are some of the great powers. Not everyone in Atlantis knew them. Very few did and very few on the excarnate side now know them. The great powers are being jealously protected. They will be used by Jesus when he comes again, because the overcoming of evil will be a power play - and then the redemption. 7317:30

Q. Has Jesus had an incarnation on Earth since his last one?

A. That Jesus of Nazareth incarnation was the climactic incarnation of that soul. It has not had a subsequent incarnation and is not scheduled to have any further incarnations. 8025:2

Jesus is that perfect person. A new incarnation might not be. The Jesus incarnation was then cut off with the manhood at full force. We believe truly it is he who shall return and be King of Kings and Lord of Lords. 7036:23

The second coming of Jesus will not be a new incarnation. It will be the same person, Jesus of Nazareth, which is the person-hood in which that soul demonstrated his complete mastery of Earth living, and personal living, of incarnations. 8025:2

Q. That would be something to look forward to!

A. Yes. It will be of God's appointed time. We think many signs indicate it can be within this generation of Earthlings. 7036:23

Q. Edgar Cayce said that Jesus would appear as he left, descending from heaven, so everyone would know him. Now I read in Ruth Montgomery's book that her guides say he will return born again as a babe to Mary. Which is correct?

A. There are various ideas of it. You must learn to use your own discretion, discrimination, and perhaps hold open various possibilities. We are of those who, such as Edgar Cayce, believe in the New Testament prophesy, that 'this same Jesus, whom ye saw ascend, will come again in like manner in the clouds with glory' to you when he comes to reign. 7036:22

The Lord Jesus will, as he himself stated, come again, himself, personally, not a new incarnation, not his influence in the hearts of people, but the person of Jesus will come from the astral into the physical plane. He will come as ye saw him go, in clouds of glory – which may have more reference to the UFO's than is generally understood or accepted by fundamental Bible students, perhaps. 7384:38

Q. Is there any artist who has seen a vision of Jesus and painted a picture of the way he really looked?

A. We think there are many artists who have seen Jesus. There have been many pictures painted which have caught some of the many faceted portions of that personality; but we think it is quite true that no one Earth artist has had presented of him the form of the risen Christ in the form of the living personality, Jesus of Nazareth. So our answer probably would be, no we do not know of any one picture. 3934:7

Q. Is the Eucharist actually to be the body and the blood of Christ?

A. This certainly would not bear out upon chemical analysis. In a spiritual way, or a symbolic way, it can really be such to some partakers. If it is not so in your consciousness, then it is not so to you; but get that which is meaningful to you, for there is so much of meaningfulness in the Mass of the Lord Jesus Christ, that however, it is conducted in formal communion, or in formal Eucharist, it has really more content than any human being can assimilate. So take that which you can. Fill your cup. You can find your cup overflowing with good even though perhaps not in the way that some other people will have their cups overflow. 7177:25

Q. If we all reincarnate whether we want to or not, then why must we believe in Jesus as our savior in order to have eternal life?

A. Jesus, the Christ, is the key, the head of that team of what may be called Lords (which are a further evolvement of souls). They are in charge at birth in the bringing of human life onto Earth. The processes of the redemption of evil are to be accomplished by this human life on Earth, helping in the salvation process. He led it in Atlantis at a time when the plans were inadequate. He leads it now at a time when we believe the plans, the preparation, the forces are, and will, prove adequate when he comes to establish his reign.

He is the leader and the savior, and his work at this salvation involves the human consciousness, which is the great battleground of evil and good. Now with this larger understanding we believe you can do some more thinking for yourself, and see how that which is presented within the pages of the Bible can be understood in a larger framework than that normally utilized as Jesus the savior is usually presented by orthodox, sometimes limited, thinkers and preachers. 7027:15

Q. Is Jesus the only avenue by which mankind can enter The Kingdom of God?

A. That depends on what one means by The Kingdom of God. There is a verse in the Bible: 'No man cometh unto the Father except by the Son.' And it is true that Jesus heads the Redemption Project on Earth. Also, that the soul was first designed and brought into being with God's permission by the Christ and the team he leads. Perhaps this is what is meant by the Biblical quotation.

However, to come close to God and to achieve that which He wishes anyone of His children to achieve is not necessarily dependent upon even knowing of the one you call Jesus. The essence is to develop compatibility with God in all that one does, and to live true to one's inmost being from God. So in that sense the answer would be no.

The religious leaders whom you have heard who have raised this question probably are working from and enhancing the authority of the Bible and of themselves; so you would not get this answer from them. 8076:1

Q. What exactly did Jesus mean by The Kingdom of God?

A. The establishment of the knowledge of God's Way and the acceptance of it in human living upon planet Earth.

Q. What is The Kingdom of Heaven?

A. The teaching is true that the Kingdom of Heaven must be entered in by the door, and Christ is the door; but put that in the cosmic framework of understanding where the Christ not only has the connotation of a person but the Christ is a state of being-ness. It is a state of totality over many lifetimes, over much experience and personal growth. The soul comes at last into wholeness and maturity as a grown-up child of God through the doorway of love, through the development of the Christ nature. 3935:10

Q. Is it a little kingdom of government, or is it literally within us as a higher state of consciousness?

A. Both, because the actual coming of Jesus to reign when "the governments shall be upon his shoulders" is to establish within human consciousness and human acceptance the knowledge and the ways of God. 7127:39

Q. I have never read a satisfying definition of "Christ." Jesus said we were all expected and required to attain his level of spiritual development. Then shall we all become "Christ?" What does being Christ, mean?

A. Expand the word "Christ" to the term Christhood, a state of being-ness. In that framework, yes, all are expected to come into the estate of Christhood. 4004:18

Just exactly what a Christ is, is another big question. Jesus was called The Christ because he was The One sent to come, and sent for many purposes: the chief revelation of God, the finest living of human life in the consciousness of spiritual citizenship.

Obviously, this is not going to be attained by others unless they, too, become chosen to go into some plane of consciousness where the knowledge and the Kingdom of God had not yet been accomplished and they have reached such a state that they are the anointed ones, then to be as a Messiah, the One sent to that stage of consciousness, that plane of existence, to bring the higher knowledge. 7071:4

Q. How does one be born again and enter it?

A. This is a symbolic thing which is exactly this way for one person, and approximately this way for another person, and a different way for another person. 7127:39

Q. How can we best serve the Christ here and now until he comes again?

A. It is the same answer as the answer has been through near twenty centuries for Christians:

1) First, seek and know him better through that which has been written, through that which you find good and can study. Through that spiritual knowledge I've shared with you; and by the spiritual groups and teachings that you have found good.

2) In your own being live more and more by the truth you know, not as a constant striving, but simply because you want to know and live by the reality of the Creator. Those qualities which God possesses and wants us to possess in which to grow – qualities of honesty, justice, of prudence, of strength, of intelligence, of being on guard against that which is wrong, but being ready to share in the enlargement of that which is wrong, but being ready to share in the en-largement of that which is good in the lives of yourself and those around you.

Following the likeness of Jesus you will increase in wisdom and in stat-ure and in favor with God and man. There is no quick bound to Heaven, excepting that every incarnation is really a short-step, what may be a long-step in its attainment, but time-wise is not long.

Five score years are not long in the eternity of God when it is lived without pressure, with a constant striving for improvement, ever seeking the "read the mind of God." Align with the others of spiritual groups who are compatible with one-self. Find the teachings which resonate with your own mind, heart and soul. These are ways of increasing the Kingdom of God which the Christ is ever bringing upon planet Earth. 8076:8

Q. If wanting to attain a greater Christ Consciousness and a spiritual deepening, what would you suggest as to bringing these two concepts into relationship?

A. To attain the Christ Consciousness you must know the Christ; and to know the Christ, you can find the Christ by observing and knowing him as he was expressed in Jesus, the greatest exponent and revealer of the Christ. There is your field of study. To know the Christ is more than a principle, also more a study of the religious, spiritual and mystical literature experience. 1659:11

Now the Master who said, "Lo, I am with you always," meant it. He is your friend. As you say, "Oh, no, this cannot be. You are too important to visit me. You are too busy to take time for me." You are closing doors to your friend, and it saddens him. He is Master of time and of space. He is The Master, the Super Scientist of this plane of being, which you call planet Earth, and of your existence as incarnate humans upon it. He reaches out as your friend.

The Father, the Creator, the Father/Mother God, enfolds you, surrounds you at all times with the great flow of His Being-ness and His purposes. 8029:9

One has only to look at the other leaders whom Earth-lings have considered the teachers of God: Buddha, fine; Mohammedan, not so fine; Confucius, not so spiritual; then into the lower echelons of the teachers.

Where does one find a being, who in his being-ness and his doing, stands anywhere near the stature of that being known best as Jesus, the Christ?

To be the Christ is not simply a position of honor and power to which certain respect certainly is due. It is a position of responsibility even more. If the Christ, the beloved Child of God as he is, should fail in redeeming Earth, he would be demoted. He does not expect to be demoted. We who serve him certainly serve him well. Knowing that his success is dependent upon our efforts as well, and if we do not serve him successfully in our place and to our capacity, we shall be demoted - and that is correct.

The God of Love loves souls as His children, and works with them in all good ways to procure their growth, so that they can receive more of His love and return it. They can enter more fully into His companionship and discover their own development, their own potentials, and thus grow in God-nature and in God-powers.

Think that over: to grow into increasing God-like-ness, or Godhood. They will never catch up with God; they will enter into the knowledge of God, the companionship, grace and the being-ness like unto God. That direction is best set for Earth, we feel, in the person and the teachings of the one best known in human history as Jesus, the Christ. 7011:7

I might add that the general body of faith in the person of Jesus Christ, which has extended over two thousand years, would not have been allowed to extend this far were it false. Too much of the plan of God for the destiny of mankind is wrapped up in the person of Jesus, the Christ, and his saving work, and major falsities are not in the well-accepted picture. 8039:2

Q. If Jesus has forgiven our sins and we have no karmic carryover, could this be interpreted as no necessity for further Earth-lives?

A. One of the very basic, and root understandings, in human thought of Earth-living and of the whole purpose of reincarnation is the imperfection of the individual and the necessity to return again and again to the experiences of Earth-living, becoming purified and growing beyond the ability to make mistakes, which creates what humans think of as bad karma, necessitating a return to the Earth framework.

This is a true concept, but it is a concept, and not 'the' concept, not the whole purpose of, and understanding of, Earth-living.

When the concept of Earth-living is expanded away from the rather limited concept of Earth as an area of punishment, the concept of using Jesus as an escape from Earth-living will be changed. The soul who had the experience of being Jesus demonstrated the development and holding to total soul consciousness within personalized expression, which is the learning and the attainment for every soul in Earth-living.

The attainment of Christhood belongs not to the personality Jesus, alone, but belongs to every soul who has ever taken on personality experience. Now, the concept of salvation, or let us say, the concept of forgiveness of sins, is valid. There is a supreme authority in the universe, a supreme law, in and through which those single and separated consciousness who, in their individual experiences have mated with that which is less, with that which is negative, with that which is evil, can be given a sense of release and freedom.

But at the point of their realization of release and freedom, they are not permanently taken away from the possibility of being again contaminated with that which is lesser than the supreme good. Rather, they are given the opportunity to again, in the making of contact with the lesser, prove what they have learned, and thus in essence, affect their own escape. 3909:10

Q. Is there to be a complete destruction of the Earth?

A. The doctrine of the ultimate destruction of the Earth is a false doctrine. Jesus came preaching salvation. It is in that plan that a soul will find the ultimate expression of its personalized developed God-being-ness. 3907:4

Christ is the Lord of Earth, and with those many souls gathered under the banner of Christ in God's plan of salvation, all levels of life in the planet Earth are to be raised to the level of conscious knowledge and co-operation with spiritual forces.

The Earth is not to be destroyed. The Earth is a valuable school of learning for souls. It is as much a cosmic school as any other plane of experience. God sent His son to the Earth to redeem the Earth, that the world through him might be saved. 3910:3

The very heart and core of the message of the greatest avatar of all, known as Jesus, the Christ, was salvation for Earth, not doom.

There are many what we might call "cosmic teams" made up of souls grouped together in various planes of existence who use their individual and combined spiritual knowledge to initiate the pattern for the bringing of the Kingdom of God to Earth, which is raising the Earth's vibrations. 3575:3

Jesus' coming will not put to an end to Earth-life. It will not destroy evil. It will be the beginning of the redemption of evil. God does not want Lucifer destroyed. God has the power to instantly destroy evil. God wants to redeem evil, through the processes of Earth-living by souls who become aligned with His purpose. 3511:6

Q. Where is Jesus, the Christ, now?

A. That soul has continuing being-ness and contact with all planes of living; and so in that sense he is at work in the Earth plane. He is actively at work in the astral plane. All the heavens and all of Earth are accessible to him.

That soul moves easily from one plane of expression to another, and expresses in turns of the life activity of each plane. Jesus Christ can be contacted as the continuing personality expression of Jesus of Nazareth in the excarnate personality form in the astral plane. And all that he spoke of while in incarnation as Jesus, of his continuing presence with those Earth-beings who love him remains a continuing experience. He is accessible. Those who ask shall receive. Those who seek shall find, and to those who knock the door will be open. 3159:10

Q. What is his mission now?

A. One of the closing statements in the Jesus personality-life was: "In my Father's house are many mansions. I go to prepare a place for you. I will come again and receive you." - meaning, receive you into those many mansions. That continues to be a major activity, a major function of that soul known in Earth-living as Jesus. He functions in many realms of being, ministers to souls in Earth consciousness and souls in other planes of con-sciousness; but this which we have said is very central in his activity. And we, ourselves, have given our commitment to serving him in that capacity which he expressed. 3165:12

You will remember he passed through those realms, as record is given, during the three days that the body lay in the tomb; and in all realms of evil he is recognized as one who conquered. Now he is not recognized as "the conqueror" in the sense that evil has ceased to battle, but he is recognized even by evil as being one who won against them.

It is because he can walk through all realms of evil without evil attach-ing to him, that he is the savior, the protector from evil of all other souls. No other soul has won that perfection. So, by all means, keep Jesus at the head of the list, but be receptive to the much good and the demonstration of other spiritual and cosmic laws as given by other spiritual teachers. 3450:16

There are low levels of the astral world, governed by the forces of evil which imprisons spiritually un-awakened souls. When you read that Jesus, following the crucifixion, descended into Hell, he entered into the lower astral world and began the very necessary process of redemption of that kingdom. A great cleansing and redeeming program of the lower astral kingdom has continued since that time and is a necessary prerequisite to the cleansing and redeeming of the incarnate forces of evil. 4008:14

One of the purposes of the Jesus of Nazareth life was to demonstrate that the cosmic school of Earth can produce one personality perfect in human- being-ness. Because the Earth plane is the plane of expressed human-being-ness, the plan of salvation, the plan which would necessitate the sifting of the wheat from the chaff, and in that framework judgment must include the leadership of this soul. For it is this one soul who has demonstrated the perfection of the human nature, and who has taught that as one soul can perfect human-being-ness, so also all souls can perfect human-being-ness.

Therefore it is important for those of like interest to look for the place of the leadership of Jesus, the Christ, within any framework of spiritual teaching being brought forth as a plan for the establishment of the Kingdom of God on Earth. 3575:4

Q. When his work is done on Earth, where will he go?

A. His work is to establish salvation upon Earth. When that is done, he will go on in his further progression into the higher realms. He actually is beyond the realm of the Elohim now, but comes back to function from that realm as Lord of Lords and King of Kings of Earth. 8025:2

The particular soul who acts as the adjutant to the Jesus-soul, who is the chief assistant, and who will truly be in a general charge of the outworking of the Jesus Plan of Salvation for Earth, is the Moses-soul. This one has been adjutant to the Jesus-soul through many millennia. He has been proved capable, humble, completely loyal, dedicated and consecrated - not always as perfect as the Jesus-soul, but of increasing Earth achievements.

So that soul will be in general charge, will be in charge of the various lieutenants, and all will be of the Melchizadek priesthood as Earth could and should understand this. 7011:4-5

It is expected by us that the Jesus-being will complete his particular responsibility for Earth within the next thousand or so years in the establishment of the Kingdom of God upon Earth. That does not mean that, all that is to be done, has been done. It means that the human society becomes the better instrument for souls, young God-children, in which to grow. They will be more protected. They will accomplish in fifty incarnations in what might have taken seventy before. There will not be the number of aborted incarnations through disease, miscarriage and infant death and such. There will not be the degradation that has come to the Children of God upon planet Earth through all the centuries past. There will be a new understanding of the real significance and holiness of human life. There will not be the simplistic roadblocks put in the way that some groups erect when they have a small part of an answer – and become part of the problem instead of part of the answer because of their simplistic littleness.

So the whole human society will continue for a long time thereafter and will need constant help and direction.

Then there are the animal and plant kingdoms; and that realm of consciousness associated with minerals, with bare matter itself.

The establishment of the Kingdom of God with the knowledge of the way of God within all of these other areas will take quite a while.

It is expected that the Jesus-God-child completes his appointed task and fulfills his responsibility and attains what he was sent to attain - then probably the Moshe soul will come into the position of major responsibility for planet Earth. The Jesus-soul will continue to take an interest but should be freed to go on to its expansion, too.

In time, if the Earth has not been completely "saved," the Moshe-soul will go on and rejoin this good friend, the Jesus-soul, on the upper track, and some other soul will take a major responsibility for planet Earth. 8031:21

The great task Jesus faces is that of redeeming common human practice. This was done in the very early stages of humanity in what is generally called the Garden of Eden experience. Here a superior level of life – the soul – had been formulated and brought into incarnation. This was an agent who had eaten of the tree of the knowledge of good and evil, and knew the difference between right and wrong, good and evil. Such a being has a higher level of consciousness than do the other animals and plants and can know the difference between good and evil and then choose only the good.

The next coming of Jesus will clarify that whole process, vivify, and invigorate it as well. You, as a human-being are a battleground. Every incarnation of a soul is a battleground between good and evil. The victory is won or lost in a hundred million experiences. New ways will be made known to assist humans in discriminating, in making the right choices, and in the effectuation of those choices. There will also be a sustaining great camaraderie of those involved in this great project so those involved will be helpful to each other. 8071:3

The preparations are much more tremendous than anyone realizes. Preparations upon Earth involve the enlargement of consciousness, the enlightenment of the mind, science with its increase in knowledge, public education, television – which can make it possible for all to see it together – and the preparation of thousands upon thousands and millions of incarnate human-beings upon Earth to know, to some degree, what is coming, and to have, to some degree, a part in that coming. 8004:3

Jesus will make himself known. The angels at his ascension assured his followers that "this same Jesus will come again, even as ye saw him ascend in clouds of glory."

There will be signs and wonders "and the whole Earth shall see it together" – which was indeed a marvelous prophecy 2,000 years ago; but perfectly plausible now with communication satellites ringing the Earth.

There will be such signs and wonders that every television and radio organization of world-reaching capability will rush its best cameras, microphones, and personnel to the site.

The Third Testament, the Covenant of Understanding, will be established – testifying to a third element of the Covenant relationship of God with man. The first Covenant, the Covenant of Law, announced by Moses, assured the chosen people that God could be counted upon, but did require that they discover and live by His rules. Jesus announced the Second Covenant, that of Love, that indeed this God under whom we live is a God of Law, but also that He is as a beneficent parent unto us. God is responsible. God is reliable. He is a God of cause and effect, with His abiding value system expressed as His Law by which we must live. But also He has a great affection, an abiding love, for all His creation: the Covenant Relationship of Love. 8135:16

+ + +

There are various levels of experience in which a person can be involved after so-called death. Jesus, then a fourth-degree initiate, worked closely with his Master, the Christ, and his fellow initiates on the inner planes during seven years. For a part of that time he was in Pralaya – a kind of equivalent to the Christian idea of Paradise, a state of constant bliss.

He was not seen in any special form by any humans during those seven yeas because he did not walk the Earth. Ghosts, or spectral, forms are the exception rather than the norm; and they occur only with relatively un-evolved individuals, tied to the physical plane by some strong desire or emotional experience such as violent death, etc.. The normal thing is for people to leave the physical plane completely, soon after death. M.M. 249

MORE SAINTS

There are saints; and there are saints - and there are more saints. At one time I wanted to read the lives of all the saints – until I learned how many saints there were; so I began by reading a book titled *The Lives of the Saints*.

When we were young my brother James used to tell a joke about Saint Anthony, and that is all I ever knew about Saint Anthony until I read a short biography of him. I had always visualized Saint Anthony as an old man; I expected his story to be sort of dreary, like something out of mothballs, but I immediately associated with Saint Anthony because of his youth. He was a boy of eighteen, living in Alexandria, Egypt, when his parents died, leaving him the family fortune; but the family wealth did not compensate for the loss of his parents.

One Sunday he was strongly influenced by the sermon of the priest reading that part of the gospels where Christ commands a rich merchant to sell his belongings and give the money to the poor if he would enter the Kingdom of Heaven. Anthony did what I have heard of other people doing; he accepted the sermon as a direct message from God and sold his possessions, giving all the money to the poor; and he moved into a cave on the outskirts of town, eventually moving deeper into the desert where he remained for the rest of his life. History now regards Saint Anthony as the first Christian monk, the father of Western monasticism.

It was my loss for having thought of Saint Anthony as only being a ninety-year-old man; for it was during the full energies of his youth that he made the decision to follow the Christ within. I read of other saints but it was Saint Anthony that remained in my mind. I visualized the majestic figure of that ninety-year-old man with long, white hair and a long, white beard, wearing a black robe and sandals, being brought before the church fathers in Alexandria to answer the question that was splitting the church: Was Jesus God, or the Son of God?

"I have seen him!" roared Saint Anthony.

The saint I looked forward to reading about the most, the popular Saint Francis, surprisingly had limited appeal to me.

One saint that did become a favorite was Saint Joseph of Cupertino, a simple and humble brother who possessed the gifts of ecstasy and levitation, gifts that held me in awe. When Saint Joseph entered the ecstatic state, the brothers would slip needles under his fingernails to test the depth of his ecstasy, causing him to awaken in excruciating pain.

Just when I felt I had found my favorite saint I discovered the magnificent Martin de Porres. This mulatto saint from Lima, Peru, became my very favorite for he was virtually a miniature Jesus – if there can be a miniature Jesus – possessing humility, compassion, selflessness, kindness, and generosity; he was blessed with the gifts of ecstasy, prophecy, clairvoyance, and healing. He is recorded to have been in two different places at the same time, (bi-location) making unseen voyages in the twinkling of an eye to Mexico, Algiers, France, the Philippines, and perhaps to China while spending all his religious life at the Convent of the Holy Rosary in Lima.

Following the example of their founder, Saint Dominic, Martin scourged himself with the discipline three times a night. His penances were prompt, severe, all embracing, and uninterrupted. He began them before he entered the order and death alone ended them. In Martin's eyes, suffering was the price of love, and he thought this price wholly insufficient.

His biographer wrote:

Brother Martin lashed himself with patience and ardor using not merely a knotted cord but an iron chain armed with hooks of steel. When Blessed Martin's shoulders began to flow with blood, he was glad to increase the pain by rubbing the wounds with salt and vinegar, hoping to make reparation for his own faults and, if possible, to merit by his suffering the grace of conversion for sinners.

After his first flagellation was over, Brother Martin would go to the chapter hall to meditate before the crucifix on the Passion of our Savior. When prayer had increased his fervor, he prepared himself for the second discipline by taking off his tough serge tunic that was glued to the bloody wounds of his body. During this second scouring Martin treated himself with even greater cruelty, beseeching heaven with all the power of his soul do bring sinners from a life of sin back to the crucified Lord.

Before daybreak Brother Martin promptly arose, and before the first sign of life in the convent, he noiselessly descended to some corner underground for his third scourging. At the dawn of day a young man of Martin's selection, who was vigorous and pitiless, with the most painful whip of all, a branch of a wild quince tree, beat long and with unflagging cruelty upon his back. It was wielded by an executioner who was urged on by the voice of his groaning victim begging him to strike with all his might, to strike until the gate of heaven was unlocked.

Brother Martin showed no trace during the daytime that he had undergone such severe penances. His smile was ever cheerful, his tenderness and solicitude for the suffering, his industry and patience in performing his duties just as unflaggingly keen and wholehearted, going about his errands with ever joyful countenance, distributing gifts to the needy and curing ills of body and soul. Few would have guessed that about his loins he wore a tightly girded iron chain. On his bleeding shoulders he wore a penitential hair shirt.

Twenty-five years after his death his body was found entire, exhaling the sweet perfume of sanctity. His flesh was fresh and tender. Men of science examined the marvelous body and each time they pierced it with their surgical needle, drops of bright red blood oozed forth. Thirty years after his death he appeared to his lifetime friend.

In religious terminology self-hypnosis, or the trance state, may be termed "ecstasy." Ecstasy is an expansion of consciousness brought about from within, as in the case of Ann Catherine Emmerich. Regardless of the term used, ecstasy or trance, a reading of the Immortal Truth, or the Akashic Records, will occur. The Akashic Records is referred to in the Bible as the Book of Life, or the Book of Judgment, or the Book of God's Remembrance. Brother Martin possessed the ability to read the Akashic Records.

Martin had used his sister's home as a hospice for Martin's sick and dying patients. Discord was about to disrupt his sister's domestic life. His sister had never told Martin of her troubles with her husband. They lived a mile and a half from Lima, and this crisis in their life took place before their home became a hospice for Blessed Martin's sick and dying.

On a particular day the quarrel between the two had risen to the highest pitch; harmony was completely, even perhaps irreparably, broken. Wrangling had been followed by tears. The rupture seemed imminent when Martin appeared on the scene.

Brother Martin began to tell in detail the difficulties which had caused all the trouble—even though he had never heard about them. He seemed to know more about the quarrel than they did themselves. He made known to them its causes, those secret causes of dispute which out of pride and self-esteem the quarrelsome try hard to keep hidden from others and refuse to acknowledge and correct in themselves. He opened up to view secret pages, and he could do so without annoyance to husband and wife because the things people try to conceal are, after all, not peculiar to anyone in particular but common to all mankind.

He undid the treacherous knots of over-sensitiveness that strangled the feelings of husband and wife and cooled their love. Then after he had encouraged them in the paths of peace, he reprimanded them severely for their foolish behavior. His sister and her husband received the shock with gratitude because they were already reconciled; henceforth they grew to know how to love each other in self-forgetfulness.

This story sounds very much like a chapter out of a life-reading from Dr. John and the Religious Research Foundation. It is the type of situation that life-readings were meant to correct; because of Saint Martin's highly developed spirituality the Akashic Records were revealed to him during ecstasy. Being aware of the Immortal Truth was only one of the by-products of Brother Martin's spiritual development. He was known to transport himself into and out of rooms that were locked. There were no barriers for Brother Martin.

In the Convent of the Holy Rosary in Lima three hundred years ago, Brother Martin is the infirmarian. An epidemic is raging, and sixty of the novices are stricken. When the door to the novitiate was locked, Brother Martin was seen to enter and leave noiselessly. He would go from one bed to another, knowing what each one wanted, arriving just in time. He responded even to the secret and unexpressed needs of the sick. There was no need to call for Brother Martin: as quick as intuition he would anticipate a request. This phenomenon was observed quite often, even outside of times of epidemic. At night Martin would be needed by a religious in the novitiate when the doors to it would be locked. Martin would be at the bedside of the sick novice, and no one could ever tell by what means the appeal had reached him.

At two o'clock one night, Francis Varesco, a novice, took very sick, so sick that he thought he was going to die. He lay helpless, desperate. Suddenly Brother Martin entered his room with all the necessities and comforts needed by the sick boy.

"Why, how did you know I was sick?"

"Don't ask useless questions," replied Brother Martin, "take comfort, for you shall not die of this malady."

Brother Francis Varesco instantly knew he was cured.

Once, when giving to a sick person a medicine unknown to Peru, Brother Martin spontaneously remarked: "This remedy is quite good. I have seen it used in France, in the hospital of Bayonne." Yet Brother Martin had never physically left Peru.

A merchant of Lima fell desperately ill upon arriving in Mexico. In the bitterness of his agony he cried out: "Oh, God! Why is not Brother Martin here to care for me?"

At that very instant Brother Martin entered the room, with a smile illuminating his face. Full of joy the merchant asked, "Why, when did you get here, my dear Brother?"

"I just arrived," replied Brother Martin. Then he walked about the room, setting things in order, rearranging everything gaily, familiarly. Then he said to the sick man, "O man of little faith, why did you think you were going to die?"

Giving the man some medicine, Brother Martin added, "Now

be assured you won't die of this fever." Martin then quietly and graciously left the room.

The merchant soon found himself in good health, and in order to thank his friend for his kindness, he hurried over to the Dominican Convent in Mexico City, where he thought Brother Martin would be staying. However, he found that Martin had never been there. The merchant inquired for Martin in all the hotels of the city in hopes of finding him. But in vain—no one had ever heard of him! The merchant had to wait until he returned to Lima for news of Blessed Martin. There, at the Rosary Convent, the Fathers assured the merchant that the good Negro had never left the Convent. The information was like a thunderbolt to the astounded merchant, who never related the incident without tears of joyful gratitude.

Blessed Martin was also endowed with the gift of invisibility. He acted at times without being seen. During certain ecstasies he would disappear from the sight of man. What is more remarkable is the fact that he could communicate this gift to others. At least they cite an example of this power. The police had tracked down two accused persons to the Convent and were about to arrest them when Martin—evidently for some good reason in accordance with the plans of God—rendered them invisible, enabling them to slip through the hands of the officers.

On occasion Martin unwittingly left open to view some of the invisible life that surrounded him. The Fathers and the Brothers declared that they saw two angels assisting him one night when, according to custom, the Little Office of the Blessed Virgin was being recited in the dormitory before matins. At another time Brother Martin was seen walking in the cloisters of the Convent in the visible company of four angels who looked like handsome young men and carried lighted torches in their hands.

What do we, as human-beings, look like on the soul level? What form do we assume beyond our physical or astral existence?

Brother Martin sometimes was seen in the shape of a ball of fire. Thus, one night when Father Barragan was very sick, the religious whose duty it was to ring the bell for Martin, saw while waiting for the appointed hour, Brother Martin traversing space in the form of a ball of lightning. He was hurled, as it were, to the bedside of the sick

Father. On another occasion the whole community witnessed a similar prodigy. Again as a sphere of light Brother Martin was transported in a flash from the chapter hall in the choir.

Just as he shared his gift of invisibility with others, so also did this "Flying Brother," as he was called, bestowed his gift of speed to thirty novices whom he had taken for a walk in the country outside of Lima. The novice master had requested Brother Martin to take the boys for an afternoon of recreation into some wooded area three miles from the Convent. They were all enjoying themselves so much that both Martin and the boys failed to notice how the time had sped by. Evening surprised them in the woods; certainly they had no way of getting back on time to the Convent.

Brother Martin was baffled for a moment. The bell of Office was about to ring, and they were far from home. The novices were afraid of being punished. Martin began to pray with all his might, as was his custom. Then his countenance brightened, and he said to the youths, "Come—follow after me!"

Perhaps they formed in line, Indian file, with Martin in the lead. No one seems to know. Perhaps Martin told them to lock hands and close their eyes—like something out of The Wizard of Oz. A few steps and all saw themselves together at the threshold of the Convent. The great distance had been covered in less time than it takes to relate the story. But that was not all. They passed through doors already locked without disturbing anyone, and at the appointed time the novices took their places in choir, ready to commence the recitation of the Rosary!

Martin understood that his great work among the poor, the sick, and the dying was an indirect means of preaching. It is scarcely necessary to add that Martin's whole life must have been a vivid and compelling sermon, touching the hearts of all those who had only to know him in order to love him and be edified by the virtues which he so wonderfully exemplified in his life.

Forty-five years have passed since my introduction to Brother Martin; and I don't remember how I became aware of him. His life was the brightest rainbow to Heaven I ever read with the exception of Jesus. The booklet telling the story of Brother Martin has gone with me, in box to box, apartment to apartment, state to state, remaining virtually abandoned on a shelf of my bookcase for decades. Now that I re-read the story of Brother Martin I find him alive and well in my present home and he will remain with me after I cross the great divide.

After the Church beatifies a saint we sometimes do what I did, put the saint on a shelf and pray to them when we need them. We look up to them as spiritual heroes and ask for their Divine intercession. The truth is, we should maintain an open door to them by emulating them in our daily living. We should see their life as worthy of being incorporated into our life. In this way we become one with them, in thought as well as in deed.

READING THE IMMORTAL TRUTH

Edgar Cayce was the first to use the term Akashic Records; which is now a staple term in the New Age. Prophets and mystics of old read the Akashic Records in accordance with their specialized gift. The Religious Research Foundation, without any awareness of Edgar Cayce, began reading the Akashic Records approximately ten years following the death of Edgar Cayce.

Cayce projected his consciousness outside of his physical body to read the Akashic Records. Dr. John, the spirit counselor-guide of Religious Research, read the records from a spiritual plane, not the physical plane as did Edgar Cayce, and then transmitted the information through a medium on Earth.

Cayce made reference to "others" who read the Akashic Records from a "different" angle. While giving a Life Reading Cayce said: "The events described here are those which made impressions upon the skein of time and space, hence they may be often viewed by others who see them from a different angle."

Dr. John read the Records from the soul level; he used the term "concept method" to explain his method of communication.

The following information was given by Dr. John Christopher Daniels to spiritual seekers who inquired as to his method of reading the Akashic Records, or the Immortal Truth. I will follow this information with a complete Life Reading from Dr. John. Numbers at end of paragraphs indicate reading and page.

Dr. John Christopher Daniels:

A. As a particular servant of Jesus, the Christ, my assignment has been to work with Earth, particularly to bring through the system of teachings expressed in these readings, and to develop the organization of Religious Research for the dissemination of these teachings. We have been given the go-ahead, as you know, as of July 1980 for the dissemination; and that is the great project in which we are now engaged. 7284:23

I come from the realm of the Light-bearers, which means that my basic commitment as a soul is to God through the agencies of Jesus, the Christ; and my commitment is to the Christ message.

I come into the excarnate astral realms to read the Akashic Records for these Readings. This is a service I am performing according to a plan and purpose set in motion many centuries ago.

Some 2300 years ago I had an Earth life in China in masculine expression, and this medium that I use for these readings, Grace Wittenberger, in that lifetime was my daughter. We established then a very close rapport; and the present relationship we have in this work has, as one of its bases, the close father-daughter relationship of that former lifetime.

I have not incarnated in the Earth realm since that time. I have access to many realms of being-ness. My major service and work during the Earth-life experience of this soul known as Grace Wittenberger is to bring through these Life Readings, although I am also engaged in other activities that affect the Earth realm but also affect other realms of being beyond your Earth comprehension. I prefer to be known and judged by the results of my Life Reading work, rather than by any claims of being-ness that I might make. 990:17

We, from our side, must work with the best we can get. A system of teaching was presented with the Alice Bailey work for which Master Kuthumi and I get probably undue credit, much of it coming from some general esoteric teaching which we might say clogged the channel; and, hence, there was a great deal of Alice Bailey in the Alice Bailey books. Likewise, they are quite ponderous as well as voluminous. It is doubtful if very many who start reading them really pursue them. Those who do, assume a certain amount of knowledge and leadership mainly because they got through the books, or say they got through the books. Frankly, I would like to be largely dissociated from that now. And why do I say that? Because now we have used a different system, different in several ways:

1) My own soul-mate has become my channel, and even though there is occasionally an element of him in the material that comes, it is true that soul-mates are close; and it likewise is true that over the years he has become, in my estimation, a very clear channel for me.

2) The whole system of transmission of the teaching has been changed.

The transmission of these teachings now may be likened to the production of the Jewish-Christian Bible in contrast with the Mohammedan Bible, the Koran. The Mohammedan scriptures are simply the pronouncements of the prophet Mohammed, whereas the Judeo-Christian scriptures are the stories of many centuries of human experience in which certain spiritual teachings were promulgated by the various prophets and teachers; and various experiences were had.

It was not so much the teachings that were promulgated, as the experiences that were had, that formed the bulk of the Judeo-Christian scriptures; and from the experiences the spiritual principles which were applied are apparent and the success or failure can be judged.

In my teachings I follow this approach. The Life Readings have brought about five thousand highly different individuals in which there is a wide range of difference in the individuals. Some are similar and some individuals are very different from all the others. The teachings that apply to the life situations of actual persons form the bulk of these readings, and are not pronouncements of a philosophical or esoteric system.

The Alice Bailey system of teachings and the Religious Research life-and-teaching readings systems are really two quite different systems of spiritual teaching.

There is truth but no human has yet attained it; humans only attain approximations of truth. If they attain a growing approximation of truth they are fulfilling their divine imperative of growing in compatibility with God. But no one will have the full truth; and I would caution not to believe that any person would stand up before his Age and proclaim the truth and demonstrate some great new advances, because he will not. Advances come in an evolutionary way.

The term "mystery school" does not apply to Religious Research because in its usage of the method of science and its appreciation of the spirit of truth which was given, which was released by the High Ones, higher even than the hierarchy, and released really by God into the affairs of man. It is no longer a mystery when new knowledge comes. You do find in Religious Research and in the teachings we have built, the modern version of advanced spiritual and other knowledge. 7270:14

The Moshe soul is deeply involved in Religious Research; this being one of the instruments that he has been very instrumental in fashioning. His best known incarnation was as the Moses of three thousand years ago. He is one of those High beings chosen by the Master and asked to join Him in the redemption project. He is the General Adjutant to the Master. When the Master's prime work is over, the Moshe soul will take over the "clean-up work" which will last some thousands of years. This gives those of us who work in this project an additional closeness to the Master. We know him as a friend and that is good. 7374:20

The basic project for Religious Research is the bringing of the tool of scientific research into the field of religion. To make this a little more distinctive in its meaning – to bring the best tool that man has of gaining sure knowledge of separating truth from error, into the field of man's spiritual nature.

Now this basic purpose can be expressed in another way, and has been: To develop religion as a science. This is a phrase which we have used officially. This is our official announcement of it: To develop religion as a science.

And what does that mean? It means to establish the knowledge of man's spiritual nature and the characteristics of that spiritual nature, upon the sure foundation of established knowledge, upon the sure foundation of researched and proved facts. This is the first, the basic project upon which we are engaged. The other projects, the other aspects, fall within this framework, to a certain extent.

The major purpose of all our projects is the service of God. The various phases of the projects and the various projects are put within that large framework. 11-12—'67

In bringing out the past lives we want you to know that this will be a selective process. Of course it always is. We seek to bring to the attention of the conscious personality those lifetimes which have meaning and understanding, those lifetimes of the past for which there is a purpose for the present personality to know. So there always is that quality of selectivity. But now, in addition to that, there is another principle of selectivity working here, in that we will not bring a full picture of the very real achievements and accomplishments by the soul in the past lives simply because we don't want the personality to dwell on those past achievements. They are there; they are good accomplishments; but we're not going to bring the full picture of the past lives for that reason. However, we do bring in what lifetimes we can as they do reflect in the personality relationship. But we do want the understanding that there are achievements and gains made by the soul more than may show up in a reading for the reason given. 3812:9

We do not operate on the clairvoyant level of reading the aura to ascertain the physical condition of the body. We are researchers into the soul history of the individual and the relating of the personality life to the soul life. 2384:2

Earth mediums can read the Akashic Records as they are reflected in the astral plane. The Earth medium can open up and, in a manner of speaking, reach into the astral plane, reach up to the astral plane and read the reflection.

When we read the Akashic Records, as we have explained, we read them from quite a different vantage point outside of the astral realm; and therefore, questions concerning the personality are not readable by those who are not in touch with the personality. We are in touch with the soul records, and when we know the condition of the personality then we can fit that into the soul's record and see whether there is purpose, or just what the situation is. This is our framework of working to which we feel we must adhere. 3211:12

On September 15, 1952, the first office of The Religious Research Foundation was opened by Reverend Franklin Loehr.

Dr. Loehr was both a scientist and an ordained minister and recognized the need for answers to spiritual questions that were based on proven facts rather than the dogma of any religion. Their motto became *Adding Facts to Faith*.

For several years The Religious Research Foundation was active in spiritual research of all types: prayer, comparative religions, life after death, psychical research, reincarnation research and parapsychology. Probably the best known work of the Foundation at that time was the prayer-plant experiment. With the combination of his degree in chemistry and his years as a minister, Dr. Loehr was the ideal leader of these laboratory investigations. He directed a controlled experiment on the effects of prayer on the growth of plants. One hundred and fifty-six people took part in this project over a three year period,

performing over seven hundred experiments, using more than twenty-seven thousand seeds with about one hundred thousand measurements.

The results were outstanding, and proved that prayer is effective.
The experiments were written up in newspapers across the country
and published in a best selling book by Dr. Loehr, *The Power of Prayer
on Plants* (Doubleday, 1959).

During the 1950s an event happened that turned the focus of
Religious Research to reincarnation.

A being in spirit by the name of Dr. John Christopher Daniels
contacted Dr. Loehr and brought messages about past lives of certain
individuals. When tested by Dr. Loehr, "Dr. John" as he called himself, proved to be a reliable source of spiritual knowledge. With this
turn of events the focus of Religious Research shifted. When asked
the reason for this change, Dr. Loehr replied: …..

. . . . . because reincarnation research is bringing us the first
direct scientific evidence of the soul. The basic teaching of
every religion on the nature of man is incarnation – that there
is a spirit, something not of flesh, which is in the flesh, en-
fleshed, embodied, in each human being. In other words,
what we call the soul.

Every piece of evidence for reincarnation is doubly evidence of this basic religious teaching of reincarnation. For if
you have lived even once before, then that which was you in
that former embodiment, and which carried over during the
time of embodiment, between that life and your present life
and now is you in this incarnation, this embodiment, that is,
de facto, your soul.

Through study of past lives, Religious Research began researching
the soul and its many facets. In the 1960s the primary focus of Religious Research became the Life Readings, channeled from Dr. John,
the spirit teacher and guide for Religious Research. Life Readings are
soul histories of real people who wrote and requested information
about their past lives and the purpose of their present life.

Responses from these people about their Life Readings were overwhelmingly positive. The Readings had increased their understanding of themselves and helped them to know who they were and why they have their own unique life circumstances. Knowing this enabled them to accept themselves, make constructive changes in their lives, heal or release relationships, more fully pursue their life's purpose and find inner peace.

As the number of Readings climbed into the thousands, it became apparent that not only were individuals being helped by them, but that a body of spiritual teachings was being built – teachings not based on the dogma of any church. These teachings, based on studying the lives of human beings, and observing the various results of different human actions, portray an orderly spiritual universe with a spiritual law of cause and effect.

From the early 1950s to her retirement in 1978, Reverend Grace Wittenberger was the key channel for Dr. John, with Dr. Franklin Loehr as alternate.

The 1960s, 19070s and 1980s were devoted to the giving of Life Readings, lecture tours, the writing of books, and the conducting of classes on reincarnation, death and prayer. Early in the history of the Life Readings, numbers were assigned to each Reading. The number identification of each Life Reading enabled it to be studied without disclosing the client's name. Because much of the material in a Life Reading is personal, care is taken to protect all identities. Thousands of Life Readings are all on file at religious Research headquarters and are still being researched today.

Following the retirement of Reverend Grace Wittenberger from Religious Research in 1978, Dr. Loehr became the only channel for Dr. John. When Dr. Loehr died in 1988 more than five thousand Readings had been given. By studying the Life Readings of ordinary people we are able to study the soul and answer questions such as:

What is a soul?

What is its purpose on Earth?

What makes one person more material-minded and another more spiritual?

Why are there lives of limitation for some and lives of privilege for others?

What determines when and where a person is born? Are marriages made in Heaven?

Life Readings provide answers to these and many more questions.

SPECIAL QUESTION READING #2241
February 25, 1964

Medium: Reverend Grace Wittenberger
Conductor: Reverend. Franklin Loehr

Dr. John:

A. When I first made contact with you in the present lifetime, some years ago, through this channel (Grace), I identified myself to you by my soul name. And for sometime in our contacts with each other we knew that name. We used it, and you know only that name. You knew really the double name, the soul name of the masculine half of the soul, and the soul name for the feminine half of the soul; and this is the way I identified myself to you.

We were still using that name when I first began bringing through the Life Readings and working for the development of this channel's mediumship for this particular service. However, rather quickly, we changed the name; and the reason we changed it was given, and it is no secret – it is in the records – and we believe that you have referred to it occasionally through the years in your reports and your lectures, the soul name.

As the Readings became established in what we were confidently expecting to be a framework of very practical and specific helpfulness to Earth-beings, we wanted to use a name for the purpose of identification which would have, more or less, a familiar ring to the people getting the Readings, a name that would not give the flavoring of the esoteric, because we were not casting the Life Readings in esoteric terms. And, therefore, I chose and brought through to you – and you did not make it up – I suggested that you use the name John Christopher Daniels. Use it mainly as any identification point, so as this one explains so charmingly in her lectures, you wouldn't have to say, "Hey, you!" when you wanted to talk with me.

I explained quite in detail – which is a matter of record and can and has been and can continue to be given publicly – that the name John Christopher Daniels is a name I expect to use in a future Earth incarnation. It is not the name of a personality expression of my own soul in a past life; it is the personality name of a future personality expression I will have.

Q. I know you have been perceived and have occasionally sent Grace greetings and messages through certain other psychics close to us: Brenda Crenshaw, Tony Conardo, and Ruth Mathias.

A. I can upon occasion identify myself to the psychic responsiveness of other mediums, yes.

Q. Have you ever brought Life Readings or portions of Life Readings through any other medium?

A. Yes, somewhat, portions of them; not in this framework but thoughts about past lives, etc., through an Earth personality with whom there is a particular close bond. She is not established in Earth in the framework as a medium. It is a spontaneous happening with that personality. Occasionally she senses past life relationships, or pieces of past lives; and this comes from my very close association with her. But she does not do it professionally.

Q. Is this Caroline?

A. That's right; but I have not worked through any so-called established medium, except on two or three occasions when I have given verification of my presence to the personality-Grace, or to the personality-Franklin through another medium. And then of course I have used the name of Dr. John Christopher Daniels, although the two of you know the soul name.

Q. If any workers from the other-side want to establish a connection with you, if they use only the name John Christopher Daniels, or only John, in one sense they know you by reputation; but if there is a real working relationship they will bring through the double soul name?

A. Yes. If there were a reason – and we do not know of any now – but it is conceivable that a situation would develop where it be of benefit for my identity to be established in Earth through another medium by another guide. And if that should develop, then it will be the soul name that is used, for the purpose of your own (yours and Grace's) verification; because you have a right to this. You are the ones whom I have very carefully trained and disciplined over a number of years, as I have frequently told you. You two are my major purpose, my project for your present lifetime. However, I am identified in every other realm of being, except the Earth realm, by my soul name; and those who know me personally, so to speak, know me as the soul, not as the personality I am to be.

There are many in the psychic realm who know of me, know of my work. I do not – let me say here – have a corner on the Life Reading market, as you Earth beings would say. I do not claim to have a monopoly. It is my particular field of expression at this time. It is a field of study in which I have engaged for a long, long time in preparation for this particular Earth-life which is a time of service being rendered by me to the Earth plane, as I am discarnate.

The service of a soul to Earth is not, of course, limited to when that soul is in Earth. I have been prepared – as far as Earth time goes – through centuries for this particular service in which you two and I work as a team. It is a service by you. You are my essentials. It is a cooperative service and would not be rendered except in that framework.

There is this service of Life Readings being developed by other souls as well; and those other souls, some of them, do know of my work. They know of me as John Christopher Daniels, the reader of the Akashic Records, the giver of Life Readings.

Those who know me personally identify me, have conversed with me, companioned and fellowshipped with me, by my soul name.

Q. We on the incarnate Earth plane have a word for it. We call it "name dropping," somebody who is seeking to establish himself. This is a legitimate pursuit, and will quite often allude to others whom he knows or with whom he has studied, or with whom he has personal friendship or something like that. And these others, being an already established point of reference in the knowledge and consciousness of his hearers, help to establish the person speaking by association.

A. Yes. This does not necessarily discredit the other. It does not discredit the work. I do not discredit the work of another in the field of giving Life Readings. I do not know the work being done in this field by every soul. I know of some of it, and I am in the same position of this other. I have heard of others who are being developed in this work. I have heard of their work. I make no judgment of the quality of the work, of the sincerity of those working with it, of their qualifications. It's none of my business. I do not discredit them. Now you have a right to know, should a part of my work involve contact through other mediums, or through other guides.

Q. We'd be quite willing for that to be, if it should be. We don't claim a monopoly on you.

A. That's right; and frankly speaking you don't have much say in it anyway. So if plans develop in such a way that I should have this further contact, you would know of it, not only probably, but I would come through and tell you. You would hear of it from other Earth beings, but you will hear of it by my soul name and by the use of both names.

Q. Well, this helps. I have been a little bit concerned because I do know the extremely careful preparation that you and Glenn Clark and I put into Grace's development. And I am a little bit concerned when somebody – you might say with a 4th grade education in psychism (of course that's a whole lot farther than most people are) but a 4th grade education, as it were, starts into practice on the professional level. We do not allow medical doctors to practice. We do not allow a lot of surgeons to practice without pretty careful education and tests and the experience of interning.

You are becoming rather well known now and you probably will become famous during our lifetime. There already is an increasing number of people informing us that you have brought messages to them. We have mainly asked them to send us some of the messages and in every case so far we have found elements which we felt were directly contrary to some of your basic teachings. But now we have another touchstone and I can see quite a plan in this, going back twelve years or so.

A. Well, we have given you in this conversation a basic framework of reference which you are certainly free to refer to in your handling of these cases.

There is this to be said: as some of the other guides develop in the profession, let us say, of giving readings, reading the Akashic Records, it may very well be that I will have a certain part to play in their training. I may give them some guidance on occasion. We will put this into the framework that you understand it. As you know, a teacher in a classroom will occasionally have the principal walk in and sit down in the back of the room and listen to her teach. This is part of his responsibility to check up on the teacher. A substitute teacher will have an established teacher very often in the classroom who will give her a lift from time to time.

Now it may very well be that at a time when a guide is bringing a Life Reading through an Earth medium, I may, as it were, wander in and take over the reins and perhaps give a portion of the reading; and if I did so it would be as John Christopher Daniels. I would be identified in that way.

I doubt very much that anyone I worked with in that framework would report it to the Earth-beings. If it were reported, the content of the message could be checked. It might be I and it may not be I. We are not saying that this cannot happen and will not happen. In general we do not expect it to. It is simply a possibility.

Now let me give you a further illustration which will pinpoint this whole subject. Some time ago, when I was giving a Life Reading through this particular medium, I opened the door for another to give a portion of the reading. And this medium instantly recognized that other one as a well known Earth personality who is now in the discarnate realm, as one whom she knew well in Earth personality, one who was established enough in Earth-living so that if the name were given there would be thousands of people who would recognize that this well-known Earth personality was giving a reading through her.

In the first place, he wasn't. He simply wandered in and saw what was going on, and I gave him a little experience in it and then he went on. It's not his field. But he was interested in it. He tried it out; but he's not giving them. And, further-more, there was the discipline on the part of this medium not to make claims to the Earth greatness of discarnate personalities working through her; and this is a good spiritual lesson for every Earth medium.

This is one which is so often missed, that to make claims to the greatness of another is to invalidate really the genuineness of one's own medium-ship, or one's own accomplishment in any realm. To make claim to the greatness of another is the quickest way to cause people to lose confidence in what does come through any medium.

This is what we, who are teachers of others in the discarnate plane, who are going to make contact with the Earth plane, constantly emphasize to them. It is the fruit of their contact with the Earth medium rather than the identification of them, rather than the personal identification with them, which is of lasting importance.

CONTACT
A Public Reading Explaining The State of Communication in a Life Reading

This was a public reading bringing the explanation of how Dr. John uses Mrs. Wittenberger and Dr. Loehr as his primary channels. The transcript begins with Mrs. Wittenberger explaining the procedure used for introducing trance which, as most Religious Research members know, is built around a count of ten.

Grace Wittenberger: Each count represents a step in this process of moving the normal every day consciousness out of the way. The last three steps – 8 and 9 and 10, will also have a finger snap. Each finger snap is a further step in the removal of the every day consciousness.

That is what I am doing in the process of putting Franklin into the state of communication in which Dr. John can talk with you. He sometimes has something he wants to say at the start of these open question periods; but after that he will be open to questions and will be glad to handle those for you. We begin with prayer:

Unto Thee w4e turn, our Father-Mother God, and with joyous knowing that there are sources of intelligence beyond our reach, and these sources of intelligence are loving, and they are wise.
We ask now to attune to the one we know, we love, we trust, that is Dr. John.

Ready: 1-2-3-4-5-6-7-8-9-10.

Q. We ask for John. Is John here?

A. Yes, I am here. I will begin by speaking of the method of communication that we use, and illustrate three different methods of trance communication.

Lettering

Perhaps the ancient phrase "lettering" will be of significance to some of the members here; I would hope so.

In this system the information is brought one letter at a time. I will bring you now a word which will not be known to the channel as a word before I complete it. The word itself does not have any particular significance at this time. I will begin the lettering:

S-y-m-p-h-o-n-y – symphony.

This is a way we have used in teaching our two Earth expression points, the two presently incarnate members of our Council of Seven, how we can communicate with them. It helped them to understand and I trust it has helped you to understand.

It is basically the method used on Ouija Boards. Even though the Ouija can move with quite some rapidity, it still is a relatively slow method of communication.

So I will give you a second method.

Word by Word

"Word," hyphen "by" hyphen "word."

Let me give you now a sentence, no fore-glimpsing of which has been allotted to our channel – even as would be the case when this word-by-word method of psychic communication is used:

When – there – is – harmony – a – symphony - of - souls – and/or - persons - can - develop.

This method of communication is, you note, more efficient. We can get more of a message in an allotted period of time. It is a more efficient use of the particular psychic energies upon which we draw in the com-

munication state you know as trance. I would add here that the communication state we generally use would be classified as a light trance, within
which psychic energies are drawn upon as heavily as in deeper or heavier
state of trance.

We do not use either of these first two methods. Instead, we use the
method of:

Concepts

In the concept method we, as it were, strike a key and a concept, or a
sub-concept, falls into place in the communication process and is spoken
by the channel's voice mechanism.

Possibly you have seen typesetters of the old "hot lead" system in
which type is set for printing by the typesetter's fingers working a typewrit-
er-like keyboard. As he hit a key, a piece of metal carrying the appropriate
letter would fall into the slot before him, then another, and another, until
a line of type of the desired length was formed. The operator would then
check it, perhaps, space it, possibly correct it, then press a lever and this
line of metal components would move upward and sideways and more
mechanism and processes were set in motion, and then a lead "slug," an
actual line of type ready for the printing machine would be formed.

To a certain extent this is an illustration of what we mean by the concept method of psychic communication. It means I will strike a concept
key, as it were, in the mind of whichever channel I am using and that concept will fall into place to be communicated in the instance, spoken.

As a result of the extensive training and experience of my two channels, and of myself, I am now able, nearly always, to keep the concepts
flowing at the same rate as the words are spoken or written, or in the case
of personal messages, understood.

This means I must use the concept bank within the mind of the channel. I cannot press a key for a concept which is totally lacking. I would
have to resort to another and slower method of communication, two of
which I have mentioned at the start of this explanation of how I work with
Franklin and Grace. I can use sub-concepts, however; I will give you an
example, but perhaps you can see now why I will "sound" differently as I
come through the different channels and why I will prefer to use Franklin's
mind bank in preference to Grace's mind bank for scientific and general
readings, for instance.

Now I am not dependent upon finished, completed concepts, of course. If that were true I could never bring through anything new. No. I can and do use sub-concepts, and interestingly enough this is illustrated at times by the occasional grammatical error found in my messages. I may strike the key, for instance, for the concept or sub-concept "There is a" – and it is spoken. Then if the next word begins with a consonant, as is usually the case with words, everything is grammatically correct, such as "There is a new idea I want to bring."

This is not only the cause for the occasional grammatical error found but also it is an evidential of the honesty and truthfulness of any communications through these channels. It is not simply "the sub-conscious mind of the medium" speaking in my name. They wouldn't make such a mistake. And I don't either. It is the "concept method" of communication which produces these few significant anomalies. Do I make myself clear? I have not quite clarified it for some.

It has been said, especially when I have come through Franklin, "Well that sounds more like Franklin speaking than Dr. John."

A more and longtime observer would say, "Franklin is sounding more like Dr. John each year as he does through life."

After all, he and I are from the same soul and share its nature as well as its purpose in this and other incarnations and other expressions. He and I have lived and worked consciously together since he first came into the consciousness of psychical realms in 1948. Because of the close rapport, especially with Franklin but also with Grace, with who she and her soul-mate and I are very close, it has been possible for us who guard and guide them, and Religious Research, to establish a continuing rapport with them, a mode of thinking, if you will, whereby we can reach them – usually easily and quickly – without taking them into a trance state of communication.

The tone of voice used in the trance communications, such as this one, is more characteristically that of the channel then any tone or timbre or resonance of voice that might characteristically be mine. In fact, as I dwell customarily in a realm where words are not spoken, I do not have a characteristic tone or quality of Earth voice. In this realm vibrations of thought are not spoken in what you know as Earth sound – vibration in the air falling upon an eardrum. Vibrations of thought are perceived, in other words, in our realm. We are not limited to ears and that receptive mechanism. So what would the tone of my voice be? Some may expect a different tone of voice. Perhaps I should be more impressive. But please excuse me if I do not bother with those trappings. There is, of course, such a thing in psychic phenomena known as "independent voice." Please do not expect it from me. That would require a great deal more psychic energy, the use of which would be rather non-productive for simple communication purposes.

Will you please release the channel, Grace?

✛ ✛ ✛

Once you have attuned to the world of spirit beyond your own consciousness, the world represented by departed love ones, the world represented by ascended masters, the world represented by angel beings, some of the power of those realms becomes yours, and you are lighted. 8133:1:6

✛ ✛ ✛

A. In operating the mechanisms of medium-ship from the astral plane we must accommodate ourselves even as the medium must be prepared. This is a principle of psychic communication and this is why some genuine psychics have very poor quality guides.

There is a compatibility on the soul level between the medium and the guide. (This "on the soul level" is a rather general statement, meaning more a matter of spiritual attunement of guide and channel). This is a vibrational matter, or as you would perhaps prefer to say, a matter of correlated energy patterns. The word "homogenous" was used in the Reading, not because it is the best word but because it was a word which could very quickly express the situation.

"Vibrational attunement" may be compared to your "scrambler and un-scrambler" methods of protecting communication. With us it is not a matter of protecting a communication, not a matter of a code which only the proper ones could decode and hence read. With us it is rather that we must be able to set up a sympathetic vibration or a resonance between the sender and the receiver; hence if a chord on Earth is stretched to produce an "A" sound, then if we can produce a correlative "A" on the astral plane, and in close astral proximity to the Earth chord, that Earth chord will vibrate to our "A."

It is true that certain other vibrations will produce nodule vibrations but these are not as accurate which is why some psychics pick up messages which contain inaccuracies. Too many psychic message inaccuracies are produced by inadequacies in the Earth medium, but also an incomplete attunement of the sending and receiving is a factor. 12-21-0'66-3

Q. How would you go about working with those Earthlings who were assigned to you as your Earth partners?

A. We have certain difficulties even before we come to the individual. I should not say difficulties, but requirements. It is not a difficulty to put a car into gear; it is not a difficulty to start an engine to run, but there are requirements before the car itself can be put into motion. There are prior requirements, certain things which must be done before we can establish any work with those on Earth.

One such prior requirement is that we must establish an anchorage in space. We who are not confined by space must learn how to operate at certain points in space. For this we must establish, as it were, anchors, or buoys, in space. These are not only identification points in space but points to which we can tie-up, can make a contact which, in turn, will hold us to that point in space for such time as we should work with that point in space.

How is this done? Emotions are an anchorage. If an emotion is centered at a point (that is, in a person with whom we work) it can then act as a beacon, as a homing radio signal if you will, and as a magnetic attraction whereby we can find that point, "lock onto it" to use your radar terminology, and also be held to it as by a gravitational force. So an investment of love is made in those persons who are the Earth points through whom you will be working.

Now let me clear my terminology. I have been using the word "you" to indicate what you would do if you were in our place. Of course I am also teaching a number whom you Earth partners do not see but who are attending this lesson and demonstration. These emotions are established as beacons and as anchorage points for us as we work from this side with those persons on Earth.

Workers from our side must learn the procedures that work, too. It is recognized here that instruction is needed, even as it is needed on each and every plane of consciousness for the consciousness to be expanded and for learning to take place. Since I have had a certain amount of instruction and experience in making these Earth contacts, one of my functions here is, somewhat, to teach classes and, somewhat, to teach teachers in this realm the things which I have been taught, and which I have learned. Then we all must learn from experience concerning making contact with Earthlings.

To establish this point in space we plant a person there, where we want him or her. Our space anchorage on Earth is a person on Earth. The emotion which gives us that homing beacon, that lock-on point, is the love (usually love, though not always) which we have for that person and that person has for us. This draws us to him or her and thus identifies that point in space where we are to work, and to bring about those functions which are ours to bring about from time to time in the realm of space-lings.

Also, it goes without saying, we must not only lock onto a point in space, we must also lock onto a moving point in time, that point which you Earth-lings call 'the present.' Once we have locked onto a person, an incarnate egoic-personality, we have locked onto the moving point of the present in the dimension of time. So once again the personal contact is, you see, the key.

Now the larger question: Once our anchorage is secured, and having familiarized ourselves well with the functional techniques of thus making entrance into time and space (and that is somewhat as a surgeon making an incision into a body) we then come to the matter of the individual who is our person in space. That person is a being, an entity in his or her own rights; and those rights must be respected. Also, we must work with individuals as individuals. I am bringing from the stand-point of one who can see that which is not seen on your side, information concerning the emotional boundaries, the emotional 'skin,' the outer limits and state of the emotional body of the individual.

This will illustrate the difficulties we do have. We never quite know what the exact response will be, even with those with whom we have worked for quite a long while – although with them, of course, we are more familiar with reactions than we are with whom we have not worked before. But even after long years of working together we will still at times run into a reaction of a little different nature, or of a different quality, of a different degree of intensity, than we had expected. We must work with each one as an individual being. Responses which we wish are implanted in a personality by karmic conditioning, by heredity factors, by the psychological conditioning of the environment of the present lifetime, and specific training and preparation.

Now not always are these responses deliberately implanted or produced. We also work with such responses as are within the individual from other sources and causes. We can utilize, when we learn how, practically every motivation or motivational possibility within a personality. If a person wishes to be rich, for instance, then that person may be reached with at least a certain rudimentary spiritual concept through the mental-ism of modern metaphysics, the 'think and grow rich' approach.

If a person is ill and comes to the time, as many are led through illness, of a very real desire for health, and perhaps a rather frightened realization that there must be some changes made, this can be used for the clearing of emotions and the combating of negatives and evils within the mind. If a person is committed in a very real spiritual consecration, then a high door is opened to that person, and high forces can reach that person and can reach that person on a high level. It does not mean that the committed person has life easy. It does mean that the committed person can be led through deeper valleys than the uncommitted can safely experience.

One of the basic ways of course in which we do reach Earth is by taking some of our own team members, some of those who are on our own level, and letting these receive all the training which we can procure for them, and preparation in counsel with us so that the full wisdom of the group is available unto them. Then they come into incarnation to bring this wisdom and knowledge, even as the Son of God came incarnate to bring the greatest wisdom and knowledge the world has yet received of God and of the true nature of mankind. These individuals then are brought to incarnation to carry the wisdom which we have and which we can procure.

Now you note I use the phrase twice, 'which we can procure.'

Perhaps you wonder at that phrase. You may ask, 'Why? Are you limited in the wisdom you can get for those who are to come as your emissaries?'

Yes, we are limited. We are all limited in several ways. We can receive and hold only that which is 'glimpsed,' is not yet received and held. But the statement was made as it was, deliberately, because when something is glimpsed, then we can gradually grow into a larger comprehension of it and a greater hold upon it. 8122:16

After the Life Reading abilities of this personality expressing as Grace

Wittenberger were perceived and recognized, it took four and one half years of development before they actually were used in the service of the other-side and in the service of Earth people. 2560:3

A talk between Dr. John and Dr. Franklin Loehr given in a Reading at the Research Center in Los Angeles, California, April 21, 1961.

Medium: Grace Wittenberger

Q. One thing that has puzzled me is the fact that I have done so little reading in these fields.

Now here we are giving Life Readings, and I have read almost nothing beyond half of *Many Mansions*; and I have read *There Is A River* and *The World Within*; but I have read very little of the Edgar Cayce reports that have come out. I have read almost nothing in metaphysics.

We are in the occult field and although we have the Alice Bailey books and many others, I have not read them. And yet the information that is coming directly, falls right in line with these books and is quite a validation.

I have seen that significance before. Also, the fact that there has not been the rather rigid preconception that could come from book study and book learning – as we call it – would mean that my mind was more open to receive directly from the research and from inspiration.

A. Right.

Q. Why wasn't the same method used as was used in the Edgar Cayce readings?

A. Because it is beyond; it takes in a greater awareness of cosmic truth than is possible when one has a closer-in, less-wide perspective. So it is quite natural and to be expected that the teachings brought in the Grace Wittenberger Readings are not the teachings of the Cayce Readings. Grace is not a repeat, or a carbon copy, in her psychic and spiritual work of Edgar Cayce. They represent different sources of cosmic contacts for quite different purposes. 3841:8

The first pioneer in this work of giving Life Readings, Edgar Cayce, presented a framework, which got results; and it was very natural that those who studied the Cayce work expect that the framework which got results at one time should continue to get results. The pattern was:

"You will have before you the body of - - - - - - - - - - who was born in - - - - - - - - - -. You will give the relation of this entity to the universe and the universal forces, giving the conditions that are as personalities latent and exhibited in the present life; also, the former appearances in the Earth plane, giving time, place, name, and that which built or retarded the development for the entity, giving the abilities of the present entity and that to which it may attain and how."

This framework of approach to a Life Reading with Grace will not get the desired results. A very major reason for this is that in such a presentation as, "You will have the entity before you, you will do this, you will do that, etc.," the conductor is speaking to the medium. Now he may be speaking to the subconscious mind, but he is speaking to the medium and the medium then must respond to that direction.

Edgar Cayce responded to that direction. He responded in several ways. He responded by reading the Akashic Records as seen in the astral plane. He responded by projecting himself to the individual getting the reading and making contact with that individual and reading the aura. To some extent, on occasion, he responded by coming into a psychical contact with the guide or teacher who knew the other person. That was a much less frequent way of response than the first two mentioned.

Now the entire training and direction of this Earth instrument, Grace Wittenberger, has been in another manner. This medium was not trained to respond to such direction. She does not have the degree of psychic openness in-channeled into these particular frameworks of reading the Akashic Records in the astral plane of making contact and reading the aura. She does have more training – or let us say – more responsiveness in making contact with a guide and teacher of the individual who can tell her about the individual. But the latter way is a way which to the extent it is used is used by the training of her by those of us on our side rather than her Earth training. 3093:2-3

As I work with her consciousness, I use a portion of the consciousness available to me and we create a certain joint consciousness which is hers and mine only, and not really to the tapped into from another angle, another person, another approach.

This is the way it works, and consciousness is not very well understood by humans or even by souls. This is an area to be explored, developed, in which much learning is to be done, even as the matters of physical matter being-ness and of spiritual, immaterial being-ness. 8028:5

She is in this particular service of the Life Readings, operating, expressing in Earth living as a psychic. She is working on and with the psychic realm. But she came into the psychic realm as a result of her emphasis on spiritual growth. The psychic realm, as a place of operation, was opened to her through her prayer work, through her hours of meditation in part.

There are other forces also that opened up the psychic realm to her; but we are concentrating our attention on the fact of the spiritual development which led to the psychic openness. 2236:7

Out of this creative mettle I will contact with her and work with her and she with me as being-ness of itself, between the two of us, which in one sense is not even available to me excepting with her. Is this understandable?

In coming through when the instrument is given over to me completely, then that which is built, is largely mine and my conscious direction and understanding; but the bridge is a different bridge. You take one bridge from Venice, let us say, and it will take you to a certain place. You take another bridge to a different place. So there is a bridge from me to Grace. There is a bridge from me to Franklin, and each is a different bridge. It is how I reach different places. When the instrument is totally given to me I am brought across that bridge with that which I bring. 8028:5

Now when the Life Readings are asked for, when they are set in motion, the conductor of them is talking directly to a guide, a teacher on the other side, not to Grace.

The one you know as my-self, Dr. John Christopher Daniels, you are asking me to present this Life Reading. Now I do so majorly by reading the Akashic Records; but I do not read them as they reflect in the astral plane. I read them from a different plane of consciousness. I can and often do contact the guides and teachers of the one getting the reading. I can if I so choose, and I do on occasion, give permission for the medium to make an auric or psychic contact with the individual. I give permission because long ago I was given permission by the medium to work with her in this way. So the medium can make contact with the person asking for the reading if I, to whom she has given the major control of her mind and her being-ness in this work, give consent.

Long ago, when the Readings were being established and you, as conductor, were trying out many different approaches. At that time you needed to be persuaded of:

1) My reality of being-ness,
2) My ability,
3) My authority,
4) My knowledge.

Then there came a time when I asked you if you were persuaded concerning me in these four areas, and you said yes.

I said to you at that point, "That is fine. From this point on I will take control. I will do the work. If there is testing and proving to be done, I will do the testing. I will do the proving."

And therefore, with all due respect to the very fine gentleman, I will not follow these directions in giving a Life Reading.

We are pleased this question is asked for it has given us the opportunity to say that which has just been said as an answer to other people. We suggest you make a record of this. 3093:3

Q. Why didn't Edgar Cayce give the teaching on the soul dividing into a feminine half and a masculine half when it comes into Earth living?

A. The answer to that has to do both with the medium and with the source of the teaching. First of all, let us point out, that in the Edgar Cayce Readings the procedure was not that of Edgar Cayce being used in a major sense as a channel of communication. The psychic abilities and qualities and temperament of that personality made it possible for him to step into a portion of his larger self, the soul self, and move away from the Earth plane into another plane of communication, into an aspect of the astral plane.

From there the personality in tune with the soul aspect had a wider view than the personality confined to the incarnate level of being. From that operational point, the larger being-ness could make contact with the physical beings of others, as he did in the physical diagnostic work. He could look upon the reflections of the Akashic Records as they would be read from that plane of being beyond the incarnate plane.

We have previously pointed out these approaches to the Akashic Records, as they can be made from the incarnate plane, as they approach, can be made from planes of being even beyond the astral. We do not use our medium, or do not allow her to give expression to her psychic being-ness in the pattern which Edgar Cayce gave.

As she temporarily takes leave of physical three dimensional consciousness in preparation for the Reading, she does not go to the physical being-ness of the person for whom she is working, nor does she go to a plane of insight where she can look upon the Akashic Records. She does not read the Akashic Records. We believe this has been emphasized in the teachings. Rather, she is taken over and used by those of us who are operating in a dimension, a plane of being-ness, over and beyond the astral plane. We use her as our telephone instrument, if you will, for carrying on our report, our conversation with the conductor who is asking the questions for the reading on the Earth plane.

From the plane in which we operate, we have an insight and an experience which would be different from another plane of operation. We have knowledge and insight into the cosmic pattern and scheme, gained from our experience and learning from this point of view. This teaching, therefore, comes from our perspective, which is beyond the immediate physical and astral plane of being-ness. 3841:7-8

There is also the matter of credentialing. The Edgar Cayce Readings, which I respect – that is the Life Readings – were credentialed by the Physical Readings brought through that source. The Physical Readings could be tested, could be proved. The fact that they could be, then credentialed Edgar Cayce and those who worked with him, as a trustworthy source.

That does not prove the Life Readings that came from him but it does prove that whatever else came from him, in addition to the Physical Readings, deserved a hearing. They were credentialed by their source.

In Religious Research we have credentialed our work we feel by our extensive research project into the influence of prayer upon plant life. This could be proved. It was proved again and again by others who replicated our work; and this credentialed the Religious Research source for the Life Readings which we believe to be a much more important aspect of our work.

Finally there are certain proofs. One of the more popular forms of proof in psychic work is what is called the cross-correspondence test, where things over here, in position 'A,' check with things over here, in position 'B.'

This has happened almost innumerable times in our Readings, as person 'A' got a Reading in which person 'A' was identified in some way or other, and then sometime later person 'B' possibly from a different part of the world or from a separation of years, got a Reading and the same truth was brought out. They corresponded with each other. 7396:27

Q. When a Life Reading is given does the soul generally share in the knowledge that it has been given and what it contains?

A. The portion of the soul incarnate with the personality generally does know. Now there is a difference in the way, or to the extent, than that knowing portion of the soul is hooked up, or hooked into, the larger soul being-ness, the larger soul individuality. In other words, the portion of the soul incarnate in personality-living may have knowledge separate from the total soul being-ness. It may have knowledge which does not become absorbed into the total soul being-ness until the personality life is completed.

The total soul being-ness does not have knowledge of the lack in the personality life as produced by that portion of the soul incarnate. If it did have knowledge, it would rush right in to give support. The individual soul intelligence connected with the personality is having this called to the attention through the device of the reading and through the continuing awareness which can be injected now by the personality intelligence. 4022:22

Q. What is the major purpose of a Life Reading according to Dr. John?

A. He agrees that although a major purpose of a Life Reading is to gain self-understanding, it is also intended to make the person live this life better.

Q. What is the general philosophy of the reason for a Life Reading?

A. How do you know where you are, and where you are going, if you do not know where you have been? How do you know you are going North unless you know which way is South, East or West?

Q. To what does this philosophy apply?

A. This applies to relationships as well as personality forces and life situations.

Q. What is the second major purpose of the Life Readings?

A. The second purpose is the more major one, which is the body of spiritual teachings being issued to Earth.

Q. To what may you compare the bulk of the Life Readings done by Grace and Franklin?

A. The wisdom taught in the Readings has been brought forth primarily in the same way as the Bible – which is the long story of people, how they lived, what happened to them, what they did, what worked in their lives, and what things did not work. The spiritual teachings in the Bible and in the Life Readings are life-centered.

Q. What are some of the things that Life Readings were never meant to be used for?

A. Life Readings are not used to find lost wills, gold mines, or relatives, nor for fortune telling, messages from departed loved one, suggested gems or metals or colors to wear nor for physicals diagnosis or treatment.

Q. How are the Readings kept confidential?

A. The research copies of the transcripts are kept under lock and key and available only to staff researchers of the Religious Research Foundation. Even the names of those getting Readings are not given out unless the person:

1) Gives special permission to use his/her name.
2) He or she publicly tells of having the Reading.

In the Readings and excerpts from Readings carried in reports and pamphlets and books, and in general research copies – which are then microfilmed – all distinctive identifying materials, names, dates, places, etc., are changed. This is one reason astrologers have had difficulty working with the published reports, for birth dates given are not the real birth date of the person getting the Reading.

Q. Who is the conductor of a Life Reading?

A. The conductor is the one who acts as your representative in the Life Reading. The more your conductor knows what you want your Reading to cover, the more intelligently he or she can represent you. The conductor studies your material and organizes it for presentation.

Q. What does a person getting a Life Reading do in preparation for it?

A. The person instructs his or her conductor in what the reading is to cover by means of:

1) A life sketch, outlining the important persons and events in their life, and why they are important.

2) The questions he/she wishes asked.

3) A brief person-sheet introducing each of the nine persons whose past-life acquaintances (if any) he wishes covered in the Life Reading.

Q. Why is it important to write a detailed life sketch when the information is to be read from the Akashic Records?

A. We will explain the purpose of the asking for a life sketch for the Reading.
It is not needful. We ask for a life sketch for two reasons. First of all

it is important in the framework of helping the client see himself in the particular framework of personality being-ness. For that it is the jumping off point for our service of helping the personality to see him-self as a soul. The personality has the inside perspective on himself, one might say, as being the one in Earth living.

The Akashic Records give the outside perspective, the larger view of the soul that is having the experience of being a personality. In my service of reading them I am not in tune specifically with the personality. I am not in touch, as for instance, excarnate guides and teachers are. Excarnate spirits are closely attuned with Earth personalities. I am not. It is not particularly needed for me to be in order to read the Akashic Records. 3847:2

In the framework of preparing for a Life Reading, the personality is asked to review his life, to look upon the patterns of growth, the areas of success, the areas of failure. This is a judgment experience which the personality undergoes in the framework of being prepared to understand the nature of its contribution to the soul. It is, if you will, a judgment upon the personality coming during the personality's incarnate life, while there is yet opportunity to increase the activity of the personality of the soul.

If all of the judgment upon the personality waited until the completion of the personality's contribution in incarnate living, the personality would not have the opportunity to add to its contribution as it does, as the judgment is made, as the personality goes along at different stages in the personality life. This is the grace of God blending with the will of God, requiring a judgment upon the personality for what it has contributed to the soul entity. 4131:10

It is helpful if the person has particular questions in the areas of likes and dislikes, in the area of dreams and ambitions. It is helpful if those are known so that I can, in a specific way, review the Akashic Records to trace out those soul qualities and those soul interests and the soul experiences as gained in previous lifetimes to see if there be a tie-in on the soul level with the present personality's specific interests or problems.

Not all of what is recorded in the Akashic Records is brought forth in a given reading. There is a process of picking and choosing. This is not done by my deliberation or choice. Some of it is done by excarnate guides and teachers who are specifically responsible for helpfulness to the Earth-being.

The suggestion that a life sketch induces the ability, either on the part of the medium or on the part of myself, to invent a story which fits, we think, has already been adequately spoken to by the fact of some thirty-eight hundred teachings already given, all of which have been recorded, all of which are open for study; and we feel we are quite safe in saying that no two of the entire body of Life Readings are alike. There is an individuality of soul being-ness; and because of that element of individuality it is quite impossible for the reading of the Akashic Records for one to fit the Akashic Records reading of another.

In the early years of training of this medium, a number of Readings were given with only the name and the birth date being given. A research into the files will indicate that these Readings gave specific helpfulness. But in comparison with the Readings of these latter years the early Readings are quite sketch in detail. They were adequate for the purpose of answering the immediate questions and problems of those getting the Readings. They were adequate for the testing and probing framework in which the Readings were first given.

The medium, her-self, needed to be convinced of the authenticity of her medium-ship; and my work as the source of the Readings had to be tested and proved. This was a demand and need on the part of Earth beings to which I, and those who worked with me, gave our-selves most willingly. But helping individuals in the framework of a Life Reading is not and never has been the major purpose for which these Life Readings were established. 3847:3

We have always been willing and desirous of lending a helping hand to Earth beings, for Earth represents a very strenuous experience. Our major purpose in establishing the Grace Wittenberger/Franklin Loehr Readings has been to bring through a certain body of spiritual knowledge. This body of spiritual knowledge, the cosmic principles and understanding, could be elucidated and clearly delineated by illustrations drawn from the actual life situations which incarnate souls experience.

These principles, this particular body of knowledge, could have been brought through in a framework of sacred theology divinely revealed. The book of Mormons was so brought and contains many principles of cosmic truth. That is but one illustration.

As we have said, that was not our purpose or desire. It was felt that there have been enough bodies of spiritual knowledge established for Earth beings in that particular way. We were interested in sending our helpfulness to the Earth plane in a way of sharing our spiritual knowledge by following essentially the process in which the principles of spiritual life as recorded in the whole Bible was established.

We would point out that those principles were established within the framework of a group of souls in a long period of Earth history having particular experiences from which the spiritual laws were drawn and by which the spiritual laws were illustrated. This is the framework we have used.

The Life Readings are people based. They are life-centered; but again, we repeat, that for the helpfulness of the individual they are secondary; for the establishment and increase of spiritual knowledge upon the Earth they are primary. This is the reason which perhaps will help you into a somewhat greater understanding. 3847:4

Q. What kind of people qualify for a Life Reading?

A. Life Readings are for people who accept that there is a continuing life after death of the Earth body, a purpose for their lives from before they were born, and that there is a God who cares.

Q. Why haven't people learned earlier about the Readings?

A. There is a cosmic guidance brought in concern to these Readings. Those who come for Readings are quite definitely guided to have them, and guided to them when those on the other-side feel that it's the right time. 2083:17

The people who are brought for Life Readings are selected for this. There were two purposes in the Readings. One is the assistance that the past life history and present life placement and purpose of the soul can bring to the present incarnation personhood on Earth now in understanding itself and its purposes, and living its life to the best. This purpose has its own integrity which I always observe. 7120:1

The second purpose is to bring through for researchers and students of the Readings, as well as for the persons getting the Readings, a fuller knowledge of what the soul is, how it operates in incarnations, and somewhat in ex-carnations and other realms, and what the plan of God is, embracing souls and persons and Earth and the material realm and spiritual realms and other forms of life. 7120:2

The incarnate human being is an interaction between two dissimilar realms of being. One is the soul, which is a spiritual form of life and is native to spirit and not to matter. By 'spiritual' here, I refer to the functional and the first definitive meaning of spiritual, which is simply that it is non-physical and non-material. Earthlings occupy, very frankly, material and physical universes but the soul occupies a very non-material and non-physical universe.

The second major component of the human being is the physical portion, which is an Earth animal which has been adjusted, or purposefully evolved, for the role of interaction with a soul to produce a person. The Earth animal part partakes of the unique nature of Earth, as well as the physical realm. 7120:3

Some persons are selected for Readings because they are at that stage in their soul development where a pertinent teaching can be brought. I am always glad for these. I tell you that even after we have given the Readings we have contemplated there still will be teachings of God which have not been brought. 7454:6

There is a lot of activity behind the scenes in the giving of these Readings. There are many guides and teachers in the planes of activity from which I operate many guides and teachers of Earth beings. Many of these guides and teachers are very eager that their Earth charges be given the opportunity of a greater understanding of the purposes of their being and of their walk in Earth living.

There are many machinations that have their origin in these planes beyond the Earth plane to bring an Earth personality into position to create that urge and outreach which results in the personality writing a letter and putting it in an envelope and sending it off as an application for a reading. When an application is set in motion, there is continued activity on behalf of that personality by his guides and teachers in these planes of operation to help that personality carry through. Because those guides and teachers see that the personality is at a point of readiness to do something. 3893:8

Life Readings are not in the psychic field. They make use of the psychic but they are not clairvoyant Readings. They do not bring in messages from departed loved ones; they do not bring through messages from guides and teachers except as those messages are given in what we called a 'round table discussion,' which takes place between the guides and teachers of the person getting the Reading; and the agent who reads the Akashic Records are beings through the Life Readings, which is the one herein speaking.

Life Readings are not basically in the pattern of a psychic reading, as some personalities expect a psychic reading to be. It is very important that a personality understands this because this in itself is cosmically designed as a way for the personality and that portion of the soul, through the personality, to take another step in spiritual growth, which is in a field allied with, but not centered in, the psychic world. 577:3

Q. Is it fair to have the advantage of knowing one's past lives and having the opportunity to correct it? Is it a bribe to throw the game of karma?

A. We think what we have brought automatically answers that in the negative. That is an affirmative negative. Yes, it is fair to know; and no it is not a bribe.

Q. I know how in the Bible it urges us to get knowledge and understanding. The Master said, "You know the truth and the truth shall set you free."

A. Yes, but with all the getting of knowledge, get wisdom! In other words, unless you do something with these Readings other than simply reading it over and having the information, you won't gain very much.

"With all thy knowledge get thee wisdom." 3220:24

Q. Can a Reading be given for an un-born baby?

A. As soon as the soul has come into the Earth plane and has assumed a body, a personality, a Reading can be given. If the doors of remembrance are wide open to that soul, it might question, "Why should these Earth beings know about me and my past?" This is if it is a young soul just starting Earth living. When the doors of remembrance have closed to the extent that they do close as a soul comes into Earth living, then more can be done.

Now this does not mean that there could never be a Reading given before the soul came into Earth expression. But it is an individual soul matter. It is very probable that where there is coming into the Earth plane a very old soul, or a soul of quite a lot of Earth development, or who has been in Earth very recently with remembrance of what it is like, such a soul probably would not have reservations. Indeed, the giving of a Reading for a soul that has not come in could be a very useful thing – not alone for the handling and training of the personality but where you have coming a soul in a service life or with a particular message, the seeds of the message could be planted; the way in part could be cleared. There could be a preparation for that soul made by bringing through a Reading. 840:2

Q. How long has the plan for the Life Readings been in progress?

A. I, Dr. John, have been preparing for this job for 4,000 years. Grace Wittenberger volunteered for the job and was trained many years in this life, as well as many past lives, for this work now.

Q. Why have certain ones singled out to receive Life Readings?

A. There is a psychic guidance and direction given for those who should have Life Readings. There are, of course, many guides and teachers on the excarnate plane of life who are responsible for the guidance and direction of their Earth personality charges. They are aware of the various cosmic influences which can be helpful to Earth beings – the Life Readings area being one. Many of them do guide and direct their Earth charges into contact with this area of counsel, and when that direction is given, although the material which I bring through is majorly that which I read from the Akashic Record of the soul, it is also true that I am in contact with the guides and teachers of the Earth beings. To some extend I am guided by their judgment on what would be helpful for their Earth charges to receive through the means of a reading. 2943:14

We do not go into a more complete explanation of the other realms because the tool Earth beings have to comprehend these other realms is limited. The human mind simply does not have the scope of intelligence to comprehend being-ness in other realms. It is a state of being-ness very different from being-ness in Earth living. Earth beings are having a hard enough time understanding themselves as Earth beings. So not having the mind tool of comprehension, we simply say there are these other realms of experience.

When we say 'we,' who do I mean by 'we?'

I am speaking of that which I see in regard to the particular Earth personality by what I read in the Akashic Records, the etheric records of that person as a soul.

Much of the information I bring through I have had given to me by his or her own teachers and guides, who have his/her welfare and growth under their care in cooperation with his or her own soul. And because much of this information comes from them, this is why I use the 'we' form. We are bringing through information from combined sources of intelligence, not from simply one source. 2194:6

Now another reason: In these Readings we do not go into much explanation of these other realms.

What do we mean by them?

Where are they?

What are the experiences a soul has in them?

There is a twofold purpose why we do not go into this. In the first place we feel that our particular point of helpfulness that we have to make to the earth beings we contact through our medium here is:

1) To help that Earth being find him or her-self in the particular framework in which they are living at this time. The very fact that he/she is in Earth living means that Earth is the important framework of learning at this time.

2) To know about the other realms and where it is going is all very interesting; but the growing edge for the soul having the experience of the present lifetime is the present life. And so we center our teachings upon that. 2194:5

In the Life Readings we have not focused attention upon the soul's beginnings in that framework, specifically because the purpose of a Reading is to give the history of the soul's Earth experience incidental to the soul's present place in Earth. There are many sources of origin for individual soul consciousness. When we speak of other cosmic schools of experience, we use that as a rather general term to indicate that the soul's individual being-ness had origin other than its beginning in the planet Earth. But we do not stress that teaching specifically, as we have indicated, because of our intent to focus upon the importance of Earth living. 4002:7

Now in preparing for these Readings we prepare on this side of life. We check up on the Akashic Records, and we also meet with the guides and teachers of the one having the Reading to determine from them what they wish, according to their responsibility for guidance of this one who is in Earth. They want to come to the conscious attention and knowledge of the personality. 2455:3

When we are prepared for the Reading – and by 'we' I include the spiritual guides of the person; and I speak of the guides as 'spiritual guides' to make a distinction between excarnate personalities who love and guide and protect their loved ones in Earth, and the soul guides, those soul entities operating in realms other than the excarnate personality realm who have a linkage with the soul of incarnate personalities and who thus might be termed 'soul guides and teachers' as distinguished from 'personality guides and teachers'; although, of course, the soul guidance encompasses, to some degree, the personality guidance as well.

Therefore, when I speak that we are prepared, I refer to, in your Earth terms, a meeting which has already taken place on the part of my-self with the soul guides, a meeting which has determined much of the soul information which is to be brought. I am the spokesperson for the group because I have the open door for Earth communication to this instrument. 3665:2

In reading of the Akashic Records we do not read the personality's aura. We do not use astrology. We do not use numerology. These things are all valid; they are all good; they can be used; but primarily the framework for these Life Readings is the acceptance by us of the personality identification through names, relationships with other people, interests, resources, attitudes, spiritual aspirations, and the linking up through the personality identification with the Akashic Records of the soul that is having the experience of the present personality pointing out how the factors within the personality life, of interests, of talents, of relationships, of attitudes and aspirations, fit into the soul's cosmic being and to what the soul has learned in past lives.

Moving on then - from that point to those constructive suggestions for the personality which will carry the soul's learning in this lifetime, a step, or general steps, further along.

This is a pretty good explanation of what the Life Readings are and why they are the way they are. 577:4

The Three Main Steps for a Reading

1) I look first for the gender of the half-soul from which this incarnation comes. The whole soul does not have incarnations. The whole soul operates in other realms; it does not operate in the Earth realm; it does not have personal expression or experience. It has individual expression and experience and it operates in other realms, as I have said. But it is the half soul which comes into incarnations, comes into vital living association with an animal body. It is the half soul that makes the Earth beings. The half souls are the masculine and the feminine, that being the particular polarization of the whole soul for incarnation purposes, and of course, whether the present incarnation is from the native or non-native gender expression is one of the significant factors that I look for in helping a client to understand his or her incarnate lifetime.

2) The next thing I look for is what is generally called the age of the soul. The soul is really only the first stage in the spiritual progression of this particular type in individuated God-being-ness. After that comes the stage of Cohesion, the stage of Elohim, the stage of the Mini-Creators, and then for those who make it, the stage of the Co-Creator with God.

In the soul stage we again have, for the sake of convenience, seven stages – well, three major divisions:

a) The young soul,
b) The middle soul,
c) The old soul.

I divide the young soul into two sub stages: the 'just beginning' and the 'well started.'

I divide the old soul into two stages: the 'well along' and the 'nearing the end' – because there are significant differences in each of these particular levels within the larger classification of young soul or old soul.

In the middle soul, sixty percent - by rough rule of thumb of the Earth experiences - the incarnations take place. Here is where the real growing is done. The young soul is just getting acquainted with Earth. The old soul swings more into a service orientation. It is the middle soul that has the great karmic lives. I do not mean retribution. I mean learning, learning by the cause and effect framework, which is the framework of incarnate and of personal experience.

3)   The third thing I look for is the placement of the present life. In other words, just where is the soul at present in its progression? And what is the present incarnation supposed to do in the growth of the soul in its progression? So this is the map of the larger purposes of the present incarnation.

These three items I usually give, as you know conductor, and as those who have read of our reports and in our books will know I usually give in the forepart of the Reading. Then we ask for the persons of whom the client is inquiring. Here I get the name and the identification, the birth date and place. 7447:2

Q. How do you know the other people are involved in the past lives of the person the Reading is for?

A. For those who have had past lives with the one the Reading is for, my customary way of working is through the name. The name is attached to a definite person, and with this I can scan the Akashic Records of the one getting the Reading to see if this other name strikes a lighted point, a lighted crossover, at any position. A bell would ring. A contact would be made, something of that sort. But if this is not done, I do not believe there is a connection from past life experiences together or from cosmic relationship. 7345:14

There are many ways of getting the names. We can go to the clairvoyant level and pick up the name from there. We do not like to do so because in working with the Akashic Records, as we have stated, we are not on the clairvoyant level. We are on a different level of work. We can send our medium on the clairvoyant level to get the name. This takes psychic energy on the medium's part that, then, we do not have available. 2762:4

The reaching out to find particular channels of truth that suits its growing edge, and then to study that truth and use it in every possible way to bring about its own growth, to expand, is something for many souls to do. The trouble is, when it does that, the soul becomes crystallized, becomes stuck in the particular study of the moment.

So we offer a different channel of truth, one of cosmic principles. Here is the opportunity for the personality to contribute to the growth of the soul and to have the joy and the excitement of learning something unique. Our pattern is different from that which it is accustomed to studying in other ways. 2455:3-4

Q. One thing I've appreciated is the fact that neither you, nor the others from the other-side working with us, claim to be either God or God's only channels for truth and guidance. 3059:11

A. Life Readings through this channel have been given over a period of years. Throughout those years there has been a witness given to the usefulness of them in the framework of individuals who find that, at the time they received their Reading, it is helpful. Ten years from that time – or two, or seven – the individual re-reads the Reading and states that it is more helpful than in the beginning; that the Reading has something in it that it didn't have the first time.

Now what has happened? It is the same Reading. The reading in content has not changed. The comprehension to the Reading has changed by the expansion of consciousness taking place in the individual over a given number of years. On a much bigger scale and a much deeper scale, this illustrates the validity of the life-centered teachings of universal truths in the Bible for those who recorded them at the time of recording, and for those who read them in these times. 3931:20

The definition of the soul identification portion of a Life Reading is channeled by the pooling of certain energies of the cosmic intelligence identified as Dr. John, with the certain energies of another cosmic intelligence relating to the person's soul. This combination of energies forms a cosmically temporary identity through whom this information, gathered together from the two parent cosmic intelligences, can then be given verbal expression, and a reality of presence through this channel. This, then, is the completion of the portion of the Reading, identified as 'the soul identification.'

For the purposes and the interest of personality researchers, as this conclusion is reached, the temporary cosmic identity, birthed by the joining together of Dr. John with the person-soul's teacher, dissolves, and Dr. John continues with the reading of the Akashic Records in the usual format. 4186:4

We would point out that in the Life Readings we work with the Akashic Records of the soul of which the given Earth personality may be expressing only one portion. At the time of the Reading we are not necessarily in touch and transmitting the ideas and thoughts and considerations of the Earth-being's teachers and guides.

Our job is to handle questions within the framework of the Akashic Records, you might say, God's Book of Remembrance of this individual soul.

In preparing for a Reading the guides and teachers are frequently consulted; but in the Reading itself my particular contribution of helpfulness to Earth-beings is that of reading the records. 3111:3

We have been endeavoring to expand the consciousness of personalities in the realization of the true nature of the soul, of how it is not simply a possession, a mysterious something which connects the personality with God.

The soul is a being. It is an entity, individualized, and in and of itself separate both from God and from the personality. It is subject to laws. It is subject to progression. It is subject to growth as every other creation of God is subject to growth. The law of evolution is one of God's basic creative laws, and it is at work in every form of creation. It is at work in the mineral kingdom. It is at work in the excarnate kingdom. It is at work in the angelic kingdom. It is at work in the kingdom of the soul-beings. 4155:13

I am building through the Readings a body of teaching which presents the truths, the realities of the spirit realm as it refers to human-beings and to souls, and the nature and destinies of souls as well as their current embroilment in incarnations.

Each teaching is drawn from the particular soul of the person getting the Reading. They are not speculations. They are life-centered, life-derived. Once in a while I will bring Teaching Readings in which further teachings are brought, but on the whole the teachings are drawn from actual life situations showing the application of spiritual principles, which are the laws of God; the truths, the realities of God as they apply to souls and to persons, human-beings, in various life experiences.

This body of teachings should be completed - not that all truth will be in them – but I say this body of teachings will be completed in the fairly near future. As I have said, I expect to bring from six to seven thousand Readings. I believe the number is approaching five thousand now. For my purposes, the purposes that have been assigned to me, there is no point in continuing these Readings after the body of teachings has been completed.

I know many persons would then say, "Oh, but the Readings are so helpful to the individuals getting them!"

I am thankful for this. To know the truth of one soul and the spiritual laws applicable particularly to it, is a cause of deep thanks. This is true. And maybe there will be other ways in which this service can be picked up and continued.

Remember that it is only recently that people have understood internal parasites and how to avoid or evict them. It is only in recent years that detailed knowledge of the heart has been secured by heart researchers. So if it takes another hundred or thousand or so years for the wide spread knowledge of past lives and their intricate pattern, the inherent pattern of human lives as the soul progresses, if it takes another hundred or thousand years for that knowledge to find other ways to express itself, that would still be in the planning of God. XVI;17-18

Q. You have spoken through a channel other than Grace Wittenberger and Dr. Loehr in the past. Is it possible, or likely, you will use other channels in the future?

A. The usual answer has been no. But in an unusual way, yes, it is possible. This is probing into what is, as yet, an uncertain future. But another may come. If that does happen, I assure you the members of Religious Research will be among the first to know.

It may be, too, that sometime in the future one or more channels will be developed for some of my advanced students. I do not have an advanced student who has reached my level of proficiency; but as they learn they can be used in some ways. XVI:17-1

Conclusion

Within the body of teachings which we have established in Earth consciousness through this channel, we have established that God's purpose for a soul basically is growth.

We have established how each individual, birthed from God's love and God's thought, has set before it a path of progression which, experienced by the soul, will evolve that individual soul in a pattern of growth which parallels the pattern in Earth living of an individual moving from babyhood to the adult status.

This process by which a child of God, while always a child, yet becomes an adult companion, co-worker and friend of God. The basic process a soul enters into from the moment of its emergence as an individual expression is a process of growth. To bring about growth requires change.

The cosmic school of Earth has a quality of uniqueness making it distinctive from all other cosmic schools, all other worlds, or all other planes which a soul experiences as it follows its individual pattern of growth. The distinctiveness of the Earth framework lies in the element of separation in unique and distinctive processes. Separation distinguishes Earth living from cosmic living. 4143:2

The process of entering into the Earth school is a process of separating the soul in its estate of soul-being-ness by requiring the soul to adopt human-being-ness. The process of a soul coming into Earth living is a process of separation in that the soul separates a portion of itself for the experience of the Earth plane of being-ness. So there is not only in the experience of a soul incarnate in the Earth plane a separation from the soul's cosmic origin, but there is also this element of separation of the soul from itself, from its total being-ness.

The very process of Earth living include experiences of separation. The growth of a personality from childhood to adulthood includes this element. The child in its first day of incarnate life, in the process of physical birth, experiences a separation from the mother as the umbilical cord is cut. As that new-born-personality moves through life it experiences separation. As the child enters educable years, it experiences a separation from its home base as it is sent into school. The very process of education is one of separation as the child moves from one grade to another.

The child as a young adult enters into the world beyond that which has been representative of its academic achievements, and that is a separation. Of course the experience of physical death represents an experience of separation. Within this total process involving the soul in Earth living, from physical conception until the death of the physical body, includes numerous experiences of separation.

A basic statement of the law of growth might be a mandatory experience of learning how to handle, how to respond to experiences of separation, separation and changes. It is well known that there are definite elements helpful to induce the processes which produce change. Some of these elements are represented as heat. It is well known that molten metal becomes malleable metal, metal that can be changed from its original shape or size, lengthy or depth of width, into a size or shape different from its origin. Heating the metal produces the possibility of change. 4143:3

It is well known in the chemistry laboratory that substances sealed in a flask and held over heat changes in characteristics. It is well known that the hard husk surrounding a kernel of wheat requires heat to break that husk so that the growth process within the kernel might be initiated. So it is mandatory that change be effected by experiences of separation.

Human personalities are not immune to these underlying processes of God's universe. Each and every soul in the process of experiencing Earth living is going to experience separation and change. We would point out that growth is an activity, an activity as distinguished from a mental decision or a mental conclusion. The processes of thought can develop conclusions, but those conclusions have in them the element of sterility unless they can be demonstrated and proved in patterns of activity.

Activities of change is emphasized in patterns of incarnation in Earth lives by being a human being, experiencing and understanding the different patterns in different times and in different places; to put down firm roots and achieve a usable understanding of how it is to assume human-being-ness 4143:4

Now a personality with intelligence may argue against the cosmic process that 'being done unto' is as valid a way of learning as the process of 'doing' by the soul. All the intellectualizing does not change the spiritual fact that this process of the soul, being the subject upon which life acts, is one of the cosmic frameworks of learning. It is what the soul allows the activities of human life upon it to do to it, which determines the amount and the depth of the growth achieved by the soul in a specific lifetime.

The personality's attitudes and the response the personality gives to the experiences of life acting upon it, can be a help or can be a hindrance to the learning of the soul. The personality can give a response of bitterness, of resentment. It can say, "I do not deserve this kind of treatment."

That attitude can hinder the gains that the personality's life can bring to the soul. Or the personality can say, "There is meaning and purpose to these things that happen to me and I can learn how to make them work for my good. I can use them to be more compassionate, to be more understanding, to be more responsive to the universe, accepting its way instead of my own will."

Such a response on the part of a personality is a positive aid and help to the soul that is learning in and through that personality.

It is true that the will of a personality may be very distinct, very different, and very separate from the will of a soul that is experiencing the life as a personality. The will of the personality may resist, and often does resist the pattern or growth the soul has set before itself for that lifetime. The personality, in the very process of being a personality, has its ideas, its aims, its goals, its desires. This is what distinguishes one personality from another personality.

This pattern of personality-being-ness may be different from the soul's will, ideas, purposes and the soul's gain. The difference does not have to manifest as conflict. It often does. The personality and the soul rather frequently appear as protagonists, struggling against each other. When they struggle against each other, instead of cooperating together, the purpose of the lifetime may well be aborted. 4143:6

The purpose is not given the energizing it needs for fulfillment if the energy it could receive from the personality, and the energy it could receive from the soul, is not flowing into it because these two flows of energies are conflicting with each other.

The fulfillment of the life purpose is majorly the responsibility of the soul that is incarnate as the personality. The personality's responsibility is to discover the purpose of the soul and put its energies into effecting a good working partnership with that soul.

Now in that statement we have just made we are starting at the point of assumption that the soul's purpose is in alignment with the cosmic pattern of growth. Occasionally, for various reasons, it may not be; but now you have the human personality with its wills and its desires. The human personality has a desire for growth and fulfillment even as a soul. But the human personality wants that achievement in frameworks of challenge, in frameworks which require effort. Personalities like to act, but they do not accept in the way a soul does the value of growth by those events or happenings which the personality considers hurtful or painful. This is what causes a conflict between the will of the personality and the will of the soul.

The personality must find its way into cooperation with the soul's way. For the soul's will is greater; it is stronger than the personality's will. Now, again, this statement is valid in the framework of the soul being aligned with cosmic purposes. 4143:7

Earth-beings aware of soul-being-ness sometimes have a tendency to abdicate their own contribution in favor of what the soul can contribute in the Earth framework. The Earth personality, as it awakens to soul being-ness, is called to a place of partnership with the soul. The soul and the personality are not to be in a master-servant relationship. Sometimes this framework is necessary as the soul is in the early learning of awakening to soul awareness in personality expression. 2585:5

A personality who becomes knowledgeable of his soul identity, and who then will use the Earth means at his disposal, as a personality, to come into partnership with the cosmic realms, that personality is the illustration of the kind that is wanted in the Earth realm. That kind of personality, which is a partner with his own soul, is honored and respected as a co-worker by the hierarchal forces because of this cooperation. In that pattern of expression in the Earth plane, which Earth-lings call "The New Age," this is the kind of Earth personality that is wanted. The personality, because it is in the Earth framework, has a perspective on Earth living which souls in other planes of expression do not have; and so their perspective of Earth is different.

The joining of these two perspectives provides the framework for bringing the Kingdom of Heaven into Earth in a more intelligent way than simply the pattern represented and implicit in the phrase of "master and servant." This is one reason why the whole field of parapsychology has come into an emphasis in Earth consciousness.

It is a beginning point in Earth consciousness for the growing of the awareness that there is more to Earth living than the animal consciousness. The increased awareness of other worlds, for example, through the phenomena of interplanetary vehicles, or flying saucers, the increased emphasis on the possibility of communication with some one or some thing beyond the Earth framework as experienced in Earth consciousness in psychical research. 2585:6

A LIFE READING

A Life Reading reveals an individual's past: the good, the bad and the ugly – to use a Clint Eastwood expression.

A Life Reading can also provide a social education by revealing a glimpse into history. I use the following Life Reading because I was fascinated by its revelations. The information in this Reading seems especially appropriate for our present time.

One never knows what another person's life will teach us. It has often been said: *As ye sow, so shall ye reap.* We may hear that phrase so often it goes in one ear and out the other. But the phrase is absolutely true. We **do** reap what we sow. Reincarnation teaches that what we do today, we answer for tomorrow.

The following Life Reading for Sarah Sanderson provides stark evidence of that fact.

Sarah had made several phone calls to the Foundation regarding her Reading. In the beginning stage of her contact with the Foundation, Sarah came across as sweet and loving, one who had been mistreated and misunderstood most of her life. The same thread of "being misunderstood" ran throughout Sarah's twenty-plus, single-spaced typed pages, telling again and again how others had misunderstood her horribly because no one had properly interpreted her motives.

It was realized that this very sweet lady had problems in communication at the very least - but more likely was not only paranoid but mentally deranged.

Sarah had a very strong desire to do the right thing, and a tendency to blame others when the right thing turned out to be the wrong thing. Her low math ability was based on her fear of the math teacher. Her typing instructor gave her an old defective typewriter which is the reason her typing was poor. Sarah was a writer for her high school newspaper but individuals who were jealous of her would not print her article in the newspaper. She always had someone else to blame.

She justified her cheating in her school work due to the fact that her parents were poor and making great sacrifices financially to send her to private high school. Her math teacher spoke too fast, and scolded her frequently. In high school she didn't know how to join in on the games with others.

Sarah came across to the conductor of the reading as homosexual, a condition Sarah did not want to admit to being. The idea of sexual intercourse repulsed her, even though her sex drive was normal. She never had a crush on boys but she did have a crush on a young lady senior in high school and looked up to her as her ideal – until she discovered her ideal young lady playing with her fingernails in church instead of praying.

Sarah decided against marriage, so she became a nun. In the convent she felt lonely and misunderstood. She was moved around frequently.

She intended to persevere as a nun to the very end of her life; but somewhere in her thirties she began to become overwhelmed with all the misunderstanding, rejection and failure that she was experiencing. There was much anger inside of her that she tried to suppress. Toward the end she became discouraged, apathetic, depressed, and found it increasingly difficult to keep the rules, and broke quite a few of them, which seemed to go unnoticed.

Sarah left the convent after eighteen years as a nun, but found difficulty getting and keeping a job.

The local employment agency sent her to a social psychologist, which proved quite helpful. For fifteen years Sarah held a good janitor's job in a large office building.

Sarah then spent some time in a psychiatric ward.

The conductor's heart ached for Sarah and the pain she had experienced. A person's life sketch had never revealed such a devastating sequence of events.

What could be the forces behind such a life?

Dr. John explores the soul dynamics behind the Sarah personality in the following Life Reading for Sarah Sanderson:

Dr. John:

A. Yes, her records are here; and this is most interesting, conductor.

Even as Jesus bore sins not his own upon the cross and suffered and died from them, and that suffering and death were redemptive, so also Sarah Sanderson bears sins not of her making; but it is a redemptive suffering. This is definitely a karmic lifetime.

First, I should say that Sarah Sanderson is an incarnation from the feminine half of her whole soul, so she is in her native gender. It's a young soul, into the second stage, the "well-started" stage, but not very far along in it. The karma, which really is the setting, the starting point and the most influential factor in her present life, comes from the immediate past-life. Since this is so important, let me go into it now.

It was in the masculine gender in Africa as a black. He was a strong man and belonged to a group in his tribe which preyed upon other blacks, seizing members of them and taking them to the coast to sell them to the slave ships that came.

It is often forgotten in the sympathy for the blacks having been slaves that it was essentially the blacks who seized other blacks and made them slaves. Had the white slave traders had to get blacks themselves, and had the blacks been united in even a rudimentary way against them, there would have been few slaves indeed. It was blacks who put blacks into slavery and sold them to far countries in servitude.

This, of course, made karma for all involved: the slave traders, the slave buyers, the slave marketers, the slave owners, and also the black slave stealers, slave procurers.

Sometimes such a karma will somewhat continue on in a small way through a number of subsequent lifetimes; or sometimes, as in Sarah's case, the karma is centered in one lifetime.

Karma can grow from a course of action but very often the details of the karma are set by some particular in the general course of action; and such is the case with Sarah.

In one of the slave raids upon an unsuspecting small village, the men were gone out hunting and so the slave raiding party was unopposed. They seized practically all of the women and children who were present.

One of these women had a daughter eight years old with her. She thought she saw a chance to escape the day after they had been captured and as they were marched away she yelled to her daughter to run; and then she started to run. But the particular slave raider man, who was the then incarnation of Sarah Sanderson, threw his club at her. He probably could have run and caught her but he had become calloused and rather brutal. Somewhat instinctively he threw his club which was rather heavy, and the heavy part of the club caught the woman from behind right at the base of the neck. She fell as though dead. I do not see if the little girl got away or not. The children did not bring as much money. If the little girl managed to hide in the confusion, she may have gotten away. Whether she got back to her own village, I do not know, and of course her own village had been decimated, had been robbed of its women and other children.

But the woman was not dead. She came to after a while. Cold water was probably thrown on her or something, but she was mentally deranged after that. In a way, the mental derangement made it easier for her to be marched away and sold as a slave. She had only very confused memories, confused emotions. She would sometimes break out into a tribal chant or she might break out into a rather fast spoken gibberish. Definitely she was deranged but she could follow simple orders such as "March," and such.

The slave raiders rather concealed the fact of her derangement as they sold her. She would be quiet at times for perhaps several days at a time without an outbreak. So she was sold and put on the ship. I do not see her after that.

Now this is that which Sarah Sanderson did not do; but the former incarnation of her soul did. Her soul was not strong enough to direct that previous incarnation successfully. It was an early incarnation. It was an early masculine incarnation for the young feminine soul and really the soul was rather close to that person and rather exulting in the masculine strength of the man, which was good; but the exaltation rather blinded it to the cruelties.

The man made quite free with the women captives sexually and with no regard for them. He really exulted in his manhood but in a rather reprehensible way. This has carried over into the Sarah Sanderson person in several ways. The sexual drives of the Sarah person are still those of that prior man. There is not really the drive towards men; there is a drive towards women. It is less intense, of course, and it is masked by the feeling, "Well, I just have a feeling of love and outreach, companionship, affection to this other woman. All I want is for her to return that."

But it comes across to the other woman and to society as a lesbian attempt, as a homosexual outreach, which it really is. Although, since it comes from the 1700s and early 1800s male, it was not homosexual then; but now that Sarah is not male but female, it is homosexual.

If she knows this it will help her to not get into embarrassing situations; for she will have a tendency to fix her attention and her desire upon a woman. Then, in rather direct ways, somewhat crude, express interest, attention, and make some gifts, and expect to have the woman respond to her in the same way.

It might be that Sarah would find a lesbian woman who would respond in the same way, and the two of them might have an interesting and rewarding love relationship. I do not know; but I see this as a possibility. A woman who is not homosexual will rather quickly sense that there is something "not normal" and "unhealthy" in Sarah and will have to take steps to protect herself - the steps being to draw away from her.

But there is an even more direct karma in that the mind-tool of Sarah is not a completely healthy or balanced mind-tool. She may realize this or she may not, but it is so. There will be times when her reaction to something will not be logical, would be more emotional than logical, or her emotional reaction may partake of a bit of a twisted mentality.

Now the Sarah-soul chose this deliberately as its way in deep penitence of making amends for what it had done to this particular woman who had been hit and deranged by the club that the man threw. The Sarah-soul was given quite a lot of training. This is one reason there has not been an intervening incarnation. The Sarah-soul was allowed to see what happened to many of the blacks whom it had helped to capture and sell into slavery.

The focus was made on this particular one so that the karmic restitution, the penitence, could be put into very practical immediate terms. So the soul chose to have a mind that was somewhat deranged - not nearly as much as the woman who had been hit suffered; but in a way the suffering is even more because that woman didn't know really what had happened to her and that she was damaged mentally.

The Sarah Sanderson person is, of course, in much better contact with life and reality than that woman was. But in a way, that makes the mental aberration even a bit more difficult because these mental aberrations have come, and Sarah, somewhat with the strength, even with a – well, swaggering, not arrogance, but a masculine strength that that man felt for whom she is making atonement now, feels that she is correct, that her attitudes are correct, her desires are correct and pure and her emotions are righteous and good, and does not realize her difficulties.

Conductor this is a very unusual reading as you will see. You might think it is a difficult reading to give, to bring to this warm and loving woman, Sara Sanderson. This woman wants things to be right and wants her life to be creative and a life of love and service and who wants companionship – to bring to her these words which sound so harsh. But conductor, I am bringing what can be light to her. Only from the Akashic Records can this part of her life and its difficulties be made clear to her.

So what is the answer?

Well there is a verse in the Holy Scriptures: *Let no man think of himself more highly than he ought to think,* which should be helpful to her.

When things go wrong let her not assume that she is in the right. If she says, "I'm okay, you're not okay," she is in trouble and others will react in ways that will rebuff her, will cause her trouble and expense and difficulties and unhappiness and sadness and so forth.

So let Sarah be a little more prone to listen to what others say, to watch how they react to her, and not try to insist upon what she thinks she is doing right - because it might be that what she is doing is wrong.

If she can see this, it will help her. If she can see how her outreach to some selected woman, or women, for love and affection really is a lesbian outreach, this will help her.

Now what about this life? She spoke in that which you read of a high-minded wish that the life be successful, be creative, have happiness.

Well, this life is something like the crucifixion of Christ upon the cross. It is not as intense, but it is longer than the crucifixion; and the crucifixion was not a time of happy fellowship. The crucifixion was a time of pain and suffering; and it was a redemptive suffering; and the soul of Jesus knew this and had accepted it and carried it through to victory.

If Sarah Sanderson can see that her life is making up for some mistakes that her soul has made in the past and that she is a redemption-point, not particularly a person destined to have artistic expression and creative achievement or even the love and affection and happiness she seeks, she will see that what she is doing is even more important and even more of an achievement, and will bring release and love and affection and creative outlet to the soul in future incarnations.

This may sound like the old charge made against religion that it promises 'pie in the sky by and by.' But in the framework of reincarnation, which Sarah understands and accepts, it is seen that the 'pie in the sky by and by' is very real and is, well, worth working toward in the present life.

This is the picture.

I have been very frank with Sarah for I feel that she does have the understanding to get this in her quiet moments and in her sane moments, and most of her time is that way. I think she has a spiritual outreach to accept this and incorporate it into her understanding. I think she will find in it many answers to questions that she has asked for a long time and for which she has found no answers anywhere else.

I hope she will find it a solace for her mind and heart in realizing that what is being done is very good, is a great service to her own soul, given at certain high costs to her personality, to her person, to Sarah Sanderson as a person in her life.

This is my hope; and this is that which I have primarily for Sarah Sanderson. Is there a question to this point?

Q. One question and then a comment. The first question is: What century was this lifetime in?

A. That was mainly in the 1700s and a little bit in the early 1800s. It was in Africa, of course.

Q. I have just a comment, mostly for Sarah. There is quite a bit of understanding in here. I want to make sure very quickly that Sarah knows that if she does have any questions she should contact me. I will be glad to help her in any understanding.

Now the picture is complete. Sarah, because of the callous actions of the 1700s personality of her soul, is paying a karmic debt.

In this day and age the sexual drives toward women might not be too difficult for Sarah to handle if her mind were normal; but because of her limited mind, Sarah does not recognize this lesbian bias. It is no wonder that Sarah often feels rejected and misunderstood, particularly by women. Our hearts still ache for Sarah, but when there is purpose in pain, that pain can lessen. And the Sarah-soul chose this way to cleanse itself from the evil slave-trader lifetime.

Sarah asked about both of her parents. Although they are deceased, during their lifetime she got along well with each of them and loved them both. There were no major problems there. Each parent was found to be a cosmic family member who had shared several past lives with Sarah. The parents were chosen to support her in this most difficult life.

Sarah has a brother who has been extremely helpful to her. Her comment about him was that he is "so good to me that he seems to be trying to make up for something."

When Dr. John was given the brother's name it was discovered that he had been Sarah's father in China in the 1600s. However, there were so many children the incarnation of the Sarah soul received little notice from that father. In this life-time she is receiving that attention . . . and most welcome it is.

Sarah asks about a friend in the convent. She only knows her as Sister Mary, does not have her given name or even her age. Sister Mary is one who was particularly kind to Sarah. Dr. John replied:

A. No I do not find her. When I have a name, a clearly identified person, I can find if that person's soul lifeline, as it were, has crossed with the soul lifeline for the person for whom I am reading the Akashic Records. Not being able to do that in this case, I will look at it in a different way, in a way of trying to sense, to pick up in this more intuitive or sensing way.

I believe they have been together in cosmic schools. I think this one of whom you inquire, this Sister Mary, which of course was not her birth name, was a teacher or at least a senior student in some cosmic school which was preparing Sarah for the present life, which was enlightening that soul. So this was a good contact.

But I do not believe there was any past-life acquaintance, or any cosmic relationship, and I do not see any future incarnation of the two together, although that might take place. There were certain good bonds established between them in the present life . . . . . perhaps stronger on the Sarah side than on the Sister Mary side, for she had more to think about, more persons.

This relationship could be used constructively in future incarnations together. But it is not yet patterned and I do not see if it will or will not take place.

Q. Now we come to whom Sarah considered the most important relationship in her life. In her preparation material and over the phone Sarah talked about her former minister – we'll call her Belinda – with love and longing but frustration and bitter disappointment:

"When Belinda came on the scene as our minister and gave her first lecture in church, the following words she spoke were words I latched on to tenaciously and they were words that told me what kind of a person she is. These are the words: *I have a lot of love to give away.*

"From that moment on I saw her as a very loving person, and I fell in love with her.

"Under her loving influence I seemed to open up like a closed bud opening up its petals to the sun. Being an introvert by nature I began to open up more to giving love not only to her personally, via gifts and personal services, but my love toward others expanded likewise simultaneously.

"Having given so much love to her and hungering for the expression of love and gratitude from her in reciprocation, and like-wise in gratitude for the expression of her love, I attempted to draw closer in friendship to her. But the closer I tried to draw to Belinda the more I seemed to be repelled by her. I even rubbed her the wrong way in class. She accused me of many things that were not true, as for example, holding on to her, threatening her, saying mean things about her and the Board members, trying to get members to side with me, of lying, all of which I believed were quite untrue. In a word I was treated unfairly by her in ways too numerous to mention; yet my affection toward her never waned, and because I felt such great love for her, I felt deeply hurt and depressed over the situation. I was advised by her and the Church Board to go for counseling therapy.

"I had made some angry remarks in class which she did not like, but I was treated unfairly by her in class. My problem with her and the Church Board seems so complex and so puzzling that it is almost impossible to put on paper except to say that, here again, as in the past, my goodness, love, devotion and words were misunderstood, misinterpreted to such an extent that it made me feel like I was some kind of criminal or something, the way I was treated.

"Last year in a conversation over the phone with Belinda I was so despondent at not being able to get her to respond to me with the same affection that I was giving her that in order to obtain more love and attention from her I expressed fear I would commit suicide. Of course I wasn't really serious about doing this, but she took it seriously and advised me to go for help. To make a long story short, after the board members also urged me to go for therapy I did go but very reluctantly. After the seventh session Belinda, the board members, and the counselor and I got together to try and resolve our mutual problems in some way. At this session basically the same accusations were made against me. At this point I buried my head in my hands and weeping, I said, 'I don't think I will live to the end of the year.'

"By this remark I merely meant to give those present to understand that the unjust accusations, the misunderstanding, the ingratitude, the lack of sympathy, the very deep hurt coming to me from the person, Belinda, whom I loved in a very special way was so burdensome to me emotionally that this itself could end my life. But the persons who were present misunderstood me and thought I would commit suicide. After weeping, a woman physician came in and tried to persuade me to take some pills. This frightened me and made me angry because I felt threatened not knowing what their real intentions were. So I got up, made some angry gestures and remarks and stormed out of the room, slamming the door behind me in anger."

(I'm exhausted reading this.)

Sarah continued in her life sketch to tell how the police came with a subpoena and took her to a psychiatric ward where she was confined for three days. The diagnosis about her made by the psychiatrist, according to Sarah, was completely wrong. She suffered very much but refused to hate anyone. *Father, forgive them,* she wrote, *for they know not what they do.*

(And neither, I might add, did Sarah.)

Fortunately for Sarah – though she probably did not see it that way – Belinda was transferred by the Bishop to a larger church too far away for Sarah to visit.

Sarah still has love for Belinda even though she feels that Belinda betrayed her.

We now go to what Dr. John had to say when Belinda was inquired about:

A. I have her. No there is no past-life acquaintance, and there is no cosmic relationship, and they will not be together in the future. (So you can relax Belinda.)

Is there a question?

Q. She had felt that Belinda had misunderstood her and Sarah has a great caring for her.

A. I would warn her again, as I have, that a great caring for a woman is interpreted by that woman and by onlookers as a lesbian outreach. Also, there is another factor here conductor that is rather interesting.

Belinda has the creativity and the attainment and the warmth and other qualities such as the Sarah person would like to have. This would make for a certain identification of the Sarah person with the other one, but that is a mistake. That is a mental trick, as it were, that the mind plays. Let her diminish. Let Sarah not come into contact with the other one anymore. If the other is a minister in the church, then let Sarah go to another church. Let Sarah break that contact completely; and in her own mind see that it was not as she saw it to be. It was something else and really held much potential for that which was not good even though Sarah would assume and claim that it was only for good.

Q. I know that Belinda has moved and there is no contact really.

A. There is the move then, so the contact has been broken?

Q. Yes.

A. Then let it stay broken.

Q. Sarah is finding this hard to do emotionally, but I believe your words will help her.

A. Well, she wanted to be a lover, and a lover sometimes has to take himself in hand and allow a certain amount of time for his love outreach, which has been blocked, to heal. But that has to be. Actually, of course, that black man of almost two centuries ago broke many a love relationship as he stole slaves away from their homes.

Q. Sarah next asks about a member of the church whom Belinda appointed to be a special friend and confidant to Sarah. This lady had been most helpful to Sarah during her "greatest trial," momentarily easing the soul-searing pain she was going through.

A. No past-life acquaintance; no cosmic relationship. They may be together in the future sometime. Sarah in a future incarnation may be born to the other as a child. Remember, they will be two different persons at that time. If Sarah makes a success of the present life, as really in a way she is doing, they will be quite different persons and she will be free from this cloud of misplaced desires, this cloud of karma, this cloud of a clouded mind, at such a time.

Sarah also asked about some spiritual leaders of a well-known national group. Their teachings had been helpful to her but there were no past-life or cosmic ties.

The Reading concludes with Sarah's questions.

Q. The first question concerns an inner message she received at a time when she was particularly upset, (again.) She was very depressed at the state of affairs between her and Belinda and she was resting on a recliner and received this message:

Gotha will guide you to freedom.

She has some questions about this message. She wants to know first of all: Is this the name of her high-self or Christ-self?

A. I don't see this message at all. You say, "Gotha will lead you to freedom?"

Q. Yes.

A. I do not see the event. It has not impacted on the Akashic Records as something like this normally would not do. I do not see it. I do not pick it up psychically.

She is psychic, but with the difficulties in the mental tool, which I have spoken of, there can be difficulties in the conscious pickup of psychic messages and such. These difficulties in the mental tool of course, are not nearly as bad as the difficulty in the mental tool of the woman who was hit by the past-life man's club.

Q. Her next question:
From what I understand, dreams can be helpful as a tool to our spiritual growth and that they usually are symbolic rather than literal. How could a person know how to interpret the symbolic meaning behind a dream, or a vision, for that matter?

A. Dreams are not always significant in this manner, but at times they are. The symbolism of dreams varies a great deal. There are some symbols which have some-what of an agreed meaning among many dreamers or dream interpreters. If an individual knows what the meaning of the symbol is, then of course, when he dreams that symbol the meaning is available to him.

The person doing the dreaming usually can interpret the dream better than another, although not always. There are others who are more skilled in dreams and perhaps have a psychic ability to interpret dreams.

This is the answer I can bring. It may not be what she wished but I am not a dream expert.

Q. She wanted to know if symbols in dreams had universal, or if they had different meanings for different persons.

A. Essentially different meanings for different persons – but different standardization can take place. If the dreamer knows the standard symbol meaning ahead of time, then it is more likely to be in that framework in his dreams.

Q. You have answered this but let me re-present it anyway: "Why have I experienced so much rejection, misunderstanding, misjudgment, jealousy, and even hatred, although I have tried hard to be straightforward and kind to people?"

A. Actually, she has deserved it - in that things which she has done, which she thought were good, came across as not good; things she has done which she interprets as being simply an expression of love and hope for affection can come across as being over-bearing, demanding, a bit domineering; and other persons will rightfully reject it.

Other than that I don't have anything more to say . . . . . except let her take some cues from the response that she gets. This may help her to see that what is coming across is not what she thinks or tells herself she is do-ing. She may be doing something else as far as it has meaning to the other person, you see.

This is part of the mental haze, which is part of the karma of the pres-ent life. It includes suffering but not as much suffering as was brought to that mother and wife separated from her family in that previous life.

(Dr. John will not let Sarah off the hook for the pain her soul's previous incarnation inflicted upon that poor mother in her past life. What a horrible pain it was! So, Sarah, quit your bitchin!)

Q. Her last question: "Who is my opposite polarity counterpart or, as you term it, soul-mate?"

A. He is not incarnate. Actually he is not very close. He is aware of what is happening in this life; but remember, he is from the same young soul. He does not have much of wisdom and helpfulness; so he wisely stands aside and lets her council of guides and teachers take more direct part in her life.

She must live her own life and achieve her own salvation, of course, but with their help.

Q. Have they had past-lives together?

A. No.

Q. Do you see his soul name?

A. No, nor hers.

Q. Is there anything at all that you know about him?

A. No.

Q. I believe this completes the questions that she wanted asked. Do you have a final word for Sarah?

A. I do not know if that which I have brought will be received correctly and used profitably or not. It may be the time has been wasted. I think it has not been wasted. I think Sarah Sanderson will get at least some information and some insight from her own Akashic Records and some guidance for her present life.

Actually she is accomplishing the purpose of this life - certainly with a passing grade - a good 'C' grade. If she continues to keep herself a productive member of society, carrying on as best she can in the way that she does, this will increase the good that this lifetime is accomplishing.

Q. Certainly, Dr. John. Just knowing that we are walking in God's path for us, no matter how difficult that path is, but knowing that we are walking in the right path can be a great comfort.

And so the Life Reading for Sarah Sanderson came to an end.

The conductor concluded:

"Dear, sweet, Sarah, suffering redemptive karma from deeds of a former incarnation of her soul - a classic textbook case of a karmic lifetime."

We are not all so lucky as to receive a Life Reading. Those who benefit from reading this material owe a debt of gratitude to Sarah for allowing her past life to be revealed to us and to learn the spiritual lessons involved. For that I am sure Sarah will receive a special blessing.

The Life Reading of Sarah Sanderson provides another good example of the sacrifice of the Paschal Lamb. Innocent Sarah is the lamb being sacrificed in this lifetime for the sins of a former incarnation from her soul. Sarah did not commit the karma, but she is the Paschal Lamb suffering the consequences of her soul's previous incarnation as a brutal slave stealer.

Blessings to you Sarah.

Printed in the United Kingdom by
Lightning Source UK Ltd., Milton Keynes
136927UK00001B/319/P